THE TWO SOVEREIGNS

T0352720

'A Simmelian – in form and content – inquiry into modernity, via its characteristic and cosmopolitan modes of reflexivity ... extraordinarily, even elegantly, written.'

Scott Lash, *Lancaster University*

This book examines modernity through the prism of the two sovereigns – of the individual and the collectivity. It is a stimulating and highly original meditation on the difficult and contradictory experiences of European modernity. It uses the collapse of communism in Eastern and Central Europe to explore why the institutions and narratives of modernity found it so difficult to deal with problems such as the meaning of freedom, the role and status of intellectuals, and the legacy of the past. The book argues that the central question of modernity is: how can the world be made a better place? The author argues that this question remains relevant and that it has never been definitively answered: the identity of the 'sovereign maker' was always open to debate.

The book is a superbly crafted examination of the collapse of communism in Central and Eastern Europe and the prospects for change. It will interest students of Sociology, Political Science and Cultural Studies.

Keith Tester is Lecturer in the School of Social and Historical Studies, University of Portsmouth.

THE TWO SOVEREIGNS

Social contradictions of European modernity

Keith Tester

Routledge
Taylor & Francis Group

LONDON AND NEW YORK

First published in 1992
by Routledge
2 Park Square, Milton Park, Abingdon, Oxfordshire OX14 4RN
Simultaneously published in the USA and Canada
by Routledge
a division of Routledge, Taylor & Francis
711 Third Avenue, New York, NY 10017

First issued in paperback 2014

Routledge is an imprint of the Taylor and Francis Group, an informa business

British Library Cataloguing in Publication Data
Tester, Keith, 1960–
The two sovereigns: social contradictions of European modernity.
I. Title
306

Library of Congress Cataloging in Publication Data
A catalog record for this book is available on request.

ISBN 13: 978-0-415-06191-9 (hbk)
ISBN 13: 978-1-138-87993-5 (pbk)

Typeset in Baskerville by
J&L Composition Ltd, Filey, North Yorkshire

CONTENTS

INTRODUCTION

This book is an essay which takes the recent history of Europe as an opportunity to try to say something about the social relationships and institutional arrangements of modernity. It is also an exercise in sociology, which attempts to see the intellectual enterprise called sociology as part of the problem of modernity rather than the source of objective and universally valid or reliable answers.

Essentially, this book is predicated on an assumption that the kind of sociological discourse which it uses, and to which it contributes, is itself a product of the modernity which the discourse ostensibly seeks to explain. In order to demonstrate this close proximity between the conditions of existence and the discourses called sociology (their narratives, their questions, their answers), I have tried to understand the discipline as a social, historical, and cultural phenomenon which should be placed in context. As such, the book does not use the narrative devices of alleged objectivity, empirical validity, and factual grounding which are conventionally found in sociological texts. Those devices are internal to sociology but it seems to me that a narrative which looks outwards might be rather more interesting. I have attempted to use a variety of illustrative figures, drawn from the worlds of literature, art, and music, in order to demonstrate that the professional area in which I work should be understood in terms of a cultural milieu, rather than as a distinctive pure science possessed of a God's-eye view of something *out there*.

Consequently, the mode of argument used in the book might seem to be rather precious, pretentious, and basically nothing more than a self-conscious effort to hide the failure of my own

1

research to provide evidence or proof for what I have to say. That is certainly not what I intended. The rather metaphorical mode of argument has been chosen quite deliberately and does not lose sight of the logic of sequential development of analysis.

The mode of argument is deliberately metaphorical for a number of reasons. Firstly, because I hope this essay can either inspire debate or stimulate some more research (if only to prove how silly Keith Tester can be). Secondly, and a lot more importantly, because if I believe that sociology is a discipline which can only appear in certain places at certain times (and I believe just that), then any 'facts' which I might use to justify my claims are themselves socially and historically dependent. The map called sociology creates the landscape relevant to the sociologist. Put another way, the facts are internal to the discourse. Therefore to use the facts to substantiate the discourse is to participate in little more than tail-chasing.

The style of the book indicates a very serious argument. To assume that sociological categories are to be taken as direct reports of reality is to *mythologize* sociology and the relationships to which it ostensibly refers. I want to suggest that the discourses of sociology are not of the status of unproblematic reports of reality (given the right methodology), but are themselves partly constitutive of the reality called society. So, this book might well work against the conventional grain of sociology, but it is no less serious – and no more precious or spurious – for that.

My deliberate decision to work without some of the conventional devices of the modern sociological discourse, which seem to me to be near exhaustion and redundancy, indicates better than anything else my sense of not working from within a condition of modernity.

This book is, then, an essay written in the knowledge, and partially in the interests, of what Agnes Heller has called a *hermeneutics of social science*. It also tries to operate in the wake of Heller's claim (which owes more than a little to Husserl), that: 'As long as social institutions or historical events are "taken for granted", we understand them to some degree. The moment we put them under scrutiny we start to understand what they are really all about' (Heller 1990: 23). It is because of the concern not to take things for granted that the book spends quite a lot of time exploring the social and historical conditions of existence of the modern intellectuals who created things like sociology.

Throughout the discussion, I refer to the intellectuals as *double strangers*. Whenever I use the phrase double strangers I am referring to those social groups which combined in their existential conditions of existence the deconstructive effects of firstly, urbanization and secondly, Enlightenment. The meanings and importance of the double strangers can be seen in the example of the character of Thomas Stockmann in Ibsen's play *An Enemy of the People* (Ibsen 1988) or, more concretely, in the real-life figures Immanuel Kant and Lenin (although, and as I try to show in Chapter 3, I am not too sure that Lenin was real). *The double strangers as I define them are only possible in the conditions of European modernity.* I am in no way seeking to postulate an ahistorical or a universal category (as such, Plato, for example, was not a double stranger). More than that, the precise characteristics of the double strangers were defined by the conditions of their espousal of what, in Chapter 4, I call, the *culture of reflexive discourse* (a term borrowed from Alvin Gouldner). It was a commitment to that culture which created the commonality of the double strangers such that it is appropriate for otherwise quite diverse individuals to be assimilated within a general category.

One of the main themes running through this discussion is how the double strangers dealt with the social worlds which they encountered. I argue that they typically employed one of two main methods of treatment. If the social world was interpreted by the double strangers *as if* it were mute, then they engaged in garden relationships. If the double strangers interpreted the social world *as if* it were already active, they engaged in allotment relationships (I define the meanings of the garden and allotment metaphors in Chapter 2). The *as if* is important: I am not saying that, to give an example, Lenin worked in a Russia which *really was* mute. I am just saying that he worked in a situation in which there was *nothing to prevent* him treating Russia *as if* it were mute.

The gardening and allotment relationships were the basis of the 'Two Sovereigns' mentioned in the title of the book. Sovereignty consisted in the ability to make the world a better place, but I argue that the identity of the maker was more than a little vague. One sovereign was the collective, which had to be led by the firm hand of the double strangers. The other sovereign was the individual, who was interpreted as able to change the world by and for him- or herself. (In accordance with academic orthodoxy, I have tried to use gender-neutral terms in the discussion, but I think it should be remembered that for the most part the sovereigns of European modernity were actually men.)

It is more or less implicit to my argument that the very ability to talk about the two sovereigns in a manner which sees them as metaphors to be interrogated rather than factual reports of reality, means that they might well be of nothing more than historical importance, or that they might be important only to the extent that they are images from the past which continue to haunt us. The narrative of the argument and the mode of the argument to some extent come together.

I would like to ask that this book be read as a sociological *commentary* upon the history and relationships of European modernity. It is not an *account*. That will explain why the discussion operates at what might seem to be an extremely high level of abstraction. The evident abstraction is a product of my effort to see the events of modernity to some extent in the round rather than in the detail.

This concern might also mean that I am guilty of reducing people and events to the status of simple abstractions made flesh. Against that charge I would strongly plead that I am not guilty. A central theme of the book is that modern abstractions only became abstractions at all because of social and historical relationships. The collapse of really existing socialism, the event which occasioned this book, shows quite clearly that it is people who make history. But they have to have the idea that history can be made in the first place. And the idea is socially and historically contingent.

As a final introductory point, I must stress that the book is about *Europe*. It does not say, and is not meant to say, anything directly about the United States of America. However, the absence of the United States from the discussion might seem to be rather curious. After all, I have argued that Europe is more a concept than a geographical area, and it can be argued in these terms that America is European in a far greater sense than, say, Bulgaria.

It could be argued furthermore that the history of America actually disproves everything I have said. Firstly, ever since Max Weber sociologists have known that it is possible to see the

United States as something like *the* expression of modernity. Secondly, the United States was founded in more or less exactly the mute terrain which I have proposed as the basic requirement for garden relationships. And yet America evidently bears as little relationship to the garden as it is possible to imagine.

As to the first objection, I can only acknowledge Weber but emphasize that my concerns are with what might be called the *old* Europe of the Rhine, the Danube, the Seine, the Thames. Moreover, it could be said that America was a European export and, therefore, to understand *there*, one must first understand *here*. On this count, I have not written about the United States because I was not concerned to do so. To have written about it would have meant a much longer book and a number of diversions along the lines of the American Exceptionalism thesis.

As to the second objection, the American continent certainly did offer a fairly close approximation to ideal garden conditions. But the point is that the opportunity to indulge in garden relationships was not taken. This is important. The ability to treat a terrain as mute did not *necessarily* mean that garden relationships would occur. There was no *necessary* connection at all. The opportunity to create gardens had to be *seized*. Once again, the crucial dimension is the big *as if*. The point rather seems to be that the founders of the United States of America did not treat their terrain as if it were mute (see Lienesch 1988).

The question of the compatibility between America and the interpretation of modernity offered in this book needs further investigation. At the moment I do not have the resources to pursue the matter. For the present, it is enough for me to be able to propose that the interpretation of modernity which this book contains holds good for the old Europe. I would also speculate that the United States does not refute my story.

I would like to thank Zygmunt Bauman and Linda Rutherford for their continued encouragement and support. All the usual disclaimers apply. Neither is to be held responsible for the analysis of the book. The responsibility is mine alone. The book is dedicated to Madeleine Tester.

1

STRANGERS

Really existing socialism – what I shall often call the Soviet-type system on the grounds that it 'extended beyond the Soviet Union as a result of Soviet military presence' (Feher *et al.* 1983: ix) – was said by its enthusiasts to be the ultimate way of ensuring a complete and total social freedom. The system which the Soviet Union exported in the years immediately after the collapse of Nazism was intended to reconcile the previously different concerns of the collective and the individual. But the system was overthrown, or at least given the final push before it self-destructed, by people who struggled in the name of freedom. One definition of freedom challenged another definition. The alleged highpoint of European history was seen by its subjects to be one of the two nadirs in the modern history of oppression.

I think that paradoxical situation is rather interesting. How could it be that the forms and experiences of modernity could be so contradictory and so opposed? How was it that the states which dominated Central and Eastern Europe for the forty years or so after the Second World War were identified as such an obscenity, and why was their collapse greeted with such pleasure? But I am also interested in the light which events in 'their' part of Europe might throw on non-events in 'my' part. I witnessed those events, which amounted to the death of the Soviet-type system, from the vantage point of an armchair in England. As I watched the television, I felt confident that anything even remotely like a mass popular uprising would not happen here. Why not? (I am not saying that a popular uprising is therefore desirable; I am merely asking a sociological question.)

Of course, it could be said that really existing socialism fell apart (whether it toppled or was pushed is something to be considered later) because it was basically an 'Evil Empire', as old Cold Warriors and Solzhenitsyn might like to argue. By extension, therefore, the Western European systems remained intact because they were not evil, because they were good. But that kind of righteous stone throwing is actually not too useful, irrespective of its rather silly secularization of the religious Armageddon. Milan Kundera has repeatedly made a point which is quite crucial if the Soviet-type experience is to be understood. It should always be born in mind: 'Communists ... had a grandiose program, a plan for a brand-new world in which everyone would find his place ... the creation of an idyll of justice for all' (Kundera 1982: 8). Really existing socialism was meant to be close to the achievement of perfect social relationships. It was intended to be the shell in which all individuals would be happy, whole, and true to both themselves and their humanity. But it would rather seem that it was not.

I want to ask you to bear one thing in mind whilst you are reading through this analysis. Although Leninism, to take a prime example, might at present seem to be a bit of a disaster if not completely abhorrent as a programme of social organization, it was also the principle and understanding of the world through which countless millions of European men and women struggled to make dreams become flesh. I am not going to spend much time blaming really existing socialism for anything. That would be a relatively pointless exercise in conceit. It would also be an indulgent distraction. As Georg Simmel said, 'it is not our task either to accuse or to pardon, but only to understand' (Simmel 1950: 424). A hard yet admirable task.

But, of course, the forms and experiences of modernity were by no means exhausted by the rise and fall of really existing socialism. After all, Western Europe also lived the relationships of modernity. Yet rarely, if ever, did it look at all like the Soviet-type system. Whereas really existing socialism defined sovereignty as some kind of collective enterprise invariably under a firm guiding hand, the Western nation-states like Britain and France have a long tradition of the formal acceptance of the sovereignty of all individuals (notwithstanding brief Jacobin episodes). In theory, but perhaps occasionally not in practice, the Western experience of modernity *always* tended to

7

uphold the meaning of sovereignty which the Central and Eastern European, Soviet-type systems attempted to demolish.

So, a curious dimension of modernity was a profound uncertainty about who or what was the true and proper sovereign of human and social history. And, therefore, to the extent that we were thrown into a world which bears the imprint of modernity, we are similarly uncertain about our own place, our own limits, our own social or personal being. As Foucault realized, there can be two meanings to the word 'subject', and it is hard to know whether one or both is applicable to us (Foucault 1982). That dilemma was at the heart of modern culture. It was the central theme of an immense amount of literary reflection and indeed implicit to the narratives of the social sciences which frequently continue repeatedly to cover the barren terrain of the futile debate between structure and agency.

Modernity was lived under the sign of *two sovereigns*. Each sovereign claimed to be the only true sovereign. The collective (usually following some vanguard) or the individual. During the twentieth century, when most of the sweet and bitter fruits of modernity ripened, different parts of Europe lived and struggled under one sign and tried to condemn the other as little more than a grotesque mask. I will try to explain why those different sovereigns developed, how they were consolidated, and why they could proclaim their own unique superiority. But by the final decade of the twentieth century, one of the definitions of sovereignty had been consigned to the wastebin of history; ironically the very bin which was intended to be the final resting place of the *other* definition.

That raises a number of rather interesting questions. Ultimately, the Soviet-type version of really existing socialism turned out to be an expensive and tragic farce. Moreover, it was to a large extent replaced by institutional arrangements which formally upheld the sovereignty of all individuals rather than that of the organized and mobilized collective. In the final instance, there is quite a lot to the partisan claim that the Central and Eastern European societies tried to become more like Western European social systems. This raises the simple but deep issue of why. Was the Soviet-type system a diseased form of modernity? Was it a digression from what modernity should have *really* been like? Is the interpretation of sovereignty as an individual affair a better interpretation than the collective one?

8

More broadly; now that most European states attempt to live by the same principles, is it reasonable to identify some tendencies towards *convergence?*

To answer all those pretty big questions, to even approach answers (and any answers in this book are tentative), it is necessary to spell out precisely what modernity actually was. Of course, many meanings could be given from the sizable literature, but in view of the specifically sociological worries of this analysis, Anthony Giddens provides a suitable beginning. 'As a first approximation, let us say the following: "modernity" refers to modes of social life or organisation which emerged in Europe from about the seventeenth century onwards and which subsequently became more or less worldwide in their influence' (Giddens 1990: 1). Giddens locates the onset of modernity in a definite historical period, the seventeenth and probably eighteenth centuries. A whole cluster of other vitally important historical events was occurring at that time. Michel Foucault has fairly convincingly shown that the structures of knowledge and indeed the foundations of social relationships were undergoing absolutely fundamental epistemological transformations (see, for example, Foucault 1970, 1977), whilst, broadly speaking, the eighteenth century was the era of the European Enlightenment.

In a nutshell, the Enlightenment involved the proclamation and practice of the autonomy and sufficiency of socially produced knowledge (reason) in place of revealed or traditional knowledge. The announcement had a profound social impact. If reason was the basis of a true and wholly satisfactory understanding of the order of things, then the Enlightenment was also the assumption that irrational (for which read religious and habitual) social arrangements should be marginalized. Men, and perhaps sometimes even women, could and should be rescued, 'from political and moral injustice and misery and set ... on the path of wisdom, happiness, and virtue' (Berlin 1981: 2). The formulation distils the problem of sovereignty. Who or what walks along the path towards Enlightenment? All people everywhere, together, or all individuals at their own pace? Moreover, who would lead the women and men along the path? Are leaders required?

Reason was meant to be the new guide of social practices and relationships. It would rescue women and men from the errors of the old and existing ways. In other words, the narratives and practices of modernity were predicated upon the belief that the social is self-sufficient. As such, it can be suggested that the experiences and the arrangements of modernity were characterized by a single but compelling *leitmotif*. In Wagnerian opera, the *leitmotif* is a short phrase which signifies some particular situation or character. A few notes represent the complete personality and biography of complex destinies. European modernity was lived through its own phrase, its own little signature which overflowed its restricted precision to potentially illuminate everything. The *leitmotif* of European modernity was the assumption that *the world can be made a better place*. The Gotterdamerung of modernity was precisely the uncertainty over who or what was the sovereign maker.

The practices and principles of European modernity all lived by the story that existing social relationships in some way owed rather too much to superstition or tradition and that they consequently needed to be made to approximate with the demands and requirements of reason. The rule and increasingly the domination of self-sufficient reason rendered the existing ways flawed and inadequate and in dire need of improvement. Indeed, the typical forms of modernity were impossible without the belief that, in the words of a once famous anthem, 'Reason in revolt now thunders, and at last ends the age of cant'. But the strains of the *leitmotif* would not be played by some extra-terrestrial orchestra. After all, if reason was entirely social, the revolt of reason had to be self-sufficient as well. To quote the largely forgotten song once again: 'No saviour from on high delivers; No trust have we in prince or peer.' The world was made a better place by the independent practices of social subjects who worked through social relationships.

Consequently, at its heart, modernity was synonymous with *freedom*. Its institutions and interpretations were founded upon the assumption that social relationships do not have to be like they are, that social forms are in no way intrinsically immutable. Indeed, if the social were unchangeable, it would be more than a little difficult to go about making it different. Modernity was, thus, the recognition and practice of a sharp distinction between the pliable realm of the social and the determined realm of the natural. As Ferenc Feher and Agnes Heller have said:

Persons living in a rigid world of seemingly unalterable personal dependence regard themselves (if they achieve that level of self-reflexion at all) as things, in that they accept their existence as parts of a process which has no alternative. But a process without alternative is nature. Anyone who does not distinguish himself or herself from nature, is not only unfree *but is also unaware of the existence of freedom* and in this sense a thing.

(Feher and Heller 1983: 213)

The statement would have been impossible outside of the conditions of European modernity. It was certainly impossible before the eighteenth century. Before that time, it was indeed understood that social relationships were the way they must be, that there was no alternative. Such a profound reification and naturalization of existing social relationships was achieved through the belief in the overwhelming power of God and His divine plan.

The sociological literature provides a good illustration of the assumption of God's all-inclusive sweep. According to Weber, the Protestant ethic implicitly assumed that all women and men were just things in God's world. In struggling for personal wealth, the subjects of the Protestant ethic were not at all demonstrating their freedom. On the contrary, they were merely showing the profound extent to which they were trapped by God, the extent to which they had been reduced to the status of wealth-creating machines for the glory of the deity. They might have made money, but the point was that they were not *free* to make money. They were compelled to do it (see Weber 1930. James Hogg's novel, *The Confessions of a Justified Sinner*, provides another discussion of the social effect of the Protestant ethic).

In opposition to this pre-modern situation of the rigid, ordained, order of things, the social subjects and arrangements of modernity understood themselves to be free. They were free because, firstly, they could reflexively distinguish themselves from nature and secondly, because they could imagine new and better worlds. Consequently, they were not *things*. Given the rule of reason, all social processes were under social control (and therefore the inability to control became the fault of the vestiges of the flawed past). Indeed, there was no other controlling agency anyway.

11

The tradition of modernity offers one leading candidate to explain the awareness of freedom which developed in Europe during, and shortly before, the eighteenth century. That candidate is the Death of God. In other words, it might be suggested that the self-sufficiency and independence of the social could be recognized and acknowledged to the extent that the extra element of the deity was seen to be of decreasing explanatory value. Of course, such an account is useful. The Enlightenment project of the rule of reason could only launch an offensive against any notions of rigidity which wrapped some relationships, and all explanations, inside mysteries and enigmas. But the line of the Death of God would lead to a simple, monocausal account for the social forms which prevailed in Europe for the two centuries or so after the mid-eighteenth century. That approach would see modernity more or less exclusively as an event in the history of ideas.

Now, whilst Feher and Heller might go a little too far, there is more than a germ of validity to their objection that a 'monocausal explanation of any kind is either a self-delusion or an ideology' (Feher and Heller 1983: 212). The interpretation of modernity as the result of disenchantment alone must be able to make a plausible leap from the history of ideas to specific social practices. But that would involve a search for some principle of action which is outside of ideas. After all, modernity involved practical attempts to make and remake the world as a better place. The narratives and hermeneutic systems of modernity involved a lot more than idle speculation. The full richness and complexity of modernity, and especially the confusion over the problem of sovereignty, can be perhaps only appreciated if monocausal explanations are indeed avoided and, instead, an account is developed which can bring together both social ideas *and* social practices. That itself can only be achieved by a concentration on the social processes which underpinned the recognition of freedom.

Feher and Heller rightly link freedom to the imagination and practice of alternative social arrangements. But, to reiterate the difficulty, it must be asked how those imaginations of the *better* world were possible and, indeed, why they proved to be so inspirational. The world could be made a better place simply because, by the end of the eighteenth century, reason was said to have created a blueprint of how society should be constructed if it were to be close to the standards of the perfect order. The world was made better to the extent that what people did got nearer to what it was said that they should do. Similarly, the social order was said to be better to the extent that it was founded upon reason and not tradition. Modernity involved the assumption of the ability of the independent freedom of social relationships to make a new and self-sufficient social order. It embodied concerns with the plan or programme.

Those few comments in part follow the lead of writers like Mary Douglas who identify social order as a social construction. The comments do not follow the lead of the social scientific orthodoxies which see order as a normative state or as a condition of equilibrium. Those approaches merely reify the question of order and, therefore, try to put some existing social features beyond question by making them beyond proper social intervention. As Douglas has said, 'Order implies restriction; from all possible materials, a limited selection has been made and from all possible relations a limited set has been used' (Douglas 1966: 94). That is, social order is *created* through the idealization of some relationships and practices, and the forcible exclusion of the legitimacy of others. It is a choice, a programme. Elsewhere, Douglas has commented that, 'Order stands for classification, the symbolic system. This dimension can vary in coherence and scope' (Douglas 1975: 217). Social order is *not* immanent within social relationships, rather it is a symbolic reality which has to be practised and made.

Social order is a social construction; a practical and a cognitive system which seeks to make the world intelligible and which is especially concerned to consolidate and confirm the definite place of men and women within the order of things. Social order is the attempt to divide the world into different intellectual categories and then practically force things into those restricted groups. Anything which cannot be fitted into a group without some ambivalence is thus rendered as an affront to normality. The system of order deals with that effrontery through strategies of exclusion which either exclude on the basis of a quasi-magical exceptionality (the exception proves the rule) or on the basis of inadequacy (the rule proves the exception).

The history of modernity tells the story of the imposition of plans which upheld the wonderful, magical status of some exceptional groups (and perhaps unsurprisingly it was usually

13

that very group which tried to impose that plan, or which promised to benefit from it), combined with attempts to exterminate the horrible exception of others. The problem of social order is one of knitting together all those who are 'the same' whilst also distancing all those who are 'other'. The techniques of distanciation will radically vary depending upon whether the 'other' is pushed outside on a basis of strength or of weakness. Social order is only totally coherent and indeed, unconsciously accepted, to the extent that there are no social groups which slide over the clear symbolic division of the profusion of things.

The point is that during the seventeenth, but especially the eighteenth, centuries, there was a profound increase in the sheer volume of those slimy, ambivalent groups and individuals which escaped clear classification. The profusion of things began to flop over the old order of things, which precisely through its antiquity was accepted as natural and immutable. Instead, the system and constructions of order became categories to be reflexively considered. This was largely due to the social process of urbanization. 'The towns are so many electric transformers. They increase tension, accelerate the rhythm of exchange and ceaselessly stir up men's lives' (Braudel 1973: 373). (For more on the impact of urbanization, see Harvey 1985.) The rigid world which was conceived as without alternative (because it had been like it was for so long), the milieu which made the social an extension of the natural, was not only predominantly rural; it was also interpreted through highly coherent and largely static, systems of order. More or less by definition, those worlds bore only a faint mark of social activity. Indeed, the universe was defined as an overbearing and tremendous power which would take revenge if women and men transgressed out of their small place in the order of things (that is, if the social became ambivalent).

Similarly, social relationships were made rigid. Most social life occurred in relatively restricted geographical spaces, where the limits of the social geography and the social order could be directly transposed upon one another. Where the boundaries of one finally encountered the unambiguously other, where the boundaries of the one were turned into high walls, so were the boundaries of the other. The alternative was simply nothingness. Consequently, there was no *imaginable* alternative. There was no freedom.

But, 'Europe's ... towns were marked by an unparalleled freedom. They had developed as autonomous worlds and according to their own propensities' (Braudel 1973: 396). Urbanization can, perhaps, be read as a representation and symbol of the Enlightenment (but I am not saying that the two were therefore entirely synchronous). Enlightenment itself was a predominantly urban phenomenon. If the systems of social order are founded upon the socially constructed discrimination of things, then with the entrenchment of urbanization, new things have to be classified. Compared to the village, the reality of urban existence is fast, in perpetual flux and massive: 'The metropolis exacts from man as a discriminating creature a different amount of consciousness than does rural life' (Simmel 1950: 410). The universe which had to be classified was no longer static. After all, the very word *urbanization* implies a continuing process whereas terms such as 'country life', 'the rural', and so forth indicate solid, definite conditions. As such, social order itself became more variable in the course of the eighteenth century. Certainly, it was still coherent, but it was also potentially more open-ended. It articulated greater degrees of freedom. It implicitly accepted that there was nothing immutable and, moreover, that if the order of things *could be* changed, it *should be* changed for the best in accordance with the demands of reason (and to repeat, reason was evidently the best knowledge because it was free of superstition and the encrustations of tradition).

All of this happened because the process of urbanization exacerbated the difficulty which all systems of order ultimately have to confront, and yet which they attempt to avoid. We know where we are in the world if we meet only friends and enemies, fellow townsfolk, or foreigners, but all our orderly understandings collapse when we are forced to meet the stranger. The stranger, she or he who should be distant but is near, is perhaps the basic unit of urbanized social relationships. All our urban neighbours are potential or actual strangers since they can change with a rapidity which would have been unthinkable in social worlds which were spatially and temporally more restricted. But, as Fernand Braudel has said: 'A town would probably cease to exist without its supply of new people. It attracts them ... They come ... because first the countryside and also other towns no longer want and reject them' (Braudel 1973: 380). The stranger is neither one thing nor the other; the stranger might be a friend, but then again the stranger might be an enemy. There is absolutely no prior way of knowing or of pre-ordering this experience. In the towns and cities of the eighteenth century, and ever since, individuals had to meet strangers during nearly every waking minute of every day. Consequently, the systems of order had to allow for legitimate alternatives. They could not claim to be the single and exclusive reality (an allowance which was increasingly necessary thanks to global communication as well). After all, the stranger has to come from somewhere, and she or he might turn out to be a friend. And when the stranger becomes a friend, the world is changed; the difficulty then becomes one of making sure that it is changed for the best. Modernity was the era and the attitude of a kind of freedom because it was also the milieu of the stranger.

In Georg Simmel's famous definition, the stranger is, 'the person who comes today and stays tomorrow' (Simmel 1950: 402). The stranger is a social contradiction; she or he should not be here, but she or he is here. The presence of the stranger can only undermine any systems of order which derive all their coherence from a time and place which is seen as essentially unchanging. 'He [i.e. the stranger] did not belong "initially", "originally", "from the very start", "since time immemorial". The memory of the event of his coming makes of his very presence an event in history, rather than a fact of nature' (Bauman 1990: 149. See also Bauman 1988, 1989).

Following Lévi-Strauss, it might be said that the historical presence of the stranger causes a *heating up* of otherwise *cold societies*. Cold societies, 'create the minimum of that disorder which the physicists call "entropy", and they tend to remain indefinitely in their initial state, and this explains why they appear to us as static societies with no history' (Lévi-Strauss 1969: 33). That is precisely the situation which broadly prevailed through Europe before the seventeenth and eighteenth centuries, and exactly the situation which was changed so much by the ideational domination of reason and the material process of urbanization. Both events, which stimulated, and were stimulated by, the presence of strangers, caused social relationships to be inserted into history. Since the moment of the stranger's arrival could be remembered, it was also the case that it was possible to imagine alternative ways of understanding and classifying the world. Urbanization freed social life from a too-close embeddedness in the landscape and from supernatural explanations of the perpetually restricted place of the social. The stranger gave social imagination the freedom to roam throughout the entire universe.

As Simmel realized so clearly, the point is that the modern stranger does not go away. She or he must be accommodated or assimilated by order. She or he is potentially always here (and potentiality itself implies a degree of freedom). Before the eighteenth century the social meaning of the stranger was fairly certain. She or he was, 'the wanderer who comes today and goes tomorrow' (Simmel 1950: 402). The pre-modern stranger of the cold societies was a transitory, fugitive figure. As soon as the stranger wandered into the wilderness beyond the town boundaries (which was depicted on the maps as a blank space where there be dragons), she or he ceased to be a difficulty for social order. The temporary presence of the stranger posed no threat to the system of order; consequently, it could maintain a very high level of internal and exclusive coherence. Indeed, anyone who lived outside of the limits of order was reduced to a questionable humanity.

The pre-modern strangeness was absolute. The modern strangeness was negotiable. Most of this can be seen in Shakespeare, and especially in *King Lear*. In the play, the heath beyond the castle walls is identified as a place where humans lose their social clothing and become mere beasts: 'unaccommodated man is no more but such a poor, bare, forked animal as thou art'. In other words, the pre-modern strangeness of strangers was quite complete. They came from, and indeed represented, a place where social order had not stretched. When social life was carried out on a relatively restricted canvas, the blank areas could be established as the realm which explained all offences against order. There was just the known and warm inside, and the barren, empty outside.

But with the onset of urbanization, the blank spaces were gradually coloured in. Ironically, as the spatial basis of social relationships was gradually massified and concentrated, the power and extra-sociality of the barren wastes diminished. Instead of being an immutable 'otherness', the wastes were redefined as places which would be socialized and ordered eventually. They did not have to be always 'beyond'. The formerly absolute outsider was turned into a potential future insider. The social world was pluralized. Certainly, urbanization represented a consolidation of social life, but it also meant that the full force of social relationships could be launched from a far firmer base, and aimed far more accurately at the chosen targets (see also Ignatieff 1984: 50).

The abilities and extent of social order was subject to a kind of capillary movement which started in the seventeenth century, but became more powerful in the eighteenth century. On the one hand, the foundations of the system of order were pulled firmly within the towns (the urban became the central site of social consciousness), but on the other hand the extent of the system spread everywhere. As such, the problem of what to do with strangers became ever greater. They were no longer outsiders; now, the strangers were actually or potentially exactly like the friends. Consequently, either the strangers were invested with special abilities, and thus confirmed in their strangeness because they were people apart, or the strangers were defined as filth and thus demanding of a forcible expulsion from the stable world.

The problem was, then, that thanks to urbanization, the proximity of strangers was an especially pressing issue by the late eighteenth century. But people were not strange simply and only because they were inhabiting social spaces where they should not have been. Many were also strangers because they upheld hermeneutic and practical programmes which were cosmopolitan and thus freed from the reifications of pre-modern relationships. Some people were not just free to come and go; some also imagined alternative worlds on the grounds that they had access to knowledge which was emancipated from any purely local embeddedness.

The cognitive universe of Europe before the eighteenth century betrayed little in the way of assumptions of the independent freedom and possible plurality of the social terrain. Indeed, it is reasonable to suggest that much the same interpretations of social relationships prevailed throughout the continent and, by their very extent, denied the possibility of any alternative systems. The same knowledge wholly saturated everything, everywhere, and thus became reified through a double process of, firstly, its extra-sociality (it must be beyond social interference because it is the same everywhere) and, secondly, its inscription in the restricted time and place (it must be embedded in the present arrangements otherwise the knowledge would be without social relevance).

For example, even during the period of the Enlightenment and pronounced urbanization, the intellectual life of rural France was profoundly restricted. A survey of the reading habits of the small number of literate peasants was carried out in the 1790s. It gave clear results: 'It shows a world of superstitious beliefs, trivial fables and long-standing prejudices' (Chartier 1988: 160). The rustic libraries were typically pre-modern; they reinforced and deepened the belief and practice that the world was quite simply the way it must be. The cognitive universe was as restricted and invariant as the social universe. For the peasants who could read, the books simply confirmed what they already knew, and told them what they had already been told.

But, for a few, books could be the tools with which different worlds might be made. And, not at all coincidentally, the circulation and internationalism of the publishing and printing industry increased hand in hand with urbanization. Rousseau's *Confessions* provide an especially clear illustration of the potential impact of books. Whilst a child, Rousseau had access to the library of his maternal grandfather who had been a Protestant minister. Rousseau believed that this library was of a quite unique sort, special even amongst the libraries of the literate: 'Luckily, there were some good books in it; in fact, it could hardly have been otherwise, for the library had been collected by ... a learned man according to the fashion of the day; ... a man of taste and intellect' (Rousseau 1931: 4–5). The library was to some extent strange in relation to the milieu in which it had been collected (and Rousseau is explicitly saying that it needed a special sort of person to possess a collection of this kind). It had a large section devoted to the ancient authors, and it was their impact, and especially the impact of Plutarch, which made Rousseau an intellectual stranger (later, of course, Rousseau became a spatial and a social stranger as well). He recalled: 'I lost my identity in that of the individual whose life I was reading; the recitals of the qualities of endurance and intrepidity which arrested my attention made my eyes glisten and strengthened my voice' (Rousseau 1931: 5). Of course, Rousseau was rather prone to hyperbole, but the effect should be clear.

19

For the peasantry, as typical and indubitably rural inhabitants, the way of things was quite unalterable. The peasants' imaginative universe merely demonstrated and confirmed the inability to define the social as anything other than an extension of the natural world. But for Rousseau, with his head full of the ancients, and indeed for people like Rousseau, the imaginative universe was free of the present and, for that matter, critical of it. As such, Rousseau became a *double stranger*. On the one hand he was to some extent the archetypal modern who comes today and stays tomorrow, whilst on the other hand, his cognitive interpretations drew upon a cosmopolitanism which continued irrespective of local circumstances. Moreover, that cosmopolitanism demonstrated the self-sufficiency of the social; its new lack of need to refer to the supernatural. The cosmopolitanism also relied upon completely social and known channels of communication. Rousseau might well have lived in Geneva, or Paris, or wherever, but intellectually he was always somewhere else as well.

The case of Rousseau perfectly illustrates the proximity of the stranger in conditions of modernity. Firstly, *recognizable* strangers are all around (thanks to urbanization) whilst, secondly, individuals might be *intellectual* strangers (thanks to cosmopolitan communication networks). This meant one thing: whilst the stranger was the representative of social freedom, of alternative, of the possibility of another world, those strangers who were *doubly* strange (because their odd spatial situation combined with a cosmopolitan imagination) were *the* representatives of modernity. In their very person they distilled the freedom of the social from the natural and the self-sufficiency of reason. These *double strangers* were outside of the orders of everyday life but they were not at all abhorrent. On the contrary they were rather magical or, at the very least, invested with unique abilities.

Intellectuals were elevated to the position of being the governors and legislators of modernity. They were *the* double strangers, and therefore they had the ability to rule. But the equation of the double stranger with a specific social position or practice (the intellectual, the person 'in the know') only added another dimension to the strangeness. After all, intellectuals actually are not necessary. Their very existence as a specific and self-conscious social group indicates the ability of social relationships to create and maintain their own realities. That is, the existence of intellectuals as magical strangers *par excellence* demonstrates nothing other than the most profound awareness of social freedom. The intellectuals were the agents of social self-reflexivity, and thus they were more free (because more strange) than any other social group.

The social position of the intellectual in modernity, the combination of exclusive abilities, strangeness, and freedom from the system of social order (and the difficulties which that freedom might create, and the qualifications it might entail to the legislative claims), is clearly illustrated in Henrik Ibsen's play, *An Enemy of the People* (1988). It could even be said that if Borges is right and, 'universal history is the history of the different intonations given a handful of metaphors' (Borges 1970: 227), then the universe of European modernity is illuminated in the different social, political, and cultural intonations which are contained in Ibsen's play.

The narrative of *An Enemy of the People* is on the surface quite simple. It tells the story of Thomas Stockmann who is employed as the doctor at the public baths of a small provincial holiday resort. The town is building a prosperous tourist industry on the therapeutic qualities of the waters, but Stockmann discovers that the baths are polluted. The play charts the downfall of Thomas Stockmann; at first he is an admired and popular participant in the community and his discovery is enthusiastically supported by the pillars of public opinion. But as it dawns on the community that Stockmann's discovery entails the closure of the baths and the collapse of the local economy, he is subjected to more and more abuse until, finally, he is thrown out of home and work. Ibsen managed to provide a parable on the hurdles which must be overcome if the world is to be made a better place, if it is to be freed from pollution.

Interestingly, however, Ibsen does not believe that the local community is able to improve itself without outside assistance. The indigenous resources are not adequate. The townspeople are presented as essentially ignorant or selfish dullards who will admit of no alternatives simply because they are too scared. The townspeople participate in the existing social arrangements because they are quite unable to reflexively imagine other forms. The locals are not free; but Thomas Stockmann is. Ibsen goes to great lengths to show that Stockmann, and the people who support him, are strangers to the existing, reified relationships.

21

As such, Ibsen created the figure of an archetypal governor of European modernity. Ibsen's point is that Stockmann's social freedom, his strangeness, allows him to practise a degree of reflexivity which rightly establishes him as an Enlightened legislator.

Thomas Stockmann's status as a stranger who has only an ambivalent connection with the restricted social system is complex and multidimensional. Indeed, Stockmann's biographical record of coming today and staying tomorrow is presented as something like the foundation and origin of his social status. Because Stockmann spent some time in the wastelands of the North, in an episode which is treated almost as a ritual purification and cleansing (Stockmann as Christ), he is able to distinguish the truly immutable and natural from the historical, social, and changeable. As Thomas Stockmann says to his tediously and stubbornly parochial brother, the Mayor:

> Well, you can't see it as clearly as I can, of course. All your life you've lived amongst this kind of thing, and it doesn't make the same sharp impression on you. But think of me, living all those years in the North, cut off from everything, hardly ever seeing a new face, never the chance of any decent conversation ... for me it's like coming to some great throbbing metropolis.
>
> (Ibsen 1988: 8)

Stockmann experiences the social world as something which is *there* rather than *here* as it presumably was for the Mayor. Stockmann is only able to uncover the truth of the baths and, as the play progresses, the truth of the local social relationships of power, because he is ambivalently free in relation to them. Thomas Stockmann experiences the strange freedom and the perpetual ambivalence of the metropolis whereas the small-minded and unimaginative townsfolk interpret exactly the same relationships through a coherent and invariant hermeneutic grid of classification which mirrors the tight and invariant world of apparently natural social hierarchies.

But Stockmann's status as a stranger goes even further than simply his own coming and staying. His proof that the water is polluted comes from outside of the local community, by post from the regional University. Meanwhile, Stockmann's only firm supporters are his free-thinking daughter, who at one point refuses to translate an English story about divine providence (Ibsen 1988: 51–52) and a sea captain who is planning a voyage to America. Indeed, throughout the play, the daughter, Petra, follows her father like a shadow. Of course, both educated young women and sailors are themselves strangers to fixed and unalterable social systems. Indeed, they threaten those very systems. Ibsen associates truth with a disembeddedness which is both geographical and intellectual; he is saying that only those who experience existing arrangements from a complex, critical (i.e. distant) proximity can stimulate any sort of movement away from habit and tradition (Thomas Stockmann openly mocks the traditional badges of the Mayor's authority (Ibsen 1988: 62)).

Stockmann, his knowledge, and his supporters, are all symbolic representations of freedom. They are the social representations of the possibility of difference. At first, their exceptional status in relation to the invariant constructions of the social order is dealt with through strategies of exclusion on the basis of quasi-magical specialness. Stockmann himself contributes to the creation of those intimations of exceptionality. Subsequently, the strangeness is met with forcible strategies of excoriation. In the opening two or three acts, Thomas Stockmann is usually some sort of *visitor* who causes things to happen. He is rarely already present. In the first act he enters his own house *after* traditional figures of social order are already in place (corrupt journalists, the Mayor, the housewife). The second act opens with Stockmann declaring a desire to do, 'things *for* the town', rather than with it or in it (Ibsen 1988: 22, emphasis added). In the third act, he adds honesty to a previously pompous conversation in the newspaper office. It is not until Act IV that he has to enter a social situation which is already vibrant without his stimulation.

The point is that before the almost Sophoclean moment of the fourth act, Thomas Stockmann is always coming and going more or less as he pleases, from a position of some authority. It is always him, and only him, who initiates and animates practices and imaginations of a new and better world. The arrivals of the Mayor are associated only with images of the arrival of more of the same. In other words, for the first part of the play, Stockmann is presented as a *historical figure* whose very strangeness forces social subjects to reflect upon the foundations of their own common-sense assumptions. Stockmann is freedom; a status which is confirmed by his title of Doctor (an achieved rather than ascribed status), a title which confirms some special and unique ability to beneficially administer to the true needs of an anaesthetized or moribund patient. Stockmann was the double and magical stranger.

That position gave Stockmann great powers which he quickly rationalized and justified as rights. The most basic of those rights was the ability to inspire, and if need be incite, the recognition of improved social arrangements. Stockmann entirely accepted the Enlightenment position of the self-sufficiency and yet practical significance of purely intellectual constructions. After all, 'if a man's got hold of some new idea he has a duty to bring it to the notice of the public'. Stockmann's brother merely reiterated the categories of the invariant order when he replied that 'the public doesn't need new ideas. The public is best served by the good old, accepted ideas it already has' (Ibsen 1988: 37). Stockmann's position was that precisely due to his distance from order, and yet proximity to lived social relationships, he was able to make the society reflect on its own history and indulge in improving practices. Both of those reflexive moments could, however, only be carried out under the guidance of the exceptional, and therefore sovereign, strangers.

All the time that the claims to magical strangeness could be made without dispute, the position of the new legislators like Thomas Stockmann was more or less inviolable. They were people apart, and what they lacked in quantity they more than made up in quality. 'I'll be damned if ... it's right that the fools should dominate the intelligent ... The majority has the might ... but it hasn't right. I am right – I and one or two other individuals like me' (Ibsen 1988: 76). The social impact of that typically modern thesis (which, however, hints at Plato) was quite immense, as the fierce language indicated. Stockmann utterly repudiated the notion, 'that the common man, and all the ignorant and immature elements in society have the same right to criticize and to approve, to govern and to counsel as the few intellectually distinguished people' (Ibsen 1988: 78).

Stockmann was magical and possessed of greater rights to govern so long as he could proclaim the independence and the freedom of the knowledge that the baths were polluted. As soon as people began to think that the claim might owe more than a little to the grinding of personal axes, Stockmann's purity was disastrously and utterly corrupted. As soon as the locals started to whisper that perhaps the freedom of knowledge was not all that it seemed to be and that, in fact, Thomas Stockmann might have said that the baths were polluted simply in order to take arrogant revenge on his successful brother, the magic of strangeness dissipated into thin air. All that was left was a troublesome outsider. As Milan Kundera has noted, it does not take too much for titles like 'Doctor' and 'intellectual' to be transformed from symbols of the magical and into slurs (Kundera 1982: 5). (George Orwell also realized that, and whenever he used the word 'intellectual', a contemptuous sneer was never too far away.) The point is that the free and self-sufficient knowledge of modernity was putatively meant to be upheld by free and independent intellectuals. But whenever knowledge was however loosely tied to self-interest, the strangers became little more than traitors to modernity.

That was exactly the fate of Thomas Stockmann. His problems began as soon as the thought arose that he had impetuously invented a story about pollution. Aslaksen the printer put the doubts plainly: 'I . . . believe there is some ulterior motive behind the Doctor's agitation. He talks about the baths but what he's really after is revolution' (Ibsen 1988: 71). The legislative implications of strangeness were thus reworked. Stockmann was accused of hiding selfish and highly volatile imaginations behind the mask of purification in the North and the cosmopolitanism of knowledge. He was accused of being an outsider who was trying to inflame social relationships simply for his own ends. He ceased to be magical and became a man much like any other; *but he could not be like any other because he was a stranger.* Consequently, Stockmann ceased to be an adequate participant in social relationships, and thus he had to be forcibly thrown out if social order was to be maintained. The old, rigid interpretations slammed shut against anyone who flopped across the reconfirmed boundaries. Cosmopolitanism and strangeness became unholy stigmata. The 'compact majority' had to be mobilized as the force which would carry out the expulsion. After all, 'Any man who wants to destroy a whole community must be a public enemy' (Ibsen 1988: 82). And no one threatens the life of a community like the unwanted stranger who lives inside it.

Ibsen's message is that any community or society which turns its back on the cosmopolitan strangers is doomed to wallow in ignorance, superstition, and stupidity. It is only the magical double stranger who can animate and guide the search for alternative, practical social arrangements. It is only the double stranger, archetypically only the intellectual, who can truly be called the sovereign legislator and governor of modernity. Only the few individuals like Thomas Stockmann and, it should be said, Henrik Ibsen, know what will make the world a better place because only they are sufficiently distant from the accepted reifications. The sociological point, however, is that with the progressive deepening and confirmation of urbanization as the central terrain in the social ordering of things, the sheer number and proximity of these strangers increased exponentially. The myth of modernity (magical strangers rule) was undermined by the material circumstances of modernity (all literate town dwellers are actually or potentially magical strangers). The two sovereigns rear their heads; on the one hand modernity accepted the claims to sovereignty which could be made by individuals like Stockmann, and yet on the other hand it accepted the sovereignty of all double strangers.

All of this talk of fictional characters might be just a little frivolous, and this analysis might be just a bit too rhetorical, were it not for the fact that the story of Thomas Stockmann bears an extremely close relationship to one of the founding texts of European modernity. Immanuel Kant's short but famous essay of 1784, 'An Answer to the Question: "What is Enlightenment?"' mirrors and anticipates many of the experiences of Thomas Stockmann (Kant 1970). In the essay, Kant tried to sketch the outlines of a new moment in the history of Europe, just as Stockmann tried to cajole the provincial town into a new era of freedom. There are more similarities; Stockmann was able to make his claims because he was a stranger, and so was Kant; Stockmann thought that the peculiar blend of critical distance and proximity made him a person apart who knew what was best, and so did Kant. The only difference is that where Stockmann ultimately foundered on the reefs of habit and self-interest, Kant did not. Rather, Kant actually became something of the legislator which he thought he should be. Immanuel Kant was able to maintain and consolidate his magical apartness. Kant possessed access to the resources which made his *oughts* so many *cans*.

The profundity of Kant's strangeness from the order he was talking to and about should not be underestimated. Kant's own social position reflected a multidimensional social freedom which perhaps inevitably led to the development of a reflexive and self-sufficient awareness. Kant was rather divorced from the everyday practices of women and men who were dependent upon traditional knowledge and age-old (and therefore reified) authority structures. He was the first of the important modern philosophers to earn a living as a university professor. That is, Kant's social role produced no wealth whatsoever. It was entirely predicated upon the assumption that the intellect can be sufficient unto itself and, moreover, that the users of the intellect (intellectuals) should be financed by other social participants. Kant was not speaking from the habitual sites of social authority which questioned everything but themselves. On the contrary, Kant's message came from the prestigious, influential, and authoritative, position of the Chair in Logic and Metaphysics at Konigsberg. Moreover, Kant was probably something of a stranger even amongst professors since he was essentially what would later be called a 'working-class intellectual' (his father was a harnessmaker; typically his mother's status seems to be unrecorded).

But Kant's strangeness went yet further. Kant was speaking to and for an emergent social class in late eighteenth-century Prussia. This class consisted in the state functionaries and embryonic capitalists who were excluded from the traditional positions of authority and power because of their lowly birth. This class was highly educated in the ways of reason. It was a class which looked beyond purely national boundaries for its wealth and intellectual stimulation, a class which the existing system was unprepared to assimilate. A class which was drenched in the possibility of alternative social arrangements and which, therefore, was aware of nothing so much that any social order is not natural and immutable. Norbert Elias noticed the peculiar situation of Kant and, rightly, identified Kant's work as representing the social imaginations of a 'stratum far removed from political activity, scarcely thinking in political terms and only tentatively in national ones, whose legitimation consists primarily in its intellectual, scientific, or artistic *accomplishments*' (Elias 1978: 9).

The emphasis upon achievement (and remember, Stockmann was a doctor), necessarily presupposes the existence and importance of freedom. In the traditional authority structures, the individual *achieved* nothing; she or he was simply what she or he was. Kant and the others were what they made of themselves. Their expressions represented relentless accomplishment on the one hand, and yet exclusion from the conventional positions of authority on the other. In their own inimitable way, Karl Marx and Frederick Engels put the matter a little more acidly; they linked Kant's work to, 'the impotence, depression and wretchedness of the German burghers, whose petty interests were never capable of developing into the common, national interests of a class' (Marx and Engels 1970: 97).

Kant was totally removed from the order and social life which he was discussing; and simply by virtue of his personal involvement with free achievement and a rising social class, he was able to make claims to a magical apartness. His magical position could be maintained in a variety of ways. Firstly, through the adoption of highly specialized manners (as Elias has emphasized), secondly, by an ostensible refusal to prejudice the prestige of being a professor by accusations of self-interest (the myth of all intellectuals: 'I did it for knowledge!'), and thirdly, by a refusal to condemn the existing authority structures too much. It should also be remembered of course that Kant was not alone. Whilst the rising social class might not have been too large, it was large enough and, importantly, rich enough, to be able to ignore certain others. By its own terms, it had quality. Thomas Stockmann was not so politically astute and he was alone. It was not too hard for his magical strangeness to be socially redefined as nothing more than a pollution which should be got rid of.

The difference in support explains why Kant could speak with a tremendous amount of authority, and for that matter claim institutional protection, whilst Stockmann (and his like) ended up as forgotten, broken, and rather bitter individuals. Essentially, Kant could get away with his suggestions that all the participants in habitual social relationships were so many ignorant fools, but Stockmann could not, simply because Kant played his cards well and Stockmann played his alone. Kant was magical because he had the ability to make unchallengeable claims of special access to reason whereas Stockmann did not. Stockmann's magic was dependent upon the definitions of others, and as such it was no magic at all.

Kant's 1784 essay plays on the distinction between those who are already free, and who owe their position to achievement, and those who remain tied to reified habits (and scorn was never entirely absent when he mentioned the latter) (Kant 1970). Kant's consolidated and richly textured magical strangeness had an immense social impact. It gave him and his like an ability to argue that they knew how to make the world a better place. That improvement basically involved the recognition and practice of self-sufficiency:

> *Enlightenment is man's emergence from his self-incurred immaturity. Immaturity* is the inability to use one's own understanding without the guidance of another. This immaturity is *self-incurred* if its cause is not lack of understanding, but lack of resolution and courage to use it without the guidance of another. The motto of enlightenment is therefore: *Sapere aude!* Have courage to use your *own* understanding.
>
> (Kant 1970: 54)

The motto of enlightenment might have well been one of freedom, and it was asserting a most profound independence, but it was also a strange motto. It is expressed in cosmopolitan and exclusive Latin, when the rest of the paragraph was originally in native and widespread German. That is of more than stylistic importance. Kant assumed that his readers would be able to translate the two key words into the vernacular (as does Kant's translator) and, as such, he was perhaps speaking to rather less people than his avowed audience of, 'the entire reading public'. But even that audience was not too large. Indeed the mere ability to read and have access to the latest despatches from Konigsberg itself signified a degree of strangeness in eighteenth-century Europe. Significantly, Kant was not appealing to people who could read but, rather, to a *self-aware reading constituency*. Benedict Anderson has made the point well: 'If we note that as late as 1840, even in Britain and France, the most advanced states in Europe, almost half the population was still illiterate ... reading classes meant people of some power' (Anderson 1983: 73). Kant thought that Enlightenment would make the world a better place because it would make social relationships free and self-sufficient, but he also thought that the sovereign act of the making was restricted to a new, urban, and *strange*, social group.

The effort to achieve emancipation from reification was quite immense. As Kant said, in a passage which is perhaps merely a

29

celebration of his own strangeness: 'only a few, by cultivating their own minds, have succeeded in freeing themselves from immaturity and continuing boldly on their way' (Kant 1970: 55). Everybody else had given up on the struggle because they were said to be either too lazy or too cowardly (Kant 1970: 54). The enlightened were, then, possessed of both a great strength and a magical insight. Indeed, it was precisely because Enlightenment required such a tremendous effort of free thought that the knowledge of what was for the best was worth having. The image of some kind of ritual purification comes to the fore once more. Again, the narrative asserts that only the double strangers, who exist in alternative intellectual worlds and in free social spaces, can free the world from habit and superstition. Only the magical strangers can make the world a better place because only they have no personal axes to grind.

Kant helped to establish a fundamental dialectic at the heart of the question of sovereignty. He equated the ability to make and imagine new worlds with the sovereign stranger who had managed to struggle free of the mundane reality of daily life. Kant emphasized the status of the doubly strange individual as the almost heroic leader of an internally anonymous and faceless collective. Yet, Kant knew that as the process of Enlightenment progressed, as more people were woken from their somnambulism, the number of those sovereign individuals would increase. Again, the problem of two sovereigns reappears; is sovereignty a collective issue under the guidance of some magical elite, or rather is it an individual affair? Kant could give no definite answer.

Kant was clever enough to argue that the exclusivity of the magical should be maintained at all costs. He argued that the state should defend the strangers so that the restricted and stupid provincials would not be able to redefine strangeness as a pollution. After all, the monarch had certain duties towards the magical strangers: 'it is his business to stop anyone forcibly hindering others from working as best they can to define and promote their salvation' (Kant 1970: 58). The state was thus put into a curious situation. On the one hand, it had to maintain one kind of exclusiveness which was incompatible with the existing system of order because of its double strangeness. But, on the other hand, it had to be able to ruthlessly seek out and destroy the other strangers who could not establish the legitimacy of their own abilities and who, instead, became merely people who were out of place.

The state was involved in a dual strategy of assimilation and expulsion; Kant and his group were to some degree eventually assimilated, or at least accommodated, because they were too powerful to be excluded, whilst the individuals like Thomas Stockmann were excluded because they were too strange (because too weak) to be included. The modern state operated in such a way as to deal with, and make intelligible, the prestige of some strangers and yet the abhorrence of other strangers. Indeed, the modern state accepted the importance of the legislative claims and resources of the magical strangers. The two different poles of the status of strangers are important sites of social dispute. The definitions of magic or filth are not once and for all. They have to be produced and reproduced. If they did not, Thomas Stockmann would not have experienced the circumstances of both within a matter of a few days. (For more on the state and strangers, see Bauman 1990.)

All strangers are confronted with the possibility of their own annihilation. As such, all have to try to make themselves magical and, indeed, put that status beyond social contradiction through practices of naturalization. This is more than a little ironic. Modernity was indivisible from the recognition that there was a sharp distinction between the social and the natural. Indeed, the practices and the narratives of modernity involved the creation of that distinction. And yet that social group which was *the* representation of social freedom could only make its position incontestable by making it seem as if it were natural. That is, the protagonists of alternative tried to reify their own position. The project of naturalization took two main forms. Firstly, the magical strangers, the intellectuals, indulged in practices of social closure against outsiders. As already indicated, they started to talk in obscure languages, adopted peculiar habits, and tried to establish that, as Russell Jacoby might have said, a faculty address in some way signifies special abilities. All of these themes gelled in the definition of the intellectual as a special type of person, an idea which reached one highpoint in the work of Nietzsche and Ortega y Gasset.

But, perhaps more importantly and seriously, the magical strangers tried to eradicate (cognitively and perhaps even physically) other, competing, stranger groups which might have been able to make social relationships reflexively aware of their own historical origins. As such, intellectuals went about such things as codifying national languages (and therefore discrediting regional 'dialects'; this perhaps explains the political importance of language in the many parts of Europe where strangers are an especially great problem (see Anderson 1983, and also Kosztolanyi 1987, Skvorecky 1990)). The intellectuals as governors also developed alleged sciences of fitness for the brave new world. Some strangers were also able to naturalize their apartness, and put it beyond any reasonable doubt, because they ingratiated themselves with the state apparatus (lest it be turned against them. Kant was not averse to indulging in a little bit of sycophancy) and because they discredited anyone else who might claim to be speaking the truth of reason and freedom. Where those projects of the naturalization of exclusivity worked, where one group was able to speak for all strangers, sovereignty was defined as a collective phenomenon in need of firm leadership. Where those projects failed, where there was no totalization of the experience of strangeness, sovereignty became an individual question.

In sum, then, modernity was born in the moment of social freedom which was created by the blending of the Enlightenment and urbanization. That freedom is represented in the figure of the stranger. But the difficulty of modernity was precisely that each and every stranger was potentially outside of the constructions of order without which social relationships and social interpretations of the world would have been quite impossible. The problems of modernity were, then, nothing if not immensely complex since all the promises of freedom and social self-sufficiency could only be realized by the very social groups which were potentially also open to anathematization. That difficulty was avoided in so far as certain groups which were doubly strange could claim to possess certain magical abilities which set them apart from everyone else, and to the extent that they could make their exclusive position and practices seem quite natural and, therefore, outside of the social realm which was in all other respects utterly changeable. When that double strangeness could not be legitimated, the strangers were subjected to violent expulsion.

Modernity was a paradox. Its practices, arrangements, and interpretations tried to change the entire universe of social relationships, and yet the sovereigns who were meant to achieve that universal and total transformation operated from a critical distance. The sovereigns assumed that everyone else was wallowing in the ignorance of reification, and so they set about animating them. The insiders could not change themselves without the outside assistance which the magical strangers promised to offer. The proof of the success of the magic was measured by the extent to which all the weak strangers, all the pollutants of the new future, had been pushed away. The arrangements of modernity strived for homogeneity; but that struggle could only be waged by sovereign groups or individuals who were in some way heterogeneous.

2

GARDENS

Certainly, modernity was lived through the *leitmotif* that the world could and should be made a better place. That was to be achieved through the free use and practical activities of entirely social resources. But that narrative confidence was frequently little more than a heavily plastered facade which shakily masked a whole collection of doubts and conflicts. The institutions and the arrangements of modernity might have known *why* to go on, yet the problems of *how* to go on, and indeed the identity of the fellow travellers on the journey, were rather harder to resolve. Perhaps the explanation is not too difficult to find. Although modernity was indeed the proclamation of social independence and self-sufficiency, it also involved a recognition that the realm called 'the social' was itself internally broken and riddled with schisms and fault lines between the Enlightened and the stupid, the cosmopolitan and the local. As such, the faults became things to be made good. But by whom?

Of course, this does not mean that pre-modern social relationships were therefore completely frictionless. That would be more than a little silly. But it is fair to suggest that pre-modern systems were not possessed of the reflexivity which would have enabled them to conceive of social questions *as* purely social. Pre-modern understanding would have assumed the existence and the great power of some extra-social element. It would have interpreted any difficulties through a classification which established that all ills were the responsibility of a few heretics or ambiguous creatures which transgressed the boundaries of the immutable order of things. Social relationships could not see themselves as the exclusive source of any fatal growths because social relationships were held to be the way they had to be.

Moreover, they had been that way since time immemorial. Their very longevity was adduced as proof of their efficacy. They seemed to be natural because they seemed to be outside of history.

But modernity was ushered in at more or less the precise moment when it became obvious that social relationships were not at all outside of history. On the contrary, the shattering impact of urbanization was an event in recent living memory and the fleeting yet permanent presence of strangers punctured any visions that the existing way of life was the only way of life. Modernity involved the awareness of the possibility, indeed the *desirability*, of alternatives which could be made here out of freely available materials, rather than found in simply another reified structure after some perilous journey. William Blake's New Jerusalem was to be built in England's green and pleasant land, not heaven, but when Samuel Johnson's Prince Rasselas, or Voltaire's Candide, wanted to find other kinds of social arrangements, they had to travel to new lands. The alternative was always elsewhere and never, even possibly, here. Those characters were produced in the eighteenth century but they were not protagonists of modernity so much as the last, dying, embers of the once taken-for-granted past.

The continued appeal of Rasselas and Candide is precisely that they come from an imaginative universe which is so like ours, and yet, when all is said and done, so unlike it. They could never be our contemporaries. For both Rasselas and Candide, but undoubtedly more for Lemuel Gulliver, alternatives could not be made, rather they had to be found. Other social arrangements could only be imagined as always and already existing. The alternative was just another reification. Moreover, the careers of these fictional heroes merely went to show that the individual who was not born of the particular set of alternative arrangements could not have any real part in them. The outsider was always an exotic, who would go tomorrow or be consumed, just like a hot-house pineapple.

Modernity was perhaps rather more Quixotic. Not so much because it was romantically idealist (although the representative statements of modernity were frequently precisely that), but rather because it assumed that the mundane world was the raw material out of which new and visionary arrangements could be imagined. It was Quixotic to the extent that it imagined richer, better worlds and, moreover, imagined that the new worlds could be *created here* rather than simply *discovered there*. The pre-modern spatial barrier was replaced with the temporal barriers of modernity. In pre-modern systems, other lands always 'belong' to their indigenous inhabitants. But in the representative visions produced in European modernity, the future at least potentially 'belongs' to us.

The narratives of modernity unceasingly repeated that rather soiled refrain, 'The future belongs to us!' They also gave the phrase an important evaluative dimension with the simultaneous declaration that the world of the future might be made better than the world of the present. But, since there was no extra-social source of knowledge or power, neither could there be any guarantee that the moment of possession would ever arrive. It was up to women and men to make sure that the moment indeed came. But here again, the grandiose claims and pretensions of modernity were fundamentally qualified. The 'us' was not an anthropological reference which equally included all humans on the face of the earth, despite how it might have seemed from the vantage point of evidently universal reason. Rather, 'us' was a social and a cultural category which included only those groups or individuals who could proclaim their exclusive practice of freedom, and proximity to the standards of improvement. 'Us' included only those who could make and perform social freedom, in contradistinction to 'them' who had to be made to be free or who were intractably awful. As such, modernity was not at all the forward and onward march of Humanity (with a very big H). On the contrary, it was the era and the attitude of highly complex strategic relationships of attraction and repulsion which revolved around the exercise of freedom by some groups and the wallowing in reification of others.

The group which was most free could, in principle, claim the right to be the maker of modernity. That is, so long as that group could make a case which would meet widespread, or at least very powerful, support. When the support was lacking, the claims were held to be little more than nonsense. The group which was most able to stake the claim to ultimate sovereignty consisted in the intellectuals. After all, the two key freedoms of modernity, freedom from rural reification through urbanization and freedom from reified structures of knowledge, were the very possibilities of existence of the intellectuals. The group was both the condition and the representation of modernity. It was the pulse, mouthpiece, and conscience, of modern social relationships. However, precisely because the intellectuals were so important to the reflexivity of modernity, because they lived in the permanent flux of the city and relied on cosmopolitan communication networks, they were also complete and utter strangers. Virtually by definition, there was always a kind of hermeneutic distance between the intellectuals and the relationships which were so close. And that was in part the reason for their freedom.

The consequences of the status of the intellectuals as *double strangers* were quite immense but, crucially, dependent upon social negotiation and renegotiation. On the one hand, the double strangers could easily be identified as the representations and representatives of modernity (an identification which the intellectuals were more than happy to encourage). Yet, on the other hand, they were always visitors, outsiders, to the worlds which, they said, they could improve. Jean Jacques Rousseau knew that very well. The strangeness of intellectuals was the source of all their strength and the source of all the powers which were invested in them. It was also the cause of all their problems. Quite simply, the intellectuals could not possibly be fully involved in the social relationships which they wrote about. Had they been, they would not have been representations of freedom, and neither would they have been able to see the social world from the God's-eye perspective of a critical distance. The intellectuals as strangers were only, and inevitably, ambivalently linked to the system of social order and meaning. They were not a definite part of the order of things; they could not be easily accommodated within the reified classifications, and so their presence had to be made intelligible in some other way.

The structures of meaning and going on responded to the double strangeness of the intellectuals through a definition which either emphasized their special difference (i.e. here today and staying tomorrow because they have something to offer), or which announced their absolute abhorrence (here today but exterminated tomorrow). Both strategies maintained the order of things because they excluded the double strangers from the realm of the 'normal', and yet also tried to take due account of the key experiences of modernity. Consequently, one of the central problems of modernity was to connect the special insights of some strangers to social relationships, whilst practising the abomination of other strangers. As the rather different careers of Immanuel Kant and Thomas Stockmann hopefully demonstrated, the practice of the one technique or the other depended upon the extent to which the group of strangers could gain access to the organizations and symbols of social power, and, importantly, maintain exclusivity through the self-imposition of strategies of closure. Kant and his colleagues very successfully achieved all that. As such, they were invested with, and announced their own, magical abilities. These double strangers were shamans. The double strangers who were too weak, who struggled alone, and who were unable to distance themselves from others through the adoption of special habits, could make no viable claims to the possession of special, magical insight. Instead, they were defined as opportunist careerists who used knowledge for their own ends (whereas Kant and his like used knowledge for the Good of Humanity), as mere filth who threatened the existing arrangements.

Social scientists have long been highly adept players of this game which says that knowledge which grinds no axes has special insight, and that the bearers of knowledge are therefore possessed of unique abilities. One of the central concerns of the social science of modernity was the struggle to divorce the proclamations of reason from any proximity to the personal interests of the scientists. That is, modern social scientists were, perhaps unsurprisingly, acutely aware of their double strangeness, and went to great lengths to ensure that it was associated with magic rather than filth. The concern is, of course, clearest in the work of Max Weber and his assertion of the importance of value freedom. As Weber told an exclusive audience at Munich University in 1918, 'it is one thing to state facts ... while it is another thing to answer questions of the *value* of culture and its individual contents and the question of how one should act in the cultural community and in political associations' (Weber 1948: 146). Weber was concerned to emphasize that the social scientists could be trusted to discover what was for the best, and feed that profound insight into actual social practices, precisely because they were fighting for knowledge and not for themselves.

Weber wrote the sign which many modern sociologists would have liked to have hung above the door to the lecture theatre:

'the prophet and the demagogue do not belong on the academic platform' (Weber 1948: 146). An analytic mind which was as sharp as Weber's could not have failed to recognize the difficult strangeness of the social scientist (especially given the structure of the early-twentieth-century German university system; Simmel's strangeness was even keener), and he tried to outmanoeuvre the possibility that strangeness might be defined as an abomination through a consolidation of the putative selflessness of the social scientist and the difficult exclusiveness of what was later called 'the sociological imagination.' Weber was aware of two things; firstly that social science was a product of the strangers of modernity, and, secondly, that social science could, given the right social and cultural chances, establish itself as the final statement of modernity. Weber's manifesto for value freedom can be read as a reflection upon the difficulties and opportunities which were faced by intellectuals in the conditions of modernity.

Of course, the same reflections are also expressed in the work of Karl Mannheim. Where Weber was happy to simply announce the need for a value- and therefore interest-free scientific method, Mannheim turned that assumption into an analytic principle. Indeed, Mannheim even went so far as to say that knowledge which bears traces of its social origins is a, 'prescientific inexact mode of thought' (Mannheim 1960). Consequently, the true intellectual became the person who could be, and who indeed actually was, evidently free of all social impediments in the search for truth. Mannheim thoroughly stated the need to maintain magic through exclusivity. For him, problems arose precisely when the double strangers either did not have, or gave up, the resources which maintained and stated their peculiar apartness.

Milan Kundera has, perhaps, provided a very useful illustration of the difficult position of modern intellectuals. He manages to go some way towards drawing together the rather different experiences of Immanuel Kant and Thomas Stockmann. Kundera talks about the symbolic and political significance, 'of the magic qualities of the circle' (Kundera 1982: 65). He compares the newly empowered Czechoslovakian Communist Party of the late 1940s to a circle. The circle is a source of great strength to those who are part of it, but it maintains an outstanding exclusivity. 'Leave a row and you can always go back to it. The row is an open formation. But once a circle closes, there is no return' (Kundera 1982: 65). Kundera once was a good member of the magic circle, but he was expelled from the Party and, consequently, forced out of the arrangement to which he could never return. As such, Kundera's old allegiances, old certainties, old intellectualism, were redefined.

All the time he was dancing in some Matissian circle, Kundera was powerful, happy, special, and able. Indeed, the circle-dance was once so powerful that one participant, the poet Paul Eluard, even rose above the chimneys of Prague! But when that exclusivity turned its back on Kundera, his fate was sealed. If the authorities had the chance, Kundera would be forced into the same end as Eluard's erstwhile friend, Zoris Kalandra. 'Like a meteorite broken lose from a planet, I too fell from the circle and have been falling ever since.' Kundera continues to remark that he would never be in a circle again: 'I knew I belonged to Kalandra, not to them, to Kalandra who had also broken away from the circular trajectory and fallen, fallen, fallen into a convict's coffin' (Kundera 1982: 66, 67).

Of course, this is an extremely prosaic illustration of the relationship between the double strangers and existing systems of social order. But Kundera has given a very useful metaphor. The point is that when the individual can participate in a circle, she or he becomes an integral part of something which is both powerful (see, the poet flies!) and exclusive (circles always close up). The circles maintain their abilities precisely to the extent that they consolidate their strangeness, and make it seem to be almost natural. However, when an individual stranger can-not gain access to a circle, or is thrown out, that individual becomes, merely, a simple stranger. Now, the epithet 'intel-lectual' is turned into a term of abuse which means that the individual could never be a full participant in social relationships. Like Kundera but of course in rather different circumstances, Saul Bellow has also realized that intellectuals are capable of only a strange relationship to the existing order of things. Bellow's character Charlie Citrine was so interested in books that he was unable to form reciprocal relationships: 'I had talked all the time about my Modern Library books, of poetry and history, and she was afraid that she would disappoint me' (Bellow 1975: 76; see also Kundera 1982: 5).

As a mere stranger, the lone intellectual becomes a problem to

40

be forced out of social relationships. For a while, Thomas Stockmann indeed participated in a circle, but like Milan Kundera, he too said something which would have been better left unsaid. And, like Kundera, Stockmann too plummeted from the orbit. Meanwhile, Kant was always able to participate in a circle. He was thus able to maintain his own exclusivity and, moreover, perform apparently magical feats. Immanuel Kant never ceased to be a benign wizard of modernity. Whilst some intellectuals danced the social circle, other, single, intellectuals, took on the dull inertia of natural objects. Kundera's illustrative metaphor pulls the careers of Kant and Stockmann into a single biography. It also shows quite how much the modern double strangers walked a tightrope between excellence and irrelevance.

Ralf Dahrendorf has stressed the importance of the assumption of 'makeability' in the history and the arrangements of nineteenth- and twentieth-century Europe (Dahrendorf 1990). He was right to do so. The assumption of makeability represents the most deep and profound social freedom. But Dahrendorf does not pursue the matter; he just assumes that makeability meant much the same thing for everybody. But, as the illustration from Milan Kundera might show, it did not. On the contrary, the experiences and practices of modernity demonstrated that social relationships could be made anew only by the highly specific social group of the double strangers who danced in a circle. The reason was, perhaps, simple. The practice of makeability was impossible without a relationship of domination and, indeed, freedom. Consequently, the ability to make, and the confidence to embark upon such an ambitious enterprise of potentially turning the world upside down, could be assumed only by that group which was able to establish itself as the most free and the most dominant. Just as freedom is one expression of a critical distance, so distance opens up possibilities of new freedoms. According to many of the modern expressions of scientificity, the further away we are from a thing, the greater are our abilities and chances to do what we want with it. And, due to the social fact that some groups were evidently more removed from any reification than others, those strangers were more able to make the world than the 'natives.'

Modernity could only involve practices of the makeability of the world to the extent that it threw up social groups which could draw clear demarcations between the social, the active, and the subjective on the one hand, and the natural, the passive, and the objective on the other hand. Again, the double strangers, the intellectuals, step into the limelight since they could claim to be *the* expression and condition of a free and subjective, entirely social, existence. The intellectuals were the embodiment of activity. As such, their own situation and patterns of behaviour rather inevitably became identified as something like *the* representation of the social. They were able to make and remake the realms of the natural and the social to the extent that they were able to rip apart any identity between themselves and reified structures or practices. The double strangers achieved precisely that if they had the power to define other social groups as some kind of intermediary between the social and the natural; those other groups consequently became not natural but not social either. They were ambivalent in various ways and in need of either reconstruction or annihilation depending upon the depth of their commitment to natural reification.

It is important to note, then, that the social determination of 'the natural' stretched beyond the boundaries of that which is 'nature'. In the conditions of European modernity, the natural included all social relationships and arrangements which were not subjected to the reflexive dialogue and, thereby, inserted into the realm of freedom and the self-sufficient. The natural was simply a wastebin into which was thrown everything that the social did not want.

In other words, the double strangers were able to exclusively practise a free and independent makeability because they were able to deny any identity between themselves and reification. The double strangers were potentially able to define the existing and seemingly timeless forms as a kind of barrier zone between their purely social existence and the purely natural. As such, they were able to demolish any immediate connections between the social and the natural. Jean-Paul Sartre makes the point well but, typically, a little unclearly:

> Immediacy is the absence of any mediator; that is obvious, for otherwise the mediator alone would be known and not what is mediated. But if we can not posit any intermediary, we must at the same time reject both continuity and discontinuity as a type of presence of the knower to the known. In fact we shall not admit that there is any

continuity of the knower with the known, for it supposes
an intermediary term which would be at once knower and
known, which suppresses the autonomy of the knower
in the face of the known while engaging the being of
the knower in the being of the known ... To be sure,
the separation between two discontinuous elements is an
emptiness – *i.e.*, a *nothing* – but it is a *realized* nothing, – *i.e.*,
in-itself. This substantialized nothing is as such a non-
conductive density; it destroys the immediacy of presence,
for it has qua nothing become *something*. The presence of
the for-itself to the in-itself can be expressed neither in
terms of continuity nor in terms of discontinuity, for it is
pure *denied identity*.

(Sartre 1958: 178)

This important passage has a number of implications.

Pre-modern social relationships operated through direct immediacy; there was no mediator between them and their earthly
or supernatural conditions of existence. As such, there was a
complete collapse of the knower into the known. There was a
profound reification and an impossibility of reflexivity. However, the processes of urbanization and the Enlightenment
created an emptiness between the conditions of social life and
the conditions of natural life *but only those groups which combined
urbanization and Enlightenment could realize that emptiness and thus
become a free in-itself.* The existing and indigenous social relationships became the representation of the substantialized nothing
which destroyed any immediacy between the double strangers
and nature. Consequently, the intellectuals as double strangers
were able to deny identity between themselves and reification.
Indeed, they could even suggest that free and independent
social relationships looked exactly like their own relationships.
The suggestion was made frequently and powerfully.

It is thus possible to identify three main sites of social
grouping within modernity. They all embody various degrees of
the denial of identity with, or proximity to, the incontrovertibly
non-social realm of the intrinsically natural. Firstly, modernity
was driven by, and in its own definition at least, crystallized in,
the group of the double strangers who could make claims to the
possession of magical abilities. This group was *entirely social*; it
had the practical and cognitive resources to deny any identity

whatsoever between itself and reification. Consequently, it was the representation of what everyone else still had to achieve. Secondly, modernity contained a 'non-conductive density' (to use Sartre's phrase which clearly anticipated Baudrillard's 'silent majorities': Baudrillard 1983) in the form of the social insiders who lived through reified relationships but, precisely because of their proximity to intellectuals in towns and perhaps even the reading rooms, could in principle be educated and led to a free and self-sufficient social existence (the leading role being reserved for the magical strangers). Thirdly, there was the group of the lonely and dirty strangers who were unable to proclaim their own magical exclusivity and who were, therefore, a problematic intermediary which blurred the otherwise firm distinction between the social and the natural. The dirty strangers might have well possessed knowledge but because the group had no chance of establishing any degree of consensual legitimacy (because it was ghettoized and denied access to the sites of social prestige), it could be dismissed as a barbarous dilution of social independence. Moreover, any particular forms of behaviour carried out by the dirty strangers was defined by the powerful as nothing other than a product of a reprehensible immediacy to the world of pre-modern reification. Consequently, they could not be reformed like the presently reified insiders; instead they simply had to be pushed away or, at the very least, marginalized.

I propose that *all* the social struggles of the two hundred years or so after the middle-to-late eighteenth century fit into the contestable hierarchy of identity and difference to the ostensibly reified, and therefore non-social, world of the natural.

To put the matter extremely schematically, it might be said that the history of modernity was the history of the various projects which the double, magical strangers imposed upon the improveable insiders and which were measured by the extent to which the dirty strangers or dirty ways were eliminated. Only the intellectuals who were the double strangers could carry out such an ambitious remaking of social relationships because only they could establish themselves as sufficiently social and independent. Moreover, only the double strangers, like Kant, went about deliberately seeking institutional support and defence on the grounds that they were the unique possessors of the self-sufficient truths of Enlightenment. Furthermore, precisely because of the social exclusivity which meant that no other groups behaved like the double strangers, the struggles of modernity were fought under the banner of the increasing social domination of human existence and, therefore, under the banner of *civilization*. The actual meaning of that struggle tended to be simple; the double strangers argued that everybody should be made to look and act exactly like them. Anyone or anything which did not could be dismissed as tradition, habit, and beyond the pale of the new, improved, versions of social relationships.

The social impact of the coincidence of urbanization and Enlightenment was felt and represented through the development of *projects of improvement* which were intended to transform the societies by making them more commensurate with the values and interpretations of the double strangers. The word *project* is used in the sense of an organized undertaking to 'throw forwards' social arrangements and understanding. The project, and there were many projects in modernity although the surface differences hid many hermeneutic similarities, was both historical ('forwards') and ethical ('improvement'). It was, then, ostensibly a reflection of self-sufficient freedom. But because actual social relationships only matched the categories of the project with some ambivalence, there was, firstly, a need to make sure that the criteria of the blueprint generated by the project and the practices of actuality were brought together. Secondly, it was easily suggested that the possibly enforced change of social arrangements would be for the *real* best interests of all (real interests which could only be known by those who could see beyond immediate, selfish interests).

The onus on the shoulders of the double strangers was immense indeed. After all, they were evidently carrying out a plan of world-historic importance. What they did today had major implications for what could, or should, be done tomorrow. And everybody should have been grateful for the efforts which were expended on their behalf, despite any short-term costs. As Edmund Burke said, 'The public interest requires doing today those things that men of intelligence and goodwill would wish, five or ten years hence, had been done.' In other words, the legislators of the project were *in advance* of all their contemporaries. They had to have the freedom to be able to imagine the needs of the future, they had to have the ability to ignore their own interests and relentlessly impose anything which was required by social freedom. Again, the vision of the selfless intellectual who fights only for knowledge and independence steps onto the centre of the stage.

It would seem that Kant recognized most of these themes when he wrote his 'What is Enlightenment?' essay. He was extremely aware that Enlightenment was not at all an all-inclusive, general, social process. Instead, Kant argued that Enlightenment involved vanguardism. 'If it is now asked whether we at present live in an *enlightened* age, the answer is: No, but we do live in an age of *enlightenment*.' Kant went on to suggest that thanks to the tolerance of Frederick, 'the obstacles to universal enlightenment, to man's emergence from his self-incurred immaturity, are gradually becoming fewer' (Kant 1970: 58). Kant must have defined himself as *already* free, mature, and enlightened, else those comments about the requirements of Enlightenment would have been quite impossible. Kant's social strangeness, allied with the possession of symbols of social prestige, led him to rework apartness as historical superiority. He was already that which most others remained and aspired to become. If Immanuel Kant had been as immature as most of his contemporaries were said to be, he could have hardly said what maturity was like. For Kant, the existing relationships were merely a silent density which had to have life and a truly social existence breathed into them. Kant and the other double strangers of late eighteenth-century Prussia were saying little more than that the individuals of European modernity should be reconstructed in their own image. To this extent, the project *is* vanguardism.

But, of course, this Kantian vanguard was not struggling only for itself, even though the condition of Enlightenment seemed to bear a remarkable similarity with the social hegemony which the new class of the state functionaries, embryo-capitalists, and intellectuals believed was their rightful destiny (for some indication of the reasons of that belief see Gouldner 1985). Any practices which that class frowned upon were identified as an out of place vestige of nature, as an unreflexive, habitual practice. It was therefore a practice which needed to be fully subordinated by the imposition and interpretations of the project of making the world a better place. The maturity of some was indivisible from, indeed required, the compulsory abandonment and forgetting of the cultural resources of others (for more on this point, see Bauman 1987: 51–67. For examples, see Tester 1991, Yeo and Yeo 1981). Simply because the much-heralded event of Enlightenment was, even for Immanuel Kant, a social and not at all an anthropological process, this aspect of the development of modernity meant rather different things for the different social groups. Slavery could indeed be freedom, so long as the slaves of modernity and the free legislators of modernity were kept firmly apart.

At least, that was something like the promise of the faith in projects. The promise was possible only because the powerful and prestigious double strangers were in a socially and a historically unique situation which had not existed before and would never exist again. Due to their cosmopolitan communication systems, and urban oriented understanding of the order of things, they were more or less identified as freedom incarnate (not least by themselves). Their special status and abilities were possible because they could exploit their lack of a deep, social embeddedness and turn it to their own advantage. Similarly, it was asserted that the milieu of social relationships could be qualitatively improved if the old, traditional, reified ways were wiped from the slate. The projects of modernity involved not just general improvement tomorrow. They also involved a new beginning today.

That new beginning represented the moment of the imposition of the project of the double strangers. It was both a condition and a resource of social freedom. Just as the intellectuals owed their odd separation from taken-for-granted social arrangements to the physical and mental flux of the city and the cognitive impact of cosmopolitanism, so the modern stress on new beginnings reflected the collapse of the old reified structures. In European modernity, the emphasis took one characteristic form. Indeed, 'the revolutionary spirit of the last centuries, that is, the eagerness to liberate *and* to build a new house where freedom can dwell, is unprecedented and unequaled in all prior history' (Arendt 1963: 28; a fine discussion of Arendt on revolution is offered by Feher 1987). The desire to build a new 'house' was predicated upon the certainty that alternative arrangements could, firstly, be formulated, secondly, used as a critique of existing arrangements, and thirdly, used as a guide for new forms. In other words, the typically modern belief in the desirability and mere possibility of a revolution was impossible in social contexts where all relationships were interpreted as timeless, unalterable, and simply, the way they must be.

Perhaps it is not too surprising, therefore, that most of the clearest and most pragmatic of the modern theories of revolution all gave some privileged place to the impact and influence of the urbanization of social relationships. Revolution would have been hard to imagine had not generalized urbanization, allied with a rather more restricted cosmopolitanization of interpretation systems, thrown the old orders into disarray. Hannah Arendt recognized this origin of the new in the perished shell of the old, and believed that it had important implications for the revolutionary experience. She suggests that the initial rapid success of all revolutions was due to the fact that the revolutionaries did not have to push too hard to knock over the old structures. They were crumbling already. The 'men who make ... [revolutions] ... first only pick up the power of a regime in plain disintegration.' As such, revolutions 'are the consequences but never the causes of the downfall of political authority' (Arendt 1963: 112).

The revolutionary experience was dialectical. It was a practical and a cognitive response to the fundamental changes of the conditions and interpretations of social relationships which were occurring during the eighteenth century. As such, although revolutions were born of the collapse of the old, they went beyond a simple act of negation or void-filling, and pushed into the imagined future to make new worlds. As such, Ernest Gellner is right to say that the French Revolution, 'was, though not the prime mover, at any rate the attempt to work out, codify, implement the new order, as it was then understood. It is unquestionably a milestone on the highway of world history' (Gellner 1990: 310).

Images of the new beginning, and the exhaustion or the collapse of the reified old systems abound in the iconography of the French Revolutionary period. One of the best known and richest of those icons is Jacques Louis David's painting of Marat, dead in the bath tub. Although the prospect of a dead man in a bath might be rather pathetic, the painting avoids bathos by means of an apparent harking back to the grandiosity of antiquity. Indeed, it partly represents the death of Marat through the conventions of Renaissance devotional art, and the picture is reminiscent of nothing so much as an especially lonely Pieta. It at first appears to have little to do with any new beginning. If anything, it is a perfect illustration of Marx's famous contention in the *Eighteenth Brumaire* that, 'the heroes, as well as the parties and the masses of the old French Revolution, performed the task of their time in Roman costume and with Roman phrases' (Marx 1942: 316). But Marat became a secular Christ, or at least a modern Jove, and the Revolutionaries imagined themselves as Caesar, precisely because they were practising freedom. The French Revolution indulged in historical fancy dress in order to give itself the confidence to push into the future. Marat was Christ because only through the categories of the past was it possible to even conceive of the new future which was being forged. The Revolution turned the past to the ends of the future; it made antiquity a resource in the service of transformation rather than a reified return of the always the same.

Norman Bryson has drawn attention to the character of the painting of Marat. 'Marat appears in the likeness of the dead Christ. But although Christian iconography is invoked, it precisely does not exhaust the image' (Bryson 1988: 91). The picture is a representation of an event from the revolutionary modernity which cannot be entirely contained by the systems and forms of the past. On the contrary, it escapes them. Marat the modern revolutionary is presented as greater than the greatest figure of the past. And, by extension, the new order is made to seem more magnificent than the reified old ways. David invoked the traditional Christian system to represent the death of Marat, but the whole point was that Marat was a thoroughly secular figure. David showed that the new beginning went beyond and exhausted the time-honoured categories. Again, Bryson: 'the juxtaposition of Christ/Marat places the viewer in a dialectical field occupied by Christianity and dechristianization, in this era when the state breaks with Christian faith and Christian temporality' (Bryson 1988: 91).

The use of the past to legitimize, to *naturalize*, the relationships of the new beginning resonates throughout the painting, not least in its dating. Whilst the canvas shows that the depicted incident occurred in Year II, Charlotte Corday's note bears the date 1793. Jacques Louis David's point seems to have been that

49

the old ways were a threat to the new, and a harbinger of *rigor mortis*. Charlotte Corday was doing rather more than killing a man; she was also trying to hold back the imposition of freedom.

There is still more to the painting. Importantly, it represents Marat as a stranger. His strangeness, his ambivalence, is multi-textured. Of course, the austerity and colours of the canvas create a distance between the granduer of the dead revolutionary and the mundane life of the viewer. But, more than that, Marat is presented as without blemish; in 'real life' Marat had a bad skin complaint, but after David, Marat's skin is perfect, the muscles are finely honed, and the dead face seems to bear an expression of quiet repose. Even the fatal wound is little more than a clean slit (all of this is so different to Madame Tussaud's very bloody depiction of the assassination). Marat was not just a great man; he even looked and died like a great man. We merely die painfully, filthily, pointlessly. Yet more; whilst the Revolution was an astonishingly *active* event, David gives us a depiction of a leading and militant revolutionary *as a thinker*. What we do today, Marat had thought and written about already. Marat might well have led 'the people', but he was not at all one of them. David made sure that the 'friend of the people' (as Marat liked to style himself) was identified as a man apart, as a magical figure who said more in death than most others said in life, as a stranger. (It is worth comparing David's representation of the stranger to Goya's pictures of the Spanish nobility. For example, whilst Ferdinand VII was a social stranger, Goya represented him as possessing the expression of an idiotic peasant. As such, all the magic collapsed.)

So, modernity can indeed be equated with the realization of the possibility that social relationships might be subjected to a new beginning. But, thanks to the ostensible capabilities created by the Enlightenment, that assumption of makeability was not carried out simply for the sake of it. On the contrary, the makeability was to be performed by the magical, double strangers, and it would represent a qualitative improvement of social relationships. Moreover, it would be guided by the demands and categories of the project which contained the blueprint of precisely how the better future would look. It might even be said that the imposition of the project was a sure sign of the revolt of the double strangers against the world as they found it.

But it is just a little vague to say that the double strangers, who were typically represented by the urban intellectuals, went about 'imposing' perfect projects on a reality which was thus interpreted as recalcitrant, flawed and inadequate. The problem is to explain precisely how that imposition was carried out, how the ideas of the blueprint could be turned into a guide for practical action. All of that was possible because the eighteenth century also witnessed the development of new and original relationships of social power. In particular, during the course of the eighteenth century, the double strangers who had managed to maintain their magical exclusivity and who had also been able to claim institutional support (or at least toleration), began to turn the state to new activities. The processes of Enlightenment and urbanization led to the trumpeting and legitimation of the *gardening strategies of the modern state*.

The word 'gardening' is used here as a metaphor. It was coined by Ernest Gellner and extended by Zygmunt Bauman (Gellner 1983: 50; Bauman 1987, 1989; see also Tester 1991). It refers to conceptual, practical, and strategic landscapes rather than geographical ones. It refers to how the conditions of social life were interpreted during the era of modernity. A garden is a land which is cultivated and managed by specialist human intervention. Gardening itself is predicated upon a sharp lack of any identity between the land which is made and remade, and the person who does the making. Gardening assumes freedom, and gardens are proof that the landscape is not at all reified. As such, they are radically different than wildernesses.

According to the perspective of gardening, when land is left to itself, the plants become knotted and entangled; they all struggle to gain light, and all the inhabitants fight one another for a share of the finite food supplies. The people who live in wildernesses are relatively powerless. They can do little to change the way of things, indeed, the way of things is apprehended as unchanging. All the native inhabitants can do is try to come to terms with their lack of influence by mythologizing the overpowering environment. They compensate for their weakness by defining the existing relationships and forms as quite immutable. The wilderness, 'appears as something much stronger than human – overt or tacit – agreement may call into being and sustain. It is seen as Nature, God's creation, as a design supported by superhuman sanctions and perpetuated by superhuman guardianship' (Bauman 1987: 53). To put all this into the terms of Immanuel Kant's important essay, the inhabitants of the wild and natural lands, where everything is the way it must be, where social relationships cannot be altered, are afraid to think for themselves. Indeed, they do not even think that free thought is possible, In other words, they are immature and lack courage.

Gardens are very different. They are ordered and orderly environments where nature is identified as a potential threat which can and must be extirpated. At best, nature is an unthinking ally in a plan which is greater than itself. The acts and practices of ordering can only be performed by active agents who are themselves in some way able to examine the minutiae of the garden from the perspective of the outside in, or, to put it more evaluatively, from the top down. The gardeners must be strangers to the landscapes they are changing. They must be free in relation to them and possessed of seemingly magical abilities to make some plants flourish and others wither (the radio programme 'Gardeners' Question Time' shows quite how magical, and yet scientific, the practice is, how exclusive and yet potentially open to all who can see the land from a critical distance).

The strategy of gardening implicitly assumed the combination of proximity and distance which is the essence of the stranger. The distance was due to the ability of one highly active social group to treat the other social relationships *as if* they were natural and passive, and yet the closeness was implied in the very possibility of treating the other, external relationships at all. Gardening was predicated upon the practical viability of a sharp division between the social and the natural orders. Indeed, the strategies of gardening would have been utterly impossible had the social continued to be seen in a pre-modern way and as an intrinsic part of a system which was itself nature because it was without alternative.

Gardening involved a relationship of *objectivity*. It inserted the double strangers into relationships of 'indifference and involvement' with the relationships they were working on. This helped to confirm, if confirmation were needed, the magical abilities of the strangers because the combination of indifference and involvement promised that what ever was done would be done for the best. The double strangers could be trusted precisely because of their cognitive objectivity: 'the objective individual is bound by no commitments which could prejudice his perception, understanding, and evaluation of the given' (Simmel 1950: 405). Mannheim merely turned this *is* which Simmel identified into the *ought* of the social scientific enterprise. Simmel continues to suggest that the objectivity of the stranger itself reflexively deepens the hold of freedom. Perhaps Simmel is just describing the self-image of the legislator of the gardening strategies of modernity: 'he is freer, practically and theoretically; he surveys conditions with less prejudice; his criteria for them are more general and more objective ideals; he is not tied down in his action by habit, piety, and precedent' (Simmel 1950: 405).

According to the problematic of the garden, a land and the life it supports will only be violent and brutish if left alone. The blueprint of the ordered garden turns nature into that which brings only disorder and, perhaps more seriously, ambivalence. The most worrying sources of the ambivalence are the other groups of strangers who have their own plans for the garden, plans which do not have the correct resources at their disposal and which might, therefore, reepresent nothing other than a misuse of hard won freedom.

As such, the strategies of gardening were both universalizing and homogenizing. Ironically, however, they could only involve such a war against difference because the war was waged by a special group which was utterly heterogeneous. The strategies were *universalizing* because they identified any traces of untamed nature, and any assumptions of unalterability, as a threat to the order of the garden. Anything which did not fit in with the improving blueprint, or which challenged it, became something to be extirpated. The garden could only sanction the viability of those things which were prepared to accommodate themselves to the new order. Ultimately, the garden fought against any and all vestiges of the wilderness. Otherwise, the garden would have been a mere ghetto; it would not have been commensurate with the proclamations of the Enlightenment and the general problem of dealing with strangers. Nothing could be left outside of the gardeners' actual or potential purview. The gardening strategies were also *homogenizing* because they sought to make all social relationships and all individuals intelligible through the same hermeneutic systems. They required a kind of radical ontological reduction in the quest for perfect clarity.

The same blueprint had to be able to legitimate itself as a

better form of *all* existing social relationships, and the systems of order dealt with all things as if they were the same. Indeed, from the point of view of the double strangers who had managed to deny any identity between themselves and the landscapes they were remaking, all insiders *were* the same because all insiders had to be re-educated. The dirty, weak outsiders merely had to be extirpated and pushed into their own little corners which became something like compost heaps which reminded all the insiders of what might happen if the re-education was hindered or did not succeed.

Gardening is a metaphor for the modern strategies of improvement which the state and the double strangers were introducing in the course of the eighteenth century in the attempt to establish a new and self-sufficient social life. Kant was a particularly skilful and ambitious gardener, and the essay 'What is Enlightenment?' can be interpreted as an important manifesto for those new relationships. The underlying theme of Kant's paper was the idea that individuals who believe in or practise the metaphoric wilderness are cowardly fools who excuse themselves with appeals to ordination and reified immutability. But, as a magical double stranger, Kant was saying that he knew differently. He was sure that individuals who were made free would flourish and become so much better, fitter, and stronger. They would become the people to live in the brave new world which was then only inhabited by Kant and a handful of circle-dancing colleagues. By extension, then, the institutions and arrangements of the state could, given adequate control and leverage, be rather like a 'greenhouse' which let the special gardeners like Kant try out their ideas of free social propagation. Moreover, the state as greenhouse also constituted a barrier which made sure that the gardeners did not collapse into any identity with the environment they were remaking.

Now, greenhouses are rather curious structures. They stand in the well-ordered garden, gathering all the benefit of the light. Inside they are hot and alive with the free and selfless activities which the duties of Enlightenment and improvement demand. The greenhouse is the administrative focus of the garden, and all the relationships which occur within it. From the greenhouse, the gardener showers benevolence on the plants which grow well and encourages others to grow better; the free interference of the gardener will help the plants develop yet more. But the gardener can be ruthless if a plant degenerates and deviates from the position which has been planned for it, if it becomes a stranger to the systems of order. The deviant species are no longer plants; now they are weeds and, as such, cut down. They are thrown out of the care of the garden, and are instead left to wither and die. Because the gardening strategy is universalizing, it cannot permit the deviant plants to grow outside of the garden's walls. Instead, the weeds are thrown out singly, without any support from their neighbours which are treated as potentially improveable. They are eliminated alone so that their exception proves the rules of the garden.

All of these relationships were managed and overseen by the double strangers who were able to claim that they were the condition and the agent of freedom. The gardeners (the magical, double strangers) were perfectly confident to use their own Enlightened understanding to encourage the growth of some plants and the withering of others which owed their existence to time immemorial rather than deliberate design. Cultures and resources which owed their existence to their own seeming timelessness, about which little could be done, were utterly discredited. The old was cretinized in the name of the improved future. The passage to the gardening strategies and relationships of European modernity was predicated upon the viability of social freedom, but it also heralded the development of the perfectly transparent administered society which contained no secrets, and in which strategies of power and order had a universal, or at least a universalizing, ambition. 'Deprived of authority, dispossessed of its territorial and institutional assets, lacking its own, now evicted or degraded, experts and managers, it rendered the poor and lowly incapable of self-preservation and dependent on the administrative initiatives of trained professionals' (Bauman 1987: 67).

All of the above has been an attempt to develop a model of modernity. It is that model, which emphasizes the social role of strangers and the implications of freedom, which will inform the following analysis of the curious and rather contradictory history of the question of sovereignty in European modernity. But the model should not cause a blindness to the actual forms which modernity took. Indeed, whilst the analysis cannot really be carried out if the precise meanings of modernity have not been spelt out in some detail, it is also the case that the analysis would be pointless if it paid no heed to actual social arrangements. The whole tragedy of modernity was that although the struggle for freedom was meant to be lofty and, for that matter, entirely successful, the ambitions were rarely achieved. Certainly, the double strangers were ceaselessly drawing up blueprints of new and improved social relationships, but the plans had to be used in a social setting which caused them to be reshaped and altered. Only rarely was the ideal model of gardening relationships actually a viable option, and only in a handful of cases was it imposed.

Consider the social and historical requirements if the ideal type of gardening was to be at all possible. They were highly peculiar. The imposition of a single design upon the landscape is only possible if, firstly, that landscape is not able to speak for itself, if all its indigenous resources have either decayed or been destroyed and secondly, if other gardeners can be prevented from peering over the fence and offering their unwanted advice. That is, the ideal type of gardening could only be turned into practice in those social situations where there were no alternative sites of the interpretation and understanding of freedom. All social relationships could be treated in much the same way because there was only one viable possibility of an alternative. When there was a plurality of sites or of gardeners, all of whom could claim some ability to operate in the now contested terrain, it was quite impossible for any single gardening blueprint to be imposed. Certainly, each blueprint and each project struggled to become *the* guide for action, but the viability of alternative projects could never be entirely overcome.

When the social terrain which was to be subjected to the makeability of the free double strangers was not mute, the question of sovereignty became very complex. In the ideal type of the gardening strategies, the problem of sovereignty, the problem of precisely who or what heralds freedom, is easily resolved indeed. The only sovereigns are the double, magical strangers who sharply deny any identity between themselves and the reification of nature. They are the only ones who possess the secrets of the projects of improvement and freedom. As such, sovereignty becomes a simple flow of the magical, double strangers educating the insiders whilst pushing away the dirty strangers who are too close to the natural. Historically, that situation prevailed in Nazi Germany, when the Nazis went about

56

deliberately destroying any of the Weimar institutions which might have been the source of alternative visions of the garden. (A discussion of the Nazi episode is beyond my scope, but for an analysis to which this book owes a colossal debt, see Bauman 1989.)

The single garden was also a possible option in the Russian Empire in the First World War, when the Mensheviks but especially the Bolsheviks were able to step into institutional voids and establish their own systems as the only sure guarantee of social freedom and the better world (the decay of the old arrangements is vividly portrayed in some of the better sections of Solzhenitsyn's rambling *August 1914*). It is also worth noting that the Bolsheviks and their heirs went to astonishing lengths to preserve their magical exclusivity. The only other instance in the history of European modernity of the mute landscape which gardening strategies ideally desired was to be found in Central and Eastern Europe after the Second World War, in the wake of the Nazi domination and after the subterranean activities of the Stalinists.

But it was more typically the case that the landscape which gardening was meant to improve was not at all mute and passive. On the contrary, it often possessed existing arrangements which retained some legitimacy through their longevity (England; this is essentially the case of Edmund Burke) or their replanting (post-Napoleonic France). Either the indigenous resources were still accorded some authority, or any single group of double strangers was not able to create its own exclusive claims to the exclusion of all others. It was perhaps more characteristic of modernity that the double strangers formed into a plurality of exclusive groups each of which, admittedly, pursued gardening strategies (and so it is still reasonable to identify modernity with gardening), but each of which also had to contend with the magic of others. The possibility of plurality was immanent within the social relationships which created the freedom of Kant; he was talking to and for a number of groups (capitalists, state functionaries, intellectuals) who had nothing in common other than their strangeness. It was little more than fortuitous that Kant and his colleagues were able to develop a narrative of strangeness which reflected the experience of all those different kinds of strangers and, moreover, which could not be ignored by the existing arrangements precisely because it was so well constructed.

When a plurality of double strangers had to be confronted, and when no single group could mobilize the resources to annihilate all the others, the treatment of the social as a single garden was not a terribly practical option. It might be said that in those circumstances, the single garden was replaced by the diversity of an *allotment*. Each gardener worked her or his own plot of land, but could easily see what the other gardeners were doing. And, since each gardener thought that her or his own activities were the best and the surest guarantee of the perfect landscape, they looked on the other plots as inadequate. They offered well-meant or conceited advice to their neighbours, or tried to gradually assimilate pieces of the nearby allotment.

In the allotment situation, the question of sovereignty became immensely complicated. On the one hand, there was a multiplicity of competing promises of the path to freedom and, on the other hand, there was no way that women and men could be treated as if they were natural, passive, and mute, because, by virtue of their very strangeness, they might be the magical strangers of one of the competing versions of freedom. As such, the meaning of sovereignty was fractured between the competing projects, each of which struggled to speak for and on behalf of all the individuals who were seen to be potentially and equally adequate for freedom. The intention was to make all individuals into magical and double strangers through appeals to their ability to improve themselves, or be improved along with their unknown neighbours. Sovereignty was thoroughly individualized. But still, the groups which either failed to meet, or which could not match, the requirements of the competing definitions of freedom (which must have possessed a relatively high level of coincidence, else they would not have been able to struggle against each other over the same terrain and the same questions) were defined as dirty and in need of extirpation.

Antonio Gramsci recognized this very clearly indeed. He made the point that, 'the supremacy of a social group manifests itself in two ways, as "domination" and as "intellectual and moral leadership"'. But the relationship of hegemony, which attempts to control without annihilation, only prevailed when the subject group was treated as an insider or as potentially educable through moral exhortations. When the subject group was entirely beyond the designs of the blueprint, its treatment was very different indeed. 'A social group dominates antagonistic groups, which it tends to "liquidate", or to subjugate perhaps even by armed force; it leads kindred and allied groups' (Gramsci 1971: 57). The moral leadership or solidarity of the insiders by the double strangers ('People like us') was at the same time the basis for the destruction of the dirty outsiders ('People like them').

The question was, then, one of the resolution of the question of sovereignty *given that* within the context of European modernity, social relationships could be treated and interpreted only occasionally *as if* they constituted a garden. The programmatic projects of modernity involved the leadership of some kind of privileged group which had no identity at all with the natural world, a subordinate group which was presently identified with traces of the natural, but could be made different, and another group which was quite beyond all help. But all too often, the circumstances of modernity rather disturbed that clear picture. The basic problem, which reverberated for the two hundred years or so after the eighteenth century, was how and by whom alternative social arrangements might be made here. How and by whom might freedom be practised and confirmed?

Ideally, modernity went on through the practice and institutionalization of gardening relationships. The whole purpose of gardening was to confirm and consolidate the assumption of social freedom from reification through the identification of a sharp distinction between the natural and the social worlds. As such, modernity was also the sovereignty of that group which could claim to be the most free, the most social. Inevitably, then, it was an urban and an Enlightened process. Modernity was synonymous to social initiative, and so it involved rather more than a setting apart of the social and the natural (although modernity did involve precisely that). It also involved *the social constitution of the natural world as that which the entirely social repudiated.* Any social group or practice which was unable to sufficiently establish its own lack of identity to the natural thus became either something to be wiped clean and remade in a better form, or, simply, thrown away. Consequently, modernity was not a once-and-for-all recognition of freedom as the possibility of difference; it was, instead, the permanent and perpetual *practice* of alternatives. Modernity involved the permanent social creation and recreation of its 'other' by always finding new traces of nature or new dirty strangers. Had it not, modernity itself would have had no reason for continuing. If there was not always something more to be done, there was little point in doing anything at all. And so, the social would regress to just another reification.

The projects associated with European modernity aspired to achieve much the same definition of sovereignty which Plato established as the Republic of the Philosopher Rulers. Essentially, Thomas Stockmann merely repeated Plato when he shouted out the rights of the intelligent to the positions of social power. Plato's point was that, 'until society is controlled by philosophers there will be no end to the troubles of states or their citizens' (Plato 1974: 298). The sovereignty of the Philosopher Rulers would, then, result in the achievement of a good society, but, more than that, it would also lead to a qualitative improvement of the citizens. After all, the Philosopher Rulers had to some extent glimpsed the beauty of the unchanging Forms, and this turned their laws into pathways by which the 'best minds' might stride towards the attainment of the highest form of knowledge. Moreover, those laws would stop individuals from 'behaving as they are now allowed to' (Plato 1974: 323). Plato did not doubt that the uneducated should be prevented from gaining positions of power because: 'The uneducated have no single aim in life to which all their actions, public and private, are to be directed' (Plato 1974: 323). The Philosopher Rulers had precisely that single and definite aim.

The necessary ground work for the coming of the Philosopher Rulers was quite immense. Indeed, it more or less anticipated the wildest hopes of the gardeners of modernity. The gardeners wanted to be given a passive landscape in which to impose their projects and blueprints of the new beginning. The Philosopher Rulers needed something fairly similar: 'our philosophic artists differ at once from all others in being unwilling to start work on an individual or a city, or draw out laws, until they are given, or have made themselves, a clean canvas' (Plato 1974: 297). Again, the question of a denial of identity arises; the Philosopher Rulers could only treat the canvas as if it were blank, because they were able to identify it as apart from themselves. Simply, if the Philosopher Rulers had been depicted on the canvas, it could hardly have been blank.

Plato's governors needed to practice and maintain a high level of exclusivity. That is why Plato spent so long discussing their education. The exclusivity is implicit to the famous simile of the cave. Unlike the ordinary people, the Philosopher Rulers had to remain in the sunlit world at the mouth of the cave; they could encourage others to come and join them, but they could never return to gaze at the shadows. They had to refuse, 'to return again to the prisoners in the cave below and share their labours and rewards, whether trivial or serious' (Plato 1974: 323). Immanuel Kant must have read passages like that with tremendous glee and excitement. His definition of Enlightenment resembles nothing so much as the perspective of a special sort of person gazing down, with a mixture of involvement and detachment, on the rather silly and misguided behaviour of the troglodytes.

But there was one major and immensely important difference. Plato's state of the Philosopher Rulers was completely and utterly speculative. Indeed, he even seems to have thought that the *practical* possibility of the ideal state was rather less important than the *intellectual* possibility of describing it. The Philosopher Rulers would never reign here. Undoubtedly, however, for Kant and the other gardeners of modernity, Plato was indulging in a fairly pointless exercise. Kant thought that the practical likelihood of the ideal state was indeed a matter of some significance, and he proposed that the modern Philosopher Rulers (like himself) should be allowed to make special claims in order to achieve it. But still, there was an element of wishful thinking in Kant's pleas.

That is why Lenin is so important in the history of European modernity, more important even than his putative teachers. Lenin *made sure* that the domination of the updated Philosopher Rulers came to pass.

3

SEALED TRAINS

The scene was at once romantic and resonant. The train left Zurich on 27 March 1917. It contained the exiled Lenin, Nadezhda Krupskaya, and a handful of others. Thanks to the help of the German authorities, who had powerful reasons of their own for the exiles making the trip, Lenin and the others were going to the Finland Station to incite the Great Proletarian Revolution. Indeed, the Germans gave the return to Russia such a priority that they were prepared to delay for two hours a journey by the Crown Prince (Salisbury 1977: 407). Clearly, nothing could be allowed to stand in the way of Lenin and History. Throughout the journey, the returning exiles kept to themselves; legend has it that the train was sealed so that the seeds of Revolution could not be planted beside the railway lines. The locked doors also meant that intruders or pretenders could not enter the rarefied atmosphere in which lived the Makers of History.

It was accepted by all the passengers that this particular railway journey was no mere jaunt. On the contrary, the train was on the tracks to freedom. Lenin *had* to go to the Finland Station. Lunacharsky provided a picture of Lenin, just as the travellers were about to leave Zurich: 'When I looked at him standing on the platform of the outward-bound train I felt that inside he was thinking, "At last, at last the thing for which I was created is happening"' (quoted in Salisbury 1977: 406). It was the (self-imposed) destiny of Lenin to create the final new beginning of social relationships. He was a classic stranger, coming to invigorate the indigenous resources which could never go far enough if left to their own efforts. Lenin was an almost mythical magician of modernity who had managed to live in the complex spaces of freedom, and, as such, he was able to push the women and men of the collapsing Tsarist system even further than they could possibly push themselves. Certainly, the Russians had been able to topple the Tsar, but they had only succeeded in replacing him with the Mensheviks; the Bolsheviks would come from outside to take the last and yet so necessary step. The Bolsheviks were able to deny any identity which linked themselves and their message with Russian parochialism and, therefore, they could claim to both know and practise that which had to be done.

Lenin's status as a stranger was quite profound and, it would seem, not entirely coincidental. Lenin was the Grail Knight of modernity. In the pre-modern legends, the Holy Grail was an objective entity which could only be grasped by the virtuous individual after a life of hard struggle, temptation, and purification. Similarly, there was something decidedly Parsifalian about the railway journey to the Finland Station (it would be tempting to say that Lenin was living out Wagner, if it were not for his deep loathing of such 'bourgeois' art). According to Richard Wagner and Wolfram von Eschenbach, Parsifal visited the castle of Klingsor whilst he was a child, but he was forced to leave by Gurnemanz. The time was not right and the would-be hero was not pure. However, after the passage of several years, Parsifal again came to the castle; he was no longer a stupid boy. Instead he was a strong and courageous knight. Now, the time was right for him to break Klingsor's spells and grasp the Grail. But Parsifal could only reach that moment of destiny after Kundry had washed and ritually reclothed him as a Knight of the Grail.

The story of Parsifal bears a close narrative similarity to that of Lenin (and the very name Lenin indicates a modern act of freedom; 'Lenin' was an achieved subjectivity whereas the status of Vladimir Ilyich Ulyanov was that of a putatively once-and-for-all ascription). Just like Parsifal, Lenin, too, visited the castle of his destiny before the time was right and had to go away for a considerable while. Lenin had suffered in the wildernesses, and his entire being was a monument to freedom. After all, his brother Alexander Ilyich had been executed for his part in a plot to execute the Tsar, and Lenin himself had been involved in long and arduous struggles against the false keepers of the Grail of Revolution. Meanwhile, the years of exile can be equated to

Parsifal's purifying mission (or indeed Thomas Stockmann's period in the North).

But Lenin could only achieve his destiny after he also had been reclothed in clean garments, after he too had cast off the raiments of struggle and exile. Admittedly, Lenin's ritual reclothing was considerably more mundane than Parsifal's, but the meaning is perhaps comparable. When the train briefly stopped in Stockholm, Lenin went and bought a new suit. As Harrison Salisbury comments, 'he didn't want to appear in Russia in the thread-worn suit of his exile' (Salisbury 1977: 407). The new beginning required a new suit. Lenin arrived in Petrograd as an achieved being, as a representation of freedom, as a complete stranger, who bore no traces of reification.

Indeed, Lenin's way of dress consolidated his status as a stranger who could transform indigenous social resources. He did not look like a social insider; he was at one and the same time the distillation of proximate Russianness and yet also the beacon of distant freedom. In his extremely odd tale of the *Young Lenin*, Leon Trotsky went to great lengths to show quite how ordinary and how parochial Vladimir Ilyich Ulyanov's childhood had been, quite how steeped it had been in the common sense and reification of the way of things. But Trotsky also showed that the ascribed Ulyanov was destined to become the achieved Lenin. Ulyanov–Lenin transcended any time and place through his mixed, and in any other circumstances, dirty, ethnic background, whilst his commitment to cosmopolitan and apparently *scientific* cognitive systems (which had no place for superstition) meant that Ulyanov was intellectually always somewhere else than he appeared (Trotsky 1972). In 1917, Lenin confirmed that essentially strange mixture of closeness and distance with his new suit. In the icons of the October Revolution, Lenin is presented as *close* because he wears a worker's cap, but as *distant* because he wears a bourgeois business suit. Lenin transcended class, he transcended determination; he was free to dress as he pleased because he was free to come and go as he pleased. The only compulsions which Lenin accepted were those of his own making and of modernity. He *was* the new beginning.

The whole message of Lenin was, then, that only through the denial of any identity with the indigenous, native orders of things was it at all possible to practise the makeability of social relationships. But, more than that, the making could only be carried out because the sovereign makers were in some way associated with those relationships. Lenin was not in the situation of irrelevance which Simmel identified: 'The inhabitants of Sirius are not really strangers to us, at least not in any sociologically relevant sense: they do not exist for us at all; they are beyond far and near' (Simmel 1950: 402). Certainly, Lenin had managed to deny any identity between himself and the native resources, but he was also careful to avoid tearing asunder all the relationships of the near and the far. That is, Lenin was suitably *free* of the determination of indigenous circumstances to be able to see alternative arrangements, and yet he was sufficiently *attached* to be able to do something about the Russian situation. The combination of business suit and worker's cap was some kind of sartorial representation of that careful balancing act. But it should not be forgotten that all the claims of the magical abilities of Lenin were permissible and viable because they came from a powerful and exclusive circle called the Bolshevik Party. Lenin was at the centre, and he was the stimulation, of powerful arrangements which could publicize and, later, naturalize, the special strangeness of the Revolutionary Leader.

Lunacharsky was in many ways anticipating the cult of the personality when he stressed the destiny of Lenin, the moment of the achievement of the purpose for which Vladimir Ilyich Ulyanov had been born. Lunacharsky spelt out the reason why Ulyanov was freely reconstructed as Lenin. The point was that Lenin had a unique ability because he was a unique figure. His entire being was a celebration of freedom. The construction of Lenin as the special stranger *par excellence* perhaps reached its most absurd lengths during the affair of Lenin's brain. Of course, after his death in January 1924, Lenin's corpse was made the centrepiece of a vast mausoleum, but his brain was removed and handed over to a German professor for investigation. Professor Vogt quickly noticed that Lenin's brain signified his position as a stranger since it possessed, 'important peculiarities in the structure of the so-called pyramidal cells of the third layer'. The oddities merely *naturalized* the specialness of Lenin and, by extension, the domination of the Bolsheviks. Contemporary journalists reported that the brain was, 'the reason for his [i.e. Lenin's] ingenious ideas and the ingenious tactics that Lenin devised at the most difficult stages of the revolution when many others felt the ground slip from under their feet and lost all perspective'. (This information about Lenin's brain is taken from the massive history of the Soviet Union written by Mikhail Heller and Aleksandr Nekrich (1986: 166).)

Evidently, it was not true to say that Lenin's consciousness was determined by his social being. Lenin apparently disproved one of the central maxims of the Marxist enterprise. On the contrary, and unlike everybody else, Lenin's consciousness to a very important extent determined his social being. According to the iconography of Lenin, he was a living refutation of the very systems and orders of Enlightened knowledge which were meant to be universal. Lenin was a stranger even to the project of improvement which he sought to impose. He was not a man at all; he was a contradiction. Lenin was whatever Vladimir Ilyich Ulyanov and his heirs wanted him to be, just so long as he was always the representation of an alternative and, therefore, just so long as he was the embodiment of freedom.

Trotsky went so far as to try and create a myth of strangeness around the circumstances of Lenin's death. According to the last polemic which Trotsky wrote, Lenin was aware, 'that certain of Stalin's traits were directly inimical to the party' (*Guardian* 20 August 1990: 19). A short while after the recognition of Stalin's shortcomings, Lenin had the first of the series of strokes which finally led to his death. But Trotsky proposed that strokes were not enough to kill Lenin's, 'powerful organism, supported by his inflexible will' (ibid.). Instead, Lenin only died because Stalin encouraged Henry Yagoda to poison him. Lenin could not even be allowed to die like a mundane person. His special and quasi-natural (and therefore incontestable) strangeness went to the grave and beyond. This particular train, the train of Lenin's world historic strangeness, was utterly and irrevocably sealed against any dilution or qualification of its magic.

The image of the cleanly clothed Lenin coming from the West to ignite Russia might be read as a key to the contradictions and relationships of European modernity. Lenin was a stranger who danced in a lively and enthusiastic circle. Moreover, Lenin was a classic legislator and maker of modernity; he was physically here but cognitively there as well; he was in the city but as a permanent outsider. Lenin's situation was deeply and intrinsically ambivalent. He was a Russian in Zurich, and his mere appearance combined the representations of every Russian in general and yet no Russian in particular. It is almost as if Simmel knew of Lenin when he wrote that the stranger is close because, 'we feel between him and ourselves common features of a national, social, occupational, or generally human nature,' but the stranger is simultaneously distant because, 'these common features extend beyond him or us, and connect us only because they connect a great many people' (Simmel 1950: 406). The only difference is that what Georg Simmel took to be a sociological condition, Lenin took to be a political strategy. Lenin was the freshly suited proletarian–bourgeois who came to change the lives of the ragged masses who had lived through years of war and hardship. Lenin came by a modern train to the backward world which was not yet entirely free of Tsarism. He was also well versed in the orders of things which Enlightened and self-sufficient understanding had developed in opposition to the reified structures of God and Fatherland. He arrived in what to him must have seemed like a backward and opaque world, in much the same way as a Vespucci landed on other dark shores. Indeed, Lenin did to Russia precisely what those other explorers had done to Amer ca. The only, and typically modern, difference, was that Vespucci did it *there*, and Lenin did it *here*.

Thanks to the exclusivity and strength leant by the circle of the Bolsheviks, all the layers of closeness and yet distance, of involvement and yet detachment, became a source of tremendous strength. Had Milan Kundera been watching, perhaps the exile's return to the Finland Station would have led to Lenin preceding Paul Eluard as the first levitating stranger. Lenin was invested with astonishing exclusive powers. He was the self-made and free detonator which would explode the indigenously made, and yet largely passive, bomb. There was indeed a fundamental lack of identity between Lenin and the relationships which were being remade through his lead and influence. Consequently, the myth of Lenin lived by a fairly straightforward appreciation of the problem of sovereignty. Certainly, the transition from the Tsarist Empire to the Soviet Union was carried out in the name of freedom, but it was, simply, one of the freedom of the collective under the firm leadership and guidance of the magical strangers.

After all, since Lenin was so much of a representation of the possibility of alternative social arrangements, and since his very *name* was so deeply implicated in the awareness of difference, it was impossible for any group or individual to be *as much* a sovereign as he. Moreover, since all of Lenin's multitextured access to freedom was attributable to the ambivalences which were more or less peculiar to him, he was virtually by definition *a better and a more adequate* sovereign than anybody else. Perhaps that is why the struggle for the mantle of Lenin was so important in Soviet-type systems; not because the heirs were lesser individuals (as Heller and Nekrich (1986: 166) suggest), but simply because the ability to claim a privileged access to the thoughts and self-sufficiency of Lenin also implied the possession of a special and unique measure of sovereignty. In certain situations, the deployment of the name of Lenin could be turned to any ends precisely because it represented only its own freedom (for some of the uses to which Lenin was put in the 1980s, see Smart 1990).

Lenin was able to be the centre of the vanguard which led the collective to freedom because after the arrival at the Finland Station he was operating in a historically highly peculiar situation. Single projects and blueprints could be imposed and practised because there were no definitions of freedom which already commanded high levels of legitimacy. Leninism could operate as the single and exclusive plan for the improvement of the old Tsarist garden because, firstly, the other Western European gardeners with potentially viable blueprints were trying to control their own unruly weeds and, secondly, because they were too busy looking into each others' gardens to worry about events on the Eastern fringe of the allotments. The German state did not worry because Lenin promised a safe and peaceful Eastern border, whilst Britain and France could not worry because they were too concerned with Germany and, anyway, Russia seemed far away when compared to the Western Front. Lenin was able to construct high walls to keep out the other gardeners before they even noticed that there was something going on which might have been worth some inspection and surveillance.

The garden which Leninism promised to improve was indeed largely mute and was as near to the ideal state desired by the Philosopher Rulers as modernity was likely to experience. Its indigenous arrangements had either collapsed or been unable to create new reservoirs of legitimacy, and alternative designs and definitions of freedom were at present unable to break out of their own local conditions of existence. In 1917, there were no viable or powerful alternatives to the freedom which Leninism had to offer and, as such, the Leninist offer was accepted gladly or it was merely able to step into empty spaces (it is noticeable that Leninist versions of freedom tended to be very unpopular and unsuccessful whenever they had to compete with pre-existing alternatives). The Soviet-type system of really existing socialism under Stalin exploited a similar situation in Central and Eastern Europe after the collapse of the Nazi arrangements. Stalin, too, simply walked into vacant lots as the new and universal representation of freedom. Stalin was also lucky because, until the gulag became common knowledge, *anything* seemed to be *absolutely* better than Nazism. Stalin did not have a hard act to follow.

As such, the collective could indeed only be guided from outside into the radiant future of happiness. It certainly did not have the ability or the resources to guide itself. If the existing set of arrangements did possess the powers which made it something other than mute, the Leninist scheme would have had to compete with other systems of order. It would have been unable to treat social relationships as if they constituted a single garden which could not express its own potential without outside existence. Or, put another way, *in the conditions where social arrangements already possessed some power and vitality, the Leninist enterprise was nothing more than wishful thinking.*

Modernity did not contain circumstances like those of Russia in 1917 too often. It was more usually the case that any single project for the improvement of social relationships had to operate on a terrain which either could, or did, support other blueprints. Consequently, to the extent that Lenin was indeed a magical stranger, and to the extent that Leninism reflected the combination of the impact of urbanization and self-sufficient understanding (and Leninism arguably did represent such a combination), I want to propose that the Soviet-type system which remained true to the themes or tendencies of Leninism was something like a paradigmatic expression of the ideal type of gardening relationships. The modern variant of Plato's realm of the Philosopher Rulers would have looked rather like really existing socialism as it in principle existed up to 1989. However, I am not therefore playing the exceedingly pointless game of tarring Plato, or for that matter any one else, with the brush of 'totalitarianism'. On the contrary, I am trying to unravel some of the conditions of existence and some of the typical arrangements of European modernity. Again, I want to stress that I am not throwing any stones in this essay; I am just attempting to understand.

Lenin was able to exploit the precise situation which was desired by all the gardeners who wished to practise the makeability which modernity promised. But still Lenin had to *carry out* that reconstruction of social relationships, and he was only able to do that because the way of going on which was later to be called Leninism (the epithet was first used publicly by Vladimir Sorin in 1923) constituted a very firm project for action, and expressed pragmatic and moral aspirations towards the achievement of an extremely well-drawn blueprint. Although the mute social terrain was the *condition* of the Soviet-type system, it was not the *sufficient cause* of the system. The Soviet-type arrangements had to be deliberately and consciously created and operated. To say otherwise would be to posit the efficacy of some ghost in the machine; it would be to step away from the full existential responsibilities of modernity (and really existing socialism could never do that).

The key to understanding the rise and fall of the Soviet-type version of really existing socialism is to appreciate quite how much its originator, Lenin (and remember, when I use the name Lenin I am referring to a myth more than a man), and Leninism, owed to the assumptions of modernity. Certainly, Leninism was quite impossible without the belief in *new beginnings*. The debt which Leninism owed to that assumption was even greater than the debt which was owed it by Marxism. Indeed, it is reasonable to suggest that *Leninism is more important in the history and arrangements of modernity than Marxism itself.* Marxism stressed the need for a new beginning, but it is hard not to detect in Marx's work a trace of what later became Walter Benjamin's angel of history. The trace is entirely absent in Leninism, which emphasized only the *spirit*, and wilfully forgot the *experience*, of revolution. Marx always remembered that the grandiose promises of revolutionary new beginnings often turned out to be a little misplaced. Benjamin's image of the angel of history is deep and disturbing. It was inspired by Paul Klee's painting *Angelus Novus*:

His face is turned toward the past. Where we perceive a chain of events, he sees one single catastrophe which keeps piling wreckage upon wreckage and hurls it in front of his feet. The angel would like to stay, awaken the dead, and make whole what has been smashed. But a storm is blowing from Paradise; it has got caught in his wings with such violence that the angel can no longer close them. This storm irresistibly propels him into the future to which his back is turned, while the pile of debris before him grows skyward. This storm is what we call progress.

(Benjamin 1989: 258; cf. Arendt 1963: 50)

Arguably, Marx had seen the angel. Perhaps that was why he could famously say that all historical events occur twice, 'the first time as tragedy, the second as farce' (Marx 1942: 315). But Marx pinned all his hopes on a fleeting moment when the angel had managed to peer over his shoulder and see a gleaming vision of the wonderful future, a future which would make enduring the storm worthwhile. As such, Marx *did* identify the trace of a ghost in the machine but he also tried to remain adequate to the questions and opportunities of modernity. It is the measure of Marx's brilliance that to a large extent he managed to achieve that contradictory understanding of modernity. Marx knew that revolutionary new beginnings were possible only if they were carried out when the time was right. Lenin merely understood that revolutionary new beginnings were possible.

Karl Marx believed that the moment of freedom could only be achieved when the flight of the angel of history had reached a stage where that condition was possible and permissible, when the benefits of attaining the gleaming vision compensated for the pile of debris. Especially in the *Communist Manifesto*, the contention seems to be that the process of the improvement of social relationships was something like a perfectly synchronized phalanx, where the political movement (the organized proletariat), historical progress (the flight of the angel as reflected in the transition from one mode of production to another) and the deepening of the self-sufficient independence of understanding (praxis), all fed off, and provided the measure, constituency, and proof of the other. Consequently, although Marx, and of course Engels, were typical double strangers and therefore potential legislators for freedom, they were prepared to apportion

71

some responsibility elsewhere than themselves. Certainly, Marx and Engels were special, but their point was that myriad others were potentially special strangers as well. The plurality of others constituted the proletariat, which existentially and hermeneutically experienced the shock of urbanization at its sharpest. For Marx and Engels, the experience of revolution indicated that the new beginning would only be adequate when it was led by a mass of strangers (who, however, recognized a high level of sameness through shared real interests), rather than just the elite of double strangers.

Karl Marx and Frederick Engels were perhaps quite unique amongst the legislative double strangers of modernity. They were unilaterally prepared to widen the circumference of the circle which possessed special powers, and they voluntarily diluted aspects of their own exclusivity. As the provisional rules of the Working Men's International Association put it in 1864, 'the emancipation of the working classes must be conquered by the working classes themselves' (Marx 1942a: 442). To some extent, perhaps Marx and Engels came to terms with the terrible flight of the angel of history by making it a universal problem.

But Lenin was quite unprepared to diminish his own exclusivity. Rather he pushed it to almost absurd lengths. Perhaps he could do little else. Although Marx and Engels were double strangers, they believed that the more-or-less coherent advance of the different fronts of history meant that they still retained some kind of essential bond with all social relationships. They never managed, nor perhaps even wanted, to entirely deny identity. But, on the other side of that coin, they also thought that because of the devastating impact of capitalism and urbanization, the majority of social relationships had been forced to reflect upon their own historical and hermeneutic conditions of existence. That is, Marx and Engels were in the same boat as everyone else, even though they could for a short while stake a claim to take charge of the rudder. But the claim was only exclusive for the little time until the working class was able to take control itself.

Lenin could not follow that path. He was impaled on the horns of a serious dilemma. Whilst Lenin probably did not doubt the flight of the angel of history, he was more excited by the promise of the glittering future, and paid little attention to the pile of debris which was being thrown up in the struggle for the new beginning. Lenin was stimulated by a blend of the spirit of revolution (not least through the influence on his thought of nineteenth-century Russian populism) and yet also by the self-sufficient and evidently scientific system of understanding called Marxism. He *wanted* to practise the new beginning in Russia (and the voluntarism of that phrase is quite appropriate), but, according to Marxism, the Russian Empire was not at all ready to generate the Communist revolution by itself.

Marx and Engels saw history as a definite process which was revealed in the progress from one mode of production to another. According to this logic, Communism could only come into being after the bourgeois revolution. For them, the *calendar* and the *series* were quite indivisible. The difficulty which confronted Lenin was, simply, that Russia might not have experienced a bourgeois revolution. In the preface to the 1882 Russian edition of the *Communist Manifesto*, Marx and Engels put the matter very clearly. They asked whether the peasantry, which continued to be a huge proportion of the population, could pass directly to Communist relations of common ownership, or whether it, 'must first pass through the same process of dissolution such as constitutes the historical evolution of the West' (Marx and Engels 1942: 192).

Lenin overcame the problem with some skill. He must have horrified the Marxist purists, but he was remaining true to the tenets of modernity. Quite simply, Lenin consolidated and deepened the magic of strangeness. He added a *serial* dimension to the double strangeness of urban life and cosmopolitan communication networks. Lenin turned himself and the Bolsheviks into *triple strangers*. The logic of the case was fairly impeccable. If Marxism was the absolutely free, independent, and self-sufficient story of the improvement of social relationships, then it was quite plain that at some stage in the future, Russia would be ripe and waiting for the proletarian revolution. Now, if it were possible to form a small circle which exclusively possessed the truths which had been generated in the heartlands of modernity, and possible to keep it from infection and incorrect interpretation either by 'backward elements' or other, weaker, strangers, it would also in principle be possible to speed up the flight of the angel of history, and, indeed make him more concerned with the future rather than the past. If a small and strong circle could be created which entirely lacked any identity with the social terrain, it would be able to levitate above the steeples of Petrograd and the circle could claim the historical right to lead the people into freedom.

Hence the resonance of the sealed train. The train sped through a war-torn, capitalist Europe. The occupants either were not allowed, or did not want, to communicate with the people they met on the way to the future. Indeed, had they talked too much, the pure atmosphere inside the carriages would have been sullied, and the air would have borne particles of opposition which might have tarnished the magic of Lenin, Krupskaya, and the others. Instead, the carriages remained closed. They were only opened to take on supplies and, in Stockholm, to enable Lenin to recloth himself and throw off the rags of exile. The train sped through Scandinavia and arrived at the Finland Station. In barely a week it had travelled from advanced, capitalist Zurich to backward, Tsarist Russia. And all the time, the occupants of the carriages remained immune to the temptations of the journey; they were coming from the heart of modernity, as benevolent magicians, to change the world which they found waiting for them. Lenin and the Bolsheviks on the train were, consequently, totally distanced from any too-close involvement with found social relationships; their very arrival signified the validity of alternative social arrangements. The principles of Bolshevik Party organization ensured that the train would always remain sealed, ensured that the triple strangers would always be the only real sovereigns of modernity. That is why the Soviet-type system eventually fell apart.

According to Marx and Engels, the project of improvement could be safely left to that social class which experienced the forces of the inadequate present most sharply. According to them, there would come a time when the class which capitalism treated like animals would assert its intrinsic humanity and, thus, forcibly separate the free social world from the reified natural world. That would be the only sufficient and necessary new beginning since it would be the moment when the angel of history would finally smile. The implication for intellectuals (double strangers) was that they could speak *with* but never exclusively *for* the proletariat, humanity, freedom. But Lenin could not wait for the angel to smile of his own accord; he would force a laugh. Lenin deployed the historical series, in which he lived at the peak (feudalism, capitalism, socialism, communism), over and above the calendar (Monday, Tuesday, Wednesday). Lenin and the Bolsheviks were riding on the wings of the angel of history and everyone else was forced to either cling on desperately, or just become more rubble and debris. For Lenin, the free act of the proletarian revolution could not be stimulated by the indigenous resources of Russia (has there been a bourgeois revolution? If there has, why are there so many peasants?) which was in any case being reconstructed from outside.

Lenin placed all his faith in the possibility of the project which was expressed in the texts which Marx and Engels had written in the social situation of the heartland of capitalism. The texts necessarily knew the requirements of the blueprint better than the native participants and as such their exclusivity, their magical insights, had to be rigidly and diligently defended. After all, by the Leninist criteria, the self-sufficient theses of Marx and Engels could not be vindicated by the peculiar situation of Tsarist Russia. The Party was the small circle of the initiates who possessed the correct reading of the cosmopolitan knowledge which placed them above the terrain which was to be subjected to the practices of makeability. Lenin and the Bolsheviks established themselves as the clearest manifestation of social independence and, therefore, they defined themselves as the guardian of social freedom. They were achievement embodied. Compared to them, all other people and relationships were embedded in the reifications of time and place. As such, anything which the Bolsheviks did not condone could be dismissed as 'natural' and thus put into that category of things which had to be reconstructed or annihilated.

The Bolsheviks went to great lengths to ensure that the followers of Lenin were the sole and lone gardeners. Consequently they indulged in practices which denied any identity between themselves (as uniquely triple strangers) and the terrain they were to subordinate to the project. They established themselves as the exclusive site of the social in contradistinction to all else which was unable to prevent its being treated as if it were mute and abhorrent nature. The Bolsheviks took care to ensure that the silent social garden which they fortuitously inherited would remain precisely that way without their outside intervention.

Even the working class which was the putative beneficiary of the remaking of social relationships was never fully social. It was never much more than the set of potentially educable insiders, and it perpetually threatened to fracture into a multiplicity of dirty strangers. Within the Leninist scheme, the working class was simply something which never quite measured up to the criteria of what it should be (in any case, those criteria were known only by the Party and located in the serial future; the criteria were outside of the working class itself). Famously, the working class was incapable of realizing its own freedom without the help of Lenin and the other magical strangers. The effort was always too great for the workers: 'the working class, exclusively by its own effort, is able to develop trade union consciousness ... The doctrine of socialism, however, grew out of the philosophic, historical and economic theories elaborated by educated representatives of the propertied classes, by intellectuals' (Lenin 1973: 38).

Lenin was quite prepared to do something in the 'concrete situation' of Tsarist Russia which Marx would have never countenanced; perform the revolution on *behalf* of the proletariat, and if necessary *despite* it. Indeed, as Lukács said of the Leninist system in a passage which is, perhaps, unintentionally rich, it was, 'a life-and-death question for the proletariat to have the thought and actions which *truly* correspond to its class position clearly *in front of it*' (Lukács 1970: 29, emphasis added). The truth in front of it; not within it as Marx, the stranger who did not want to be too strange, established. Lenin was happy to be, and determined to remain, in the sealed train which activated all it touched and was yet itself immune from infiltration. He always spoke for the working class, and never with it. After all, for Lenin, the working class and peasantry was so backward that it was barely capable of speech. The proletariat rarely entered into Lenin's work except as a ritual incantation or as a strategic problem. It possessed no positivity, no creativity, of its own.

The lack of faith in the mute and backward people was a continuing thread in Lenin's writing, from his days as a propagandist to the years of the leadership of the Soviet Union. The unfortunate reality which Lenin identified from his position at the head of the social and historical series was the tendency of the proletariat to refuse the obligations which the project placed upon it. In 1902, he was stating that, 'the spontaneous struggle of the proletariat will not become its genuine 'class struggle' until the struggle is led by a strong organization of revolutionaries' (Lenin 1973: 167). Lenin's very modern and terribly condescending statement can be read as a declaration that the working class could not realize any alternatives unless it received outside assistance. As Agnes Heller and Ferenc Feher have rightly suggested, classes have to be made and they are, therefore, a clear expression of the freedom of modernity. Lenin was fundamentally qualifying the freedom of the proletariat (see Feher and Heller 1983: 213).

Indeed, as late as 1923, albeit in the special circumstances of the New Economic Policy, Lenin criticized the Russians because they traded in an 'Asiatic manner,' but, 'to be a good trader one must trade in the European manner. They are a whole epoch behind in that' (Lenin 1967: 761). Lenin was emphasizing the third, self-created dimension of his peculiar strangeness. He was at least a whole historical series ahead of the Russian traders if he knew so much about their terrible backwardness. Moreover, Lenin played on the cosmopolitanism of all the strangers of modernity through the association of improvement with Europe rather than indigenous arrangements. According to the Leninist project, the Russian people was too rooted in its traditional and reified ways of doing things; consequently, those time-honoured growths had to be ripped up and annihilated if the world was to be made a better place. The Russians had to be treated as a faceless collective and held firmly by the hand, or scruff of the neck, if they were to walk the road to freedom.

Lenin placed all his faith and certainty in the ability of the peculiarly Bolshevik triple strangers to bring about the future. The confidence was positively wonderful when it was the guiding light of a revolutionary new beginning which was concerned with uprooting the reified weeds of past arrangements, but it was utterly disastrous as a principle for maintaining the social garden once the angel of history had been made to smile. The Central and Eastern European version of really existing socialism ultimately failed for exactly the same reasons that it succeeded. Lenin's project and blueprint of the perfect future was, quite simply, too clever. If the certainties of the future were known by only the Party, and if the other social participants were debarred from joining the Party (because they were not suitably strange and might, therefore, dilute the magic), then the path to the better world could only be navigated by the Party of the triple strangers. And, moreover, the Party could never be wrong if only because there were no alternative sites which could establish competing definitions of freedom (and the Party tried to make sure that those sites could never flourish). In any case, the Party could claim that the criteria of the correctness or error of its ways could not be derived from the backward world which was being improved. In other words, *when the Party of the future, which had no necessary identity with indigenous resources, became the government and the Party of the present then, from its point of view, all history ceased until the backward people caught up with it and became able to practise their own freedom. Yet the continued domination of the Party, its continued necessity to maintain a high level of exclusivity, proved precisely that the people had not caught up. And by the terms of that contract of modernity, the people never could.*

In the Leninist system, the only practical vindication of the project of the Party was the success of the project in bringing about the new beginning. Yet, if the Party had managed to do that, then it could be construed as obviously the case that the project was a true expression of social self-sufficiency (else the angel of history would have turned that particular new beginning into just another pile of rubble). The Party had taken all sovereignty upon itself and, as such, it could claim to be *always* and, more importantly, *already*, able to exercise its firm leadership over the never-ending moment of the present. Thanks to the terms of the Leninist–Bolshevik contract, the road to freedom turned out to be a treadmill. The Soviet-type system was founded upon the assumption of the unchanging and unceasing correct sovereignty of the Party.

As a theory of revolution, Leninism represented the greatest expression of social independence and the most rapid insertion of social relationships into history. But as a system of government, it represented nothing other than arrogant stasis. These particular gardeners firmly refused to accept the viability of the designs of competing gardeners. As such, the Leninist gardeners of modernity did nothing other than perpetually recreate all social relationships except their own as reified nature and in need of management as if they were passive, mute, and waiting to be made free. The Party was always and already right; and, from its point of view, the world outside the Party was full of fumbling mistakes and petty self-interests which were so many obstacles to the collective achievement of freedom.

A fine example of the strange sovereignty of the Party in the Soviet-type system, and the consequent failings of the people, is provided in Vaclav Havel's play, *The Memorandum* (Havel 1981). The play also indicates how the indigenous resources were at best irrelevant, at worst a problem, for the projects of the Party as State. One of the most interesting strands of the play concerns the debates over Ptydepe, which is intended to be the new language for an administration which is free of all interest and habitual obstacles. It is obvious to all the characters in the play that Ptydepe is unworkable, but the point is that it has been framed by the Party with the aim of helping with the administration of the project. The language has to be taught to the administrators, but, by the end of the play, all the pupils have dropped out and the teacher is giving lessons to an empty classroom. But the teacher is happy to continue without students because, since Ptydepe is required by the project, it must be taught. The fact that there are no pupils merely demonstrates how far the people lag behind the responsibilities which they ought to bear. When the Managing Director of the organization reveals an inability to grasp even the simpler rudiments of Ptydepe, the same accusation is levelled against him which proved so successful against Thomas Stockmann: 'one cannot avoid concluding that in your case it is not merely a matter of average inattentiveness or negligence, but of that particular inability to learn any Ptydepe whatsoever which stems from a profound and well-disguised doubt in its very sense' (Havel 1981: 40).

By the end of the play, Ptydepe has been recognized as a pragmatic failure, and its enthusiasts exercise self-criticism. But the campaign to free organizational communications from the old ways continues unabated. It even continues under the control of the earlier supporters of Ptydepe: 'Making an end of Ptydepe doesn't mean that we must automatically give up all attempts at finally introducing some precision and order into office communications. If we did, we would – so to speak – throw out the baby with the bathwater' (Havel 1981: 85). The decision was right and always will be; it is the human raw material which fails, and always will do.

Havel tells the story of a quite circular environment where all the individual can do to retain some shred of humanity is get out (a course of action which Milan Kundera discussed in *The*

Unbearable Lightness of Being (1984)). But that means that the individual has to renounce any role in the powerful circle of dancing strangers, and has to also give up a place in the realm of the potentially educable masses (either physically through exile or cognitively through dissent). Instead, the individual can only retain some independence through a creation of self as a stranger who is therefore dirty from the point of view of the project, but might be magical from the point of view of any alternative definitions of freedom which might, however tentatively, flourish. The single stranger might become a new gardener; but until then, she or he runs the risk of being just so much filth.

Although the attempt to introduce Ptydepe was a failure, the failure was the fault not of the initial decision (which was far ahead of the local arrangements) but of the inadequate individuals who could see only their particular interests. As such, the people needed nothing other than tighter education and a firmer uprooting of the self-regenerating capacities of their old practices. The initial decision remained quite untainted since it was part of the project of making the world a better place and in any case it was distant from any involvement in the traditional, now natural, habits. The structures and arrangements of the project were quite immutable and could never be doubted. The policy failed in the specific instance of Ptydepe solely because of the inadequacies of the native resources. But, so long as the decisions were always taken in highly exclusive social spaces, they would always be for the ultimate best and everything would come right one day. When Chorukor is introduced as the replacement for Ptydepe, all the days of the week are given the same name, so that: 'The most that can happen is that the staff will meet on Tuesday, instead of on Friday, and the matter under consideration will thus even be expedited' (Havel 1981: 83).

It might be thought that Havel was merely writing a piece of absurdist theatre, but arguably he was doing something more. Although the social arrangements of *The Memorandum* are more than a little silly, the Stalinist consolidation of the Soviet-type system actually used them as principles of systemic government. Indeed, by its own lights, perhaps the Stalinist development of Leninist themes approached something like Plato's Republic for the conditions of European modernity. (I want to stress that it is not my concern to enter into the debate about whether the gulag and the other Stalinist excesses were the responsibility of Lenin. All I will say is that it would rather seem that Leninism in no way prevented the emergence of Stalinist practices.) Of course, Stalin pushed the exclusivity of the magical strangeness of the Bolsheviks in Soviet conditions to amazing lengths. The cult of personality was intended to do nothing other than personalize all the promises and requirements of improvement, and locate them in a single figure who towered above all his contemporaries. The cult of personality served to caricature the modern difficulty of sovereignty since it turned freedom into a personal possession, and leadership into individual *diktat*. Ultimately, only Stalin was entirely social; every one else was either actually or potentially indebted to nature and, therefore, actually or potentially an anathema.

The Stalinist system could blame anybody except itself. It could therefore potentially blame everybody. Stalin was the embodiment of freedom, alternative, self-sufficiency, of modernity. He was also the heart of the Party which had successfully carried out the revolutionary transformation to the new beginning and, as such, only he could make claims which were indubitably and incontestably correct. Any failures could, from the point of view of Stalinism, only be the fault of the people which was still embedded in nature and reification. Consequently, the people had to be denied any access to the exclusive, and in the last instance entirely personal, functioning of the system. The potential causes of failure were established as actual or potential filth. It is worth quoting Stalin at some length on this point. He is speaking to the Seventeenth Party Congress in 1934, on the eve of the purifying purges, and at the moment when Kirov was a very major threat to Stalin's single-handed gardening. Stalin said:

We have smashed the enemies of the Party, the opportunists of all shades, the nationalist deviators of all kinds. But remnants of their ideology still live in the minds of individual members of the Party, and not infrequently they find expression. The Party must not be regarded as something isolated from the people who surround it. It lives and works in its environment. It is not surprising that at times unhealthy moods penetrate into the Party from outside.

And the ground for such moods undoubtedly exists in our country, if only for the reason that there still exist in town and country certain intermediary strata of the population who constitute a medium which breeds such moods.

(Stalin 1973: 275)

The Party could not be entirely detached from the environment because otherwise it would not be able to work on that terrain. But it did have to deny any *identity* to be able to define itself as the active subject in contradistinction to the passive objectivity of the existing social milieu. The problem was one of making sure that the exclusive lack of identity was not surreptitiously undermined by the terrible sites of ambivalence (and therefore filth).

The Stalinist question and strategic problem was one of making all social sites a *substantialized nothing*. Unfortunately, the 'intermediary strata' were not *no*thing; the mere act of talking about them called them forth as *some*thing and, therefore, established them as illicit sites of activity. The point was that they were too weak to answer back to the Great Leader. The only response for Stalin was to identify those ambivalent locations of the social, name them as inadequate and indebted to reification, and then treat them as if they were wild nature in the happy garden. That is, subject them to practices of 'sewage disposal' (to use Solzhenitsyn's resonant and tragic term for the gulag (Solzhenitsyn 1974)) and then cleanse the free realm of the social by the annihilation of the problematic strata.

This strategy meant that the Stalinist rendition of the Soviet-type system, and it was arguably that version which was exported through Central and Eastern Europe to fill the void left by the destruction of Nazism, was able to overcome the potential problem of the withdrawal of popular support. The people was blamed for everything which went wrong and it was consciously and rather necessarily excluded from the stable arrangements of the project. But the people still did not question the Stalinist system in any great depth. Throughout, the Stalinist arrangements were able to claim, not entirely fictitiously, that they spoke for and on behalf of the best interests of the people. Of course, terror played a major role in making sure that the domination of the Stalinist arrangements would not be questioned, but the tacit support of the people could be claimed because the people was constructed as that group of insiders which believed the promises of the good tomorrow. Everybody else, everybody who expressed some however mild doubt about the intentions of the guide to freedom, was necessarily a dirty stranger; a wrecker, a 'nationalist deviator', or a spy.

The Stalinist consolidation of really existing socialism bore an extremely close relationship with Jean Jacques Rousseau's concept of the General Will. According to Rousseau, the General Will is embodied in the sovereign government which is the manifestation of social agreement and the reconciliation of personal, selfish interests, into a common wealth. 'It follows ... that the general will is always upright and always tends to the public advantage; but it does not follow that the deliberations of the people have the same rectitude' (Rousseau 1979: 162). The Stalinist system gave the final part of that passage an especially nasty tweak. For it, any one who did not fully accept the demands of the General Will as it was known and expressed by the Bolshevik Party, was merely expressing selfish interests and was, therefore, in error and in need of correction.

Again, Vaclav Havel has made the point well. At his trial in October 1979, he evidently stated that: 'The system is based on an a priori assumption that the state can do no wrong ... then anybody criticizing their actions is logically engaging in slander, vilification, and so on' (Havel 1981: vi). That is precisely the principle which the Stalinist system of gardening relationships turned into a guide for government and an ethic for education. The State could not admit that the people did not support it, because the people by definition did. The only problems were caused by those outsiders who were either unprepared or unable to accept the sovereignty of Stalin. The system could not change until the people caught up with it (but they never could) and so responsibility for failure could only be apportioned on the basis of a perpetual definition and redefinition of the social insiders and the outsiders.

If the crop failed, for example, the failure could not be the fault of the groups of spies and wreckers who were blamed last time since they had already been sent to the sewage works, and by definition they had been sent successfully because they had been sent by the Party acting under the signature of the Leader. The fault must lie with another recalcitrant and backward group. The boundary line between the social and the natural was permanently inching inwards so that the home of freedom and independence was increasingly restricted and exclusive. The still natural, still reified, areas of life became ever greater and an increasing threat. In other words, the Stalinist system was intractably built upon two divergent and ultimately irreconcilable foundations. The blueprint was put at the head of serial history, and access to it was restricted to the small group of self-defined triple strangers who were thus placed outside of chronological history and on the wings of the angel of history, cajoling him into looking over his shoulder rather than sadly at the wake of progress. But the people were constituted and subjectively mobilized through chronological categories ('Who can we blame this time?') which were never quite up to the standards of the blueprint.

Ultimately, the sealed train was sealed too well; nobody could get in, and the occupants could not see out except through heavily curtained windows. By the 1970s, the occupants stopped looking out altogether and, instead, they merely assumed that they were continuing on the journey to the better world. Had they checked, they would have seen that the train had run out of tracks, and that the prisoners of the calendar were unable to make any more. One of the main reasons for the success and indeed failure of the Soviet-type system was that the sovereign subjects were too distant from the social relationships which they treated as mute, passive nature. Originally, that lack of identity gave the Bolshevik institutions a massive amount of room in which to manoeuvre. Lenin realized the full implications of the situation he found at the Finland Station and, thus, went some way towards practising the ideal arrangements of modernity. He could do much as he pleased and claim that it was all in the name of freedom simply because there was no alternative site for the definition of how the world might be made a better place.

But Stalin pushed those opportunities to extreme lengths and, with the massive emphasis on the domination of the series and the personalization of the future, he made sure that the lack of identity would become, simply, a lack of any contact whatsoever. The sealed train trundled along happily, but it crushed the people who were trying to cling to it. As such, the sovereigns had no contact at all with the putative beneficiaries of the march to freedom, and they were unable to command the social and material resources without which the reproduction of magical abilities was quite impossible. The gardeners failed to venture beyond the doors of the greenhouse.

Had they ventured into the spaces of the garden, the gardeners of the Soviet-type system would have seen that their very successes had created new problems which they were quite unable to resolve. It must be said that whenever the heirs of Lenin stepped into social arrangements which could be treated as if they were passive nature, they were remarkably adept at quickly establishing new varieties of social organization and new justifications for going on. *As a new beginning the Soviet-type system was an outstanding success which thoroughly vindicated some of the highest hopes of modernity.* But those initial successes could not be repeated. As the Soviet-type system of really existing socialism gradually recreated legitimate sites and arrangements of social activity which would bear the weight of the achievement of the blueprint, the system also seriously restricted its own room to manoeuvre. The blueprint could be imposed from the top and down onto a social landscape which could be treated in an entirely homogenous way, only so long as the social relationships were, indeed, all similarly silent.

But the Soviet-type system made those once silent spaces speak; and, as such, it made sure that the social landscape could not be treated as if it were all entirely the same. It was also forced to realize that perhaps the social terrain of Central and Eastern Europe, and for that matter many of the Soviet Republics, had not been as mute as was originally assumed. The quest for homogeneity merely created new forms of heterogeneity. Obviously, some attempt was made to come to terms with that rather unforeseen social construction of waste by pushing it into sewage disposal institutions, but other sites of heterogeneity could not be disposed of quite so easily. Ultimately, the Soviet-type struggle for collective freedom merely multiplied the number of strangers. The single garden needs single gardeners and an unstructured landscape; but precisely in so far as the Soviet-type system worked, it *did* structure the landscape, and it *did* create alternative gardeners. The single garden contained tendencies which would eventually lead to it becoming one allotment amongst many. And as soon as any collective definition of sovereignty has to come to terms with other interpretations of sovereignty, it falls apart. The mere possibility of plurality destroys any practice of homogeneity.

As soon as the slogan 'Socialism in One Nation!' was uttered, the Soviet-type system was flung into the wake of the angel of history. It was then only a matter of time before the angel took revenge on Lenin's effrontery. The regimes of really existing socialism collapsed because they were, firstly, out of touch, and, secondly, because they were utterly unable to deny the viability of alternative interpretations of the gifts and promises of modernity. They had to be given only the slightest of pushes, and of course the withdrawal of military assistance, to fold in upon their own irrelevance. The point is that *if* Leninism was actually what it claimed to be, it could in no way accept that it should cease at international border points. *If* the Bolsheviks were in exclusive possession of the blueprint, they could not accept the viability of arrangements which were obvious affronts to that blueprint.

But Stalin tried to show that alternative arrangements *were* viable, and indeed, necessary. For example, he told the Nineteenth Party Congress of 1952 that: 'Our Party and our country always were and always will be in need of the trust, sympathy, and support of fraternal peoples abroad' (Stalin 1973a: 508). A bigger blunder for the collective road to freedom could not have been made. Stalin said that the wellbeing of the Soviet Union was dependent upon the wellbeing of other social arrangements. As such, he was saying that those alternatives were viable and legitimate; consequently, they were also the site of alternatives which might be possible in the Soviet Union. Stalin recreated the question of freedom; all the time the Party claimed exclusive possession of the blueprint, freedom was not on the agenda since the Party knew what was ultimately best. But Stalin restricted exclusivity to national boundaries and, so, he implicitly implied that the world outside contained a plurality of alternatives. And, therefore, freedom could not be an exclusive possession. The idea of Socialism in One Country proved nothing so much that the Bolsheviks were not Plato's Philosopher Rulers. Rather, they were just self-interested strangers. They were the traitors to modernity; just like Thomas Stockmann. They suffered much the same fate.

The Bolshevik blueprint could not be naturalized as soon as it accommodated the imagination of alternatives. That is the importance of the debates surrounding the issue of human rights. The kind of opposition which Andrei Sakharov engaged against the existing power arrangements was certainly brave and selfless, but it could never be too successful. Essentially, Sakharov was a classic intellectual who took the claims and self-images of modernity entirely seriously. Isaiah Berlin has sympathetically written that Sakharov's, 'scientific outlook, unbelievable courage, physical and moral, above all his unswerving dedication to truth, makes it impossible not to see him as the ideal representative ... of the intelligentsia, old and new' (*Guardian* 20 February 1990). Sakharov's basic and unremitting point was that the Soviet-type system was a mutation of the promises of freedom and his answer to all the ills of Central and Eastern Europe was, simply, one of the *improvement* of modernity; more industry, better agricultural chemicals, more housing (this is all especially clear in an article in the *New York Times* 22 July 1968). But all the legislators had to do to deflate Sakharov's argument was suggest that indeed they were behaving in a way which was true to modernity. They could suggest that Sakharov was an impatient opportunist who had not waited long enough for the trees of modernity to bear ripe fruit. Sakharov was of course an astonishingly courageous man, but his strategy of opposition, which involved making a claim to usurp the existing gardeners, could only fail.

But the opposition on the basis of human rights was more effective altogether. Of course, the Bolshevik's exclusive claim to the position of sovereign gardeners had little or no place for any assertion that all individuals were equally morally relevant simply by virtue of their humanity. For Lenin and the others, grand anthropological categories like human rights had to be subordinated to the pragmatic demands of socialist ethics. For example, the fourth Soviet Constitution accepted the importance of the freedoms of expression, assembly, and demonstration, but it continued to qualify the broad sweep. The use of those freedoms had to be compatible with, 'the interests of the working class and aim at strengthening the socialist system' (quoted in Jarv 1987: 237–238). The history of the Soviet-type system had, however, established that the knowledge of those interests was an exclusive possession which had to be diligently defended. As such, that particular definition of freedom was thoroughly under the sway of the single gardening design. But, in 1975, the Soviet-type states signed the Helsinki Accords which established the position of human (*qua* human) rights in the legal codes of the signatory nations. The erstwhile gardeners consequently rather feebly gave up their strong and lone control of the reins of social relationships. When the notion of human rights was accepted, other definitions of freedom were also accepted as viable. The garden became some kind of allotment.

The Helsinki defence groups, such as Charter 77 in Czechoslovakia and the Movement for the Defence of Human Rights and Civil Rights in Poland, mobilized on the terrain of the restriction of the once universal project of the Bolsheviks. Certainly, the Soviet-type states could imprison or suppress the human rights groups but, solely because they had signed the Helsinki Agreement, they could never dismiss the idea of human rights. They could never dispel the forces which could bring about the collapse of the single project of freedom. The train was unsealed and new magical circles could start to dance. The once universal and homogenizing forces of socialist morality were beaten with the stick of a pluralizing human rights. For example, Charter 77 welcomed the ratification of various international human rights statements in Czechoslovakian law, but it was able to operate on the basic contradiction that although human rights was accepted in theory, it was a myth in practice. For Charter 77, the distinction between the official and the actual conditions of life was, 'a powerful reminder of the extent to which basic human rights in our country exist, regrettably, on paper alone' (Charter 77 1978: 271). Charter 77 tried to bring that contradiction into the light and effect some sort of reconciliation. It operated as an immanent critique, and was able to do so, because the formerly exclusive gardeners of the Soviet-type system accepted that other gardeners might have viable designs for the Eastern and Central European terrains and, moreover, that competing groups of strangers might themselves possess some special abilities.

For many years, the single gardening project had been imposed ruthlessly and, strictly by its own criteria, rather successfully. But that imposition was only possible because the terrain which was being gardened was itself passive and, of course, deliberately kept quiet. However, whilst the gardeners were able to maintain the lack of any identity between themselves and the relationships which they were remaking, it was impossible to keep the terrain passive. Quite the contrary. Moreover, simply by virtue of the fact that the Soviet-type systems accepted the viability of different gardening strategies (with the acceptance of Socialism in One Nation), they also gave up their own exclusive possession of the secrets of the future.

The strangers who made the Soviet Union relied upon cosmopolitanism to develop and sell their blueprints of freedom, and it was precisely that cosmopolitanism which finally forced the realization that modernity was often characterized by a plurality of blueprints. All the blueprints claimed to be true because their proof was in the eating and the eating was in the future. As such, whilst the heirs of Lenin, and more especially the heirs of Stalin, claimed to be the sole true sovereigns of human and social freedom, they gradually accepted that other sovereigns might also have a role to play. And the point is that, probably by accident rather than design, they allowed those other sovereigns to stake a claim to legitimacy within the once homogenous terrains. As such, the interpretation of sovereignty within really existing socialism was pluralized, and any sovereigns who were arrogant enough to claim a unique and a special status were simply things to be overcome and knocked down from their pedestals. In 1989, they were indeed rocked and they toppled over.

To put the matter somewhat schematically: *If* really existing socialism *were* an extremely close approximation to an ideal typical expression of the tendencies of modernity (and the Soviet-type system was precisely that), *then* modernity ideal typically led to the bureaucratic totally administered society (this point is also approached to some extent in the argument of Bruno Rizzi; see Rizzi 1985), the development of alternative blueprints of freedom (thanks to cosmopolitanism; the 'Dissidents') and, ultimately, collapse. To the extent that modernity struggled to go on, it also threw up morbid symptoms which could never be overcome without a renouncement of either the very notion of going on, or, indeed, the very resources of modernity.

4

ALLOTMENTS

The formation of the Soviet-type system can be interpreted as the proof of two things. Firstly, it was a practical vindication of the exceedingly ambitious projects which the double strangers (the legislators of modernity) occasionally created for themselves and for history. Secondly, the system could be read as an illustration of the ability of the double strangers to achieve their most desired ends, if the social and historical conditions were right. But the imposition of blueprints of qualitatively better and morally improved social relationships rarely involved a simple, or a single, leap from pre-modern reification. Rather the opposite. Whilst the narratives of modernity might have recognized no immutable no-go areas, it was frequently the case that the ideals had to exist and operate in a social context which did indeed constitute so many obstacles to what might be done.

The founders of the Soviet-type system were extremely fortunate. The reifications which they sought to demolish, or at least enter into history and thereby transform, were already showing signs of a terminal collapse. But the Central and Eastern European passage to modernity involved rather more than the *luck* of finding some circumstances as opposed to others. Such a presumption of good fortune would have been an affront to the intellectual and political legislators, and, indeed, to the reflexive self-images of modernity. It would necessarily have delimited the sphere of the social. Indeed, the ideas of fortune and fate inevitably refer to precisely the realm of some extra-social agency which is able to shape the destiny of social ambitions which modernity essentially questioned (see Giddens 1990; Luhmann 1979).

Certainly, the Bolsheviks and their heirs in Central and

Eastern Europe inherited a situation which was not of their own making (to which extent they were extremely fortunate), but they were only able to mobilize the reflexive projects of improvement because they were highly organized and solid behind their leaders. That is, the Soviet-type system was the product of the practical activity of a militant corps of magical strangers who trusted in luck only to the extent that it constituted a set of opportunities which they were capable of seizing. This raises the vitally important question of the means by which the double strangers (in the Bolshevik case, the *triple* strangers), managed to act so deliberately and cohesively. So far, the double strangers have always been referred to as if they were an internally homogeneous group. More seriously, I have tended to conflate the double strangers *in themselves* with the double strangers *for themselves*. That conflation rather naughtily implies some necessary connection between social position and social interests, and should be explained in rather a lot of detail rather than simply assumed. After all, the defining characteristic of the double strangers was precisely their lack of identity with any given standards. To the extent that the double strangers were constructed as wholly exclusive, it could well be objected that it makes little sense, and means even less, to start talking about them as if they constituted an inclusive and already identifiable social group. The exploration of the reasons why it seems fairly appropriate to make a potentially illicit conflation is of more than theoretical value; it might also go some way towards explaining why the Western European experiences of modernity tended to diverge so sharply from the Soviet-type approximation to the revised and updated rendition of the Platonic ideal.

Of course, the coherence and inclusivity of the exclusive legislators in the garden conditions out of which the Soviet-type system was made to grow, was maintained through highly developed institutional arrangements. Indeed, those magical strangers danced in a huge circle which might have got smaller over time as 'cowards and traitors' fell out, but the circle also got tighter as faint-hearts, like Milan Kundera in Prague, were forcibly pushed out. The Soviet-type system represented such an unflinching imposition of a modern blueprint precisely because the standards of social improvement were so carefully guarded and enforced by the Party. The Party not only gave the legislative, magical, strangers the organizational ability to seize the opportunities before them. The Party was also an institutional arrangement through which some inclusive identity, some shared interests, could be forged. One of the main concerns of the Party apparatus was to create some kind of identity between otherwise isolated individuals who were more or less by definition strangers to each other.

The Leninist requirement that an activist must work in a Party cell was intended to avoid the possibility of, 'a loose party mass'. Leninism ensured that there existed, 'not a mish-mash, but a firmly cast organization' (Zinoviev 1973: 89). The creation of an organization for genuine revolutionaries followed the point which Lenin famously established; the Party should comprise of professionals, 'who would serve only the revolution and not concern themselves with anything else' (Zinoviev 1973: 78; see also Lenin 1973). That is, and of course quite typically, Zinoviev and Lenin were outraged by the thought of slipping *personal* interests into the project. Such interests had absolutely no place in the workings of the institutional arrangements which wanted to bring about the apparently benign future sooner rather than later.

In the context of the Soviet-type system at least, it is viable to elide the double strangers in themselves and for themselves. The Party was a means by which an identity between strangers was constructed (on the basis of their world-historic importance), and by which that identity could be consolidated and reproduced through the exclusiveness of a largely elective group membership. To the extent that separate would-be legislators of modernity saw an expression of their interests in the Party, they joined it and started to dance in an especially magical circle. Membership of the Party subsequently reflected back on the strangeness of the 'professional revolutionaries' to transform that difference into an identity of freedom.

Now, it cannot be doubted that the Party was indeed an immensely powerful mechanism for the construction of a degree of homogeneity amongst the otherwise resolutely heterogeneous. But an emphasis upon relationships within and around the Party cannot explain that homogeneity except at the most superficial level. The point is that the 'professional revolutionaries' had *to be able* to electively associate themselves to the Party institutions, whilst the Party itself *already had to exist* as a clear expression of certain interests and blueprints in order to attract the potential members. In other words, to say that the group in itself became a group for itself through an elective affinity to the Party, is rather to beg the question of why the affinity was felt in the first place. Alternatively, perhaps it can be proposed that the affinity was constructed to the extent that the techniques of exclusivity and exclusion implied by Party membership corresponded exactly to the self-same strategies which had been already and independently adopted, or at least yearned for, by the double strangers as individuals. However, that is again to avoid the question of how it might be that some distinct identity could be made between isolated individuals who were defined precisely by the denial of any identities (i.e. how could the double strangers *as a group* possibly know that *as a group* they longed for what the Party had to offer?). The roots of the possibility of the homogeneity of the otherwise heterogeneous must have been elsewhere. That elsewhere was the *culture of reflexive discourse* which the conditions of modernity threw up, and which linked together the otherwise independent strangers.

The idea of a culture of reflexive discourse was developed by Alvin Gouldner, although he later changed the phrase to the culture of *critical* discourse (Gouldner 1975, 1979, 1985). Essentially, the reflexive discourse is seen by Gouldner as a kind of communication ethic which reflected and defined the self-definitions and legislative interests of modern intellectuals. 'The culture of critical discourse insists that any assertion – about anything, by anyone – is open to criticism and that, if challenged, no assertion can be defended by invoking someone's authority' (Gouldner 1985: 30). In other words, the reflexive discourse embodied the assumption that achievement (knowledge as a struggle of cognition) possessed an intrinsic supremacy over ascription (knowledge as a reflection of social position). It was a thoroughly modern refusal to recognize any reified structures of authority; reflexivity was an expression of freedom. The reflexive culture was the 'special ideology of intellectuals and the intelligentsia' (Gouldner 1975: 30), which established their right to speak with authority irrespective of their frequently marginal social situation. For example, the fundamental thrust of Immanuel Kant's work was that the individual agent of maturity and free thought could not be a social insider if knowledge was to be adequate to the tasks of Enlightenment.

Consequently, the reflexive culture had a quite revolutionary impact. For the intellectuals, who were staking claims for positions of hermeneutic and political legislation, it was, 'alienating and even radicalizing because it demands the right to sit in judgment over all claims, regardless of who makes them' (Gouldner 1985: 30). The culture was predicated upon, and was a means of the reproduction of, the principle that knowledge which was enlightened and not associated with the grinding of personal axes was the ruling force in the world. Inevitably, this meant that the double strangers who thought that they should be in charge, even though they were not, could be nothing other than deeply contemptuous of existing social arrangements. But this criticism was not an unfocused *angst*. Rather, to the extent that the double strangers were confirmed in their intellectual apartness by the principles and practices of reflexive discourse, they similarly shared a common trait and a shared goal. 'The "essence" of the radical intelligentsia's political striving is the removal of any social obstacle to societal rationality. This intelligentsia can be the enemy of ... *any* society, anywhere in the world' (Gouldner 1985: 48).

Of course, the double strangers were created through the dual processes of urbanization and the cosmopolitanism of communication networks. The processes established the potential universality of Enlightenment. But this did not mean that the magical double strangers constituted a group which merely *happened* to comprise of new intellectuals who were excluded from the traditional positions of authority and social order. As the examples of Kant and Thomas Stockmann indicated, a commitment to the reflexive culture was the defining trait of the double strangers *in* themselves and it was also the means by which they struggled *for* themselves. The Bolshevik Party was one manifestation of the culture, and it was the intellectual practice of reflexivity which established the elective connections between many intellectuals and the universalized and yet extremely exclusive Party apparatus. The Party was precisely the means by which the heterogeneous strangers could be confirmed in the magic of their difference and yet also assured that, unlike Thomas Stockmann, they were not alone. The reflexive discourse of modernity was the prism of the creation of the double strangers in and for themselves, and to the extent that any organization was established upon the foundations of that

94

discourse, it seemed to be the natural home of the erstwhile legislators of modernity.

In the garden-type situation of the Soviet Union, and later Central and Eastern Europe, the institutionalization of the reflexive discourse had a quite massive impact. Of course, the double strangers could be nothing other than outraged by the reified or more often collapsed social arrangements they found, and which were consequently defined as inadequate, improper, and in need of reconstruction. Through the institutions of Bolshevism, the outrage was transformed into a coherent historical destiny and, importantly, linked to a practical means of ensuring improvement. The apparatus of the Party was so attractive to so many of the double strangers on two accounts. Firstly, it consolidated exclusivity and, secondly, it turned the narrative belief in makeability into a definite practical option. The Party was the instrument which transformed the new beginning in the realm of ideas into a new beginning in the realm of social practices; it was, so to speak, an incarnation of the flight of the angel of history. It flattered the wildest hopes of the intellectuals and, perhaps more importantly, it held out the chance of *success*.

But whilst that success might have been taken as a reflection of the correctness of the hermeneutic systems of modernity, it was more deeply indebted to the fact that in garden situations the organized double strangers encountered very little which could stand in their way. Where the garden situation did not prevail, and where the double strangers indeed encountered local opposition, modernity tended to take on a number of mutated forms. This is the root of the contrast between the Soviet-type experience of modernity and of the experience of modernity in Western Europe. The inability of the Western European double strangers to either crush or ignore the traditional and reified structures of authority (that is, their inability to treat the social terrain as if it were a garden) meant that, for them, modernity meant very different things than it did for Lenin and his heirs. The point was that in Western Europe, the existing social arrangements were not in terminal decay, and the ideal conditions of the mute and passive garden which the modern blueprints presupposed could not be found.

Certainly, in the circumstances of late eighteenth and early nineteenth-century Britain, Edmund Burke knew very well that traditional reifications retained a great deal of legitimacy and were, to some extent, impervious to the full impact of the practice of reflexivity. Indeed, the hold of tradition over Burke was so great that institutions which the free protagonists of modernity would have identified immediately as superstitious and foolish were seen by him to be living and vibrant arrangements. Indeed, Burke's meditations on the lessons of the French Revolution caused him to restate the immutability, and for that matter the intellectual and social necessity, of the traditional and accepted old ways. 'When antient opinions and rules of life are taken away, the loss cannot possibly be estimated. From that moment we have no compass to govern us; nor can we know distinctly to what port we steer' (Burke 1968: 172–173). The angel of history, who, however unhappily, pointed the way forwards, is quite absent from the argument. There is not really any history at all; there is just the imagination of utter chaos.

Burke refused to accept that the indigenous social relationships of Britain constituted a mute garden. On the contrary, he identified the relationships as so many hardy and desirable growths from a self-supporting soil.

> Upon that body and stock of inheritance we have taken care not to inoculate any cyon alien to the nature of the original plant. All the reformations we have hitherto made, have proceeded upon the principle of reference to antiquity.
>
> (Burke 1968: 117)

It was precisely this continued embeddedness of the present in the past, and indeed the clear direction indicated by antiquity (the direction of a circular return), which was taken as a guarantee that the consistent social constructions of the time-honoured order of things would not collapse.

In a passage which, on the one hand, represents an attempt to turn away from the impact of modernity and yet, on the other hand, shows how the impact might be felt nevertheless, Edmund Burke tried to come to terms with his present. But the present, which involved precisely the entrance of social relationships into history, reflexivity, and modernity which Burke wanted to deny, showed only that whilst traditional structures retained habitual allegiance, they had lost all hermeneutic authority. 'Everything seems out of nature in this strange chaos of levity and ferocity, and of all sorts of crimes jumbled together with all sorts of follies' (Burke 1968: 92). Burke accepted the reification bequeathed by antiquity, and he thought that the legacy guaranteed the systems of order. But the *Reflections* prove nothing so much as the ability of modernity to escape and overflow the time-honoured ways.

However, whilst the emergence of the struggle for freedom from reification certainly prejudiced the continued existence of the institutions and the arrangements which Edmund Burke applauded, it was the case in Britain, and more broadly, throughout Western Europe, that the old forms rarely fell into a terminal collapse or a final silence. For example, even in France, where the Revolutionary new beginning had witnessed and involved one of the first battles in the Armageddon of reification, it was not too difficult for quasi-monarchical arrangements to be replanted after the Napoleonic interregnum. But in post-Napoleonic France, social order was constructed through an amalgamation of modern and pre-modern structures. The history of nineteenth-century France shows how quickly that hybrid joining together led to mutual inabilities to understand each other.

When the ideal gardening situation did not prevail, or could not be reproduced, the ideal-type arrangement of modernity (the updated version of the reign of the Philosophers) was a social impossibility. Instead, the full freedoms of modernity were compromised. When a plurality of viable social institutions already existed, independently and irrespective of the reflexive discourse of modernity, the double strangers became simply one group of ambitious legislators amongst many. Burke tried to ensure that the gardening ambitions met permanent and fundamental qualification since, 'We are resolved to keep an established church, an established monarchy, an established aristocracy, and an established democracy, each in the degree it exists, and in no greater' (Burke 1968: 188).

Inevitably, the situation of a deeply entrenched, and self-reproducible, plurality of sites of social authority, had a massive impact on the double strangers. According to the claims of reflexive discourse, the double strangers were a group of legislators who, in struggling for themselves, were also fighting to improve social relationships for everyone. In the ideal garden conditions, reflexivity was able to operate as something like a steamroller. It crushed anything which was in its way and, in its wake, left an empty, flat, and frictionless path, along which the double strangers could lead (or drag) the grateful collectivities. In the Soviet Union and Central and Eastern Europe, the practical arrangement of reflexivity was able to generate an astonishing momentum. Firstly, it was operating in a terrain which presented no local qualifications to even the wildest and most speculative claims, and, secondly, the Party organization guaranteed that the sites and agents of free reflexivity were consolidated and for a while capable of reproduction. But in the social and historical conditions of Western Europe, the steamroller effect was an impossibility.

The double strangers could not claim exclusive access to knowledge (even though they might have claimed an exclusive access to freedom and to truth), and the reflexive discourse had to operate and exist in a terrain which was found as *already* structured and *already* active. Consequently, the commitment to a narrative which paid no attention to the social location of the speaker, had to accommodate itself to a set of social relationships where the location of the speaker was indeed identified as a matter of some importance. The reflexive culture of modernity was unable to treat the social terrain as if it were a passive landscape, and the denial of any identity with local resources lost much of its appeal since it ran the risk of being charged with cosmopolitan dilettantism. The only constructive responses which the double strangers could make were to either *assimilate* concepts and patterns drawn from the local pool, or to *accommodate* themselves with local circumstances. But either response had major implications.

Quite simply, the Western European situation of the eighteenth, nineteenth, and twentieth centuries ensured that the modern interest in the new beginning could never move beyond the confines of wishful thinking. The ambition of the double strangers to universalize the practices and principles of freedom (and therefore of themselves) could not be realized. Indeed, where a plurality of legitimate social arrangements already existed, it was immensely difficult for the double strangers to identify themselves and their projects *with* a universally desirable freedom. Instead, the lack of ability to claim exclusive knowledge of the flight of the angel of history meant that the double strangers were unable to distance their ostensibly universal and selfless ambitions for humanity from charges or implications of selfishness. Where the garden situation was not fortuitously encountered, the double strangers could be easily tarred with exactly the same brush of interest and resentment which finally destroyed Thomas Stockmann.

Edmund Burke clearly realized the power of this charge. He tried to collapse all the expressions of the modern commitment to the new beginning into the ambitions of certain social groups to foster their own advancement and prosperity. 'A spirit of innovation is generally the result of a selfish temper and confined views. People will not look forward to posterity, who never look backward to their ancestors' (Burke 1968: 119). The point is that in Western Europe the double strangers had to maintain themselves in an environment where 'people' did indeed happily and actively look back to their ancestors. In other words, the double strangers were thrown into a situation where traditional arrangements retained a multitextured legitimacy. That was precisely the situation they feared, detested, and saw as an affront to all that they were and did. They were unable to claim exclusivity (since other social groups possessed legitimacy), and yet the whole *raison d'être* of the double strangers was indivisible from the emphasis on exclusivity. At another level, the double strangers derived their legislative abilities and evident right to govern from their geographical and intellectual cosmopolitanism, and yet they had been forced to reconcile themselves with purely local conditions of existence.

The sharp boundary lines which modernity had established between the cosmopolitan freedom of some hermeneutic systems and the local reification of others, were profoundly blurred in Western Europe. Consequently, the *reason for being* of the double strangers was structurally diluted, but as a distinct and self-conscious social group, the double strangers continued *to be*. They were caught on the horns of an especially serious dilemma where intellectual exclusivity was unsustainable, and yet social exclusivity was an absolute necessity. In garden situations, those two moments of apartness and distinction went hand in hand, but the linkages were pulled apart when the garden situation was not found. The Western double strangers responded to their unwanted involvement in the local, which threatened to destroy exclusivity through familiarity and the charge of selfishness, by the ritualization of strangeness. The ritual imputation of freedom and reflexivity was, 'grounded in the specialized knowledge or cultural capital transmitted by the educational system, along with an emphasis on the obligation of educated persons to attend to the welfare of the collectivity. In other words, the *ideology* of 'professionalism' emerges (Gouldner 1979: 19).

That professionalism itself became associated with participation in certain very specific occupations (the Academy), or with the positive evaluation of 'high' or avant-garde art (I understand the phrase 'high art' in a rather Nietzschean sense where high art is simply that lauded by the 'high' social groups). Frequently, perhaps even invariably, those component strands of the Western European condition of magical strangeness worked together to produce and reflect the social consciousness of an extremely specific social group which was identified as entirely free of the reproduction of mundane reality. The emergence of professionalism meant that the double strangers who could not be gardeners could still act *as if* they were gardeners. They could draw up blueprints which were meant to be the final expression of freedom, and they could create their own ritualized zones where the ethic of reflexive discourse was indeed said to hold good. The difficulty was, that outside of the restricted zones (such as the lecture theatre or the seminar room), the codes of professionalism were seen as so many peculiarities or glosses on self-interest. The interpretations of strangeness threatened to oscillate between magic and filth. However, from the point of view of the double strangers themselves, there was little doubt that the professional ethic should inform the practices and attitudes of all social groups. The professionals' problem inevitably was one of making all others more like them.

But the social requirement of the Western double strangers to emphasize strangeness through professionalization meant that the relationships of involvement and detachment which makeability supposes were pulled so far that they snapped. Quite simply, the commitment to an unhindered reflex discourse in a social context where the commitment was qualified, led the would-be legislators down a very long road of the exacerbation of exclusivity. Had they not followed that route, the double strangers would have ceased to possess any awareness of their difference from everyone else. But the further they went along the road of professionalization, the more the double strangers lost any attachment to the social relationships which were defined as in need of reconstruction. That is, the more the double strangers of Western Europe confirmed their existence, the less they became a significant social force. As such, they could not invest themselves with the last fleeting hopes for the imposition of the blueprint. The imposition had to be accomplished on their behalf.

Where the ideal garden situation did not prevail, the double strangers were eventually forced to 'shop' for an agent (Gouldner 1985: 25). The double strangers were only able to reproduce their identity to the extent that they systematized it and equated it with the possession of certain traits, or access to certain positions. But in so doing, they made themselves unable to carry out the reconstruction of social relationships which was the whole purpose of their continued existence. Consequently, they had to find some agent who would perform the making on their behalf. Alvin Gouldner's image of the act of shopping for an agent of history is extremely rich. It is worth thinking about what a shopping relationship actually involves. Shopping implies some formalized (contractual) exchange between two parties who are able to equate one thing (i.e. money) for another (i.e. a commodity). There is no necessary association between the two parties outside of the actual act of purchase, or of being purchased. The exchange relationship which is the basis of shopping occurs only in situations where it is true that, 'non-owning need on the one side must coincide with not-needing ownership on the other. If those who have what I need do not need what I have, then they will not be interested in an exchange' (Haug 1986: 13).

By this definition, the double strangers could only go shopping for an agent, firstly, to the extent that they possessed something which they did not need themselves, but which other groups did need (the blueprint of the qualitatively and ethically improved social relationships, which the double strangers *already* lived) and, secondly, to the extent that the potential sovereign agents possessed something which they did not need themselves, but which the double strangers could use (the deep involvement in social relationships which the practice of makeability required). In the ideal garden situation, the double strangers did not have to participate in acts of shopping. They themselves possessed the hermeneutic and the practical resources by which the blueprints could be imposed upon the recalcitrant way of things. As such, Lenin needed the working class only to the extent that they added muscle to what the double strangers would have attempted in any case. But in non-garden situations, shopping was indeed a crucially necessary act.

The problem is that any exchange relationship embodies a fundamental tension which centres upon the divergent interests of the purchasers and the purchased. The tension becomes especially pressing when both parties are able to speak for themselves. Quite simply, the double strangers could only successfully shop for an agent if they could offer to the potential makers of modernity something which they did not possess but actively desired. Of course, the double strangers did believe that they could offer something which any right-minded social group would deeply desire; freedom and the future. From the point of view of the double strangers, it should have been a relatively simple task to buy the efforts of a group which was in the position to transform social relationships and, consequently, become the proxy sovereigns of modernity. But the history of the attempts to indulge in shopping relationships seems to indicate nothing so much as the refusal of the proxy sovereigns to exchange their actions for the promises which the blueprints held out.

Wherever the double strangers had ritualized their strangeness to such an extent that they lost any and all identity with the social terrain, the proxy agents invariably refused to sell themselves. It rather seems that the double strangers were typically quite inept shoppers. The question is: was the inability to buy a result of the actual worthlessness of the offer, or was it the fault of the potentially bought groups who were too stupid to see the real value of the offer? The exchange relationship is predicated upon the reciprocity of buyers and sellers, and it would seem that in Western European modernity, reciprocity was elusive and extremely difficult to establish.

The double strangers were in no doubt that they could not possibly be responsible for the failure to establish reciprocal exchange relationships. After all, they defined themselves as the representation of the social and cognitive freedoms of modernity. Consequently, had the double strangers blamed themselves, they would also have been casting absolutely fundamental doubt on modernity itself. Rather, the problem seemed to be that the groups with the *ability* to make freedom were unprepared to awaken from their dogmatic slumbers and follow the lead of those who indeed knew best but were so isolated as to be unable to carry out the transformations themselves. For the professionalized double strangers of Western Europe, there was little doubt that the refusal of the potential agents to be bought was attributable to the cretinizing impact of contemporary social arrangements. More specifically, the collapse of the possibility of an exchange relationship was interpreted as an awful consequence of mass culture.

The position was clearly expressed in the work which Theodor Adorno carried out alone and, of course, with Max Horkheimer (Adorno 1989; Adorno and Horkheimer 1972). It is very easy to read Adorno as little more than a cultural elitist who was appalled by the idiotic addiction of the masses to Walt Disney and popular music (indeed, the very phrase 'the masses' is not too far away from a sneer). It is also very easy to read the notorious essay on jazz music as nothing more than a scintillating example of how even intelligent observers can totally misunderstand a cultural phenomenon of profound significance (Adorno 1989). It would be easy to do both things, but to carry out either reading would be to miss the poignancy and tragedy of Theodor Adorno's work. In his cultural criticism as least, Adorno provided a meditation on the position of the double stranger who is committed to the promotion of reflexivity and freedom (to the promotion of modernity), yet is personally incapable of turning those ideas into practices. Adorno was forced to rely on others to realize the potential of the modernity which he held so dear, and yet those others seemed to be failures or mere frauds. For Adorno, the true sovereigns of modernity were so isolated that they were quite unable to achieve their ambitions, and yet the proxy sovereigns either were too stupid, too cowardly, or too deceived to carry out the obligations which had been loaded onto their shoulders.

In the jazz essay, Adorno's point was that whilst jazz is frequently taken to be the expression of an oppositional, liberationary sensibility, it is in fact nothing of the sort. According to Adorno, the free and aesthetic promises of jazz were entirely fallacious because, 'everything unruly in it was from the very beginning integrated into a strict scheme, ... its rebellious gestures are accompanied by the tendency to blind obeisance, much like the sado-masochistic type described by analytic psychology'. The sado-masochistic tendency, 'chafes against the father figure while secretly admiring him' (Adorno 1989: 200). Jazz is widely upheld to be a new beginning in music which throws off the restrictions of the symphonic tradition, but Adorno objects that in fact jazz has a sneaking respect for the 'classical'. Moreover, Adorno makes the point that the products of jazz tend to sound much the same (Adorno 1989: 201). He says that this is due to the deep involvement of jazz in the culture industry. Consequently, 'What enthusiastically stunted innocence sees as the jungle is actually factory-made through and through, even when, on special occasions, spontaneity is publicized as a featured attraction' (Adorno 1989: 202). For Adorno, all of this was just one part of the problem of jazz.

But jazz was more terrible yet. It also had a disastrous impact on the listeners. An interesting tension runs through Adorno's essay; he clearly had some sympathy for those who believed that jazz was free and spontaneous, but he also rather seemed to despise their stupidity:

> Terrified, jazz fans identify with the society they dread for having made them what they are. This gives the jazz ritual its affirmative character, that of being accepted into a community of unfree equals. With this in mind, jazz can appeal directly to the mass of listeners in self-justification with a diabolically good conscience. Standard procedures which prevail unquestioned and which have been perfected over long periods of time produce standard reactions ... The population is so accustomed to the drivel it gets that it cannot renounce it, even when it sees through it halfway. On the contrary, it feels itself impelled to intensify its enthusiasm in order to convince itself that its ignominy is its good fortune.
>
> (Adorno 1989: 204)

The passage represents an extremely clear statement of the interests and perspective of the erstwhile modern legislators. Theodor Adorno was bewailing the fact that whilst twentieth-century music had promised so much, it had resulted in only the new barbarism of jazz. Intellectually, Adorno was operating as a gardener. He saw routinized social relationships as little more than a substantialized nothing, as little more than a wholly passive realm which accepted what it was given. Consequently,

Adorno's agenda involved the launching of a practical critique of existing social arrangements in the name of the idealized forms of the blueprint. In the essay on jazz, Adorno was able to condemn the music which *was* enjoyed from the perspective of a legislative commitment to the music which *should have been* enjoyed. The purely intellectual project of Adorno involved a reconciliation of the barbarism of the actual with the freedom of the ought. The synthesis of the dichotomy would represent an advance in the achievement of the aims of modernity.

The tragedy of Theodor Adorno was his inability to produce and reproduce the social and the practical resources which would have heralded the synthesis. Adorno certainly possessed gardening pretensions, but whilst he treated the existing social relationships as if they were mute, the very point was, of course, that they possessed viable and legitimate, reproducible arrangements of their own. After all, the social mass listened to jazz and absolutely refused to listen to the music 'they ought'. Consequently, Adorno's version of the allegedly improving aims of modernity seemed to be little more than vacuous cultural arrogance.

The story of Theodor Adorno and jazz exemplifies the Western European conditions of modernity. Since the social terrain could not be practically and cognitively treated as if it were a garden, and since the double strangers were operating in an already structured environment, they could only maintain the identity of a magical apartness through the exacerbation of strangeness. But that strategy of the maintenance of difference had extremely serious consequences. It meant that the relationships of involvement and detachment which informed the assumptions and practices of the modern makeability and reflexivity of social relationships were pulled so far that they finally broke. As such, instead of the double strangers talking *to* the 'substantialized nothing' of routine, they spoke only *about* it. The double strangers maintained cosmopolitan communication systems, and relied on external resources for their interpretation of the world, and that disembeddedness from the local and indigenous inevitably involved a transcendence of time and place to such an extent that the double strangers floated above the world and the relationships which they wanted to make anew.

The double strangers of Western European modernity spoke

to and for each other. But everyone else simply ignored them. The would-be legislators of freedom interpreted ignorance as proof of the corrupting effects of contemporary cultural forms which had made sure that the enervating messages of modernity could not get through the barriers of banal noise. The pursuits of the mass 'out there' were identified as so many enforced or gleefully accepted idiocies which made sure that the commands of freedom could never be heard. Consequently, the double strangers could not be the vanguard of freedom themselves, and so they appealed to a proxy sovereign of modernity. But that sovereign was too busy listening to jazz; the double strangers were left with no alternatives other than a retreat to the professionalized campus, exclusive social activities, and a desolate pessimism. The pessimism of Western intellectuals was certainly a disgust at the ways of the world. But perhaps just as importantly, it was also a reflection of the refusal of the world to listen to the harbingers of freedom.

Theodor Adorno was outraged at the refusal and inability of the proxy sovereigns to be bought. The problem was that the professionalization of the Western intellectuals had certainly meant that *internal* communication was immeasurably easier, but in the process the *external* channels of communication had been distorted to the point of inaudibility. Consequently, all the message receivers amongst the substantialized nothing of the mass were tuned to other channels. That was the essence of Adorno's position, but the modern reflection of Western intellectuals on their irrelevance also took another form. Theodor Adorno bewailed the tendency of the proxy sovereigns to do nothing; Ortega y Gasset bewailed their tendency to do the wrong things. Ortega y Gasset was a Philosopher Ruler who had been usurped by, 'the accession of the masses to complete social power' (Ortega y Gasset 1932: 9).

He was in no doubt that the usurpation of authority was a terrible thing and thought the situation essentially meant that a constituency which should have been a pliable and empty nothing was, in fact, a firm and active agent in its own right. The implications were apocalyptic. Ortega y Gasset sounded more than a little like Thomas Stockmann when he announced that: 'The characteristic of the hour is that the commonplace mind, knowing itself to be commonplace, has the assurance to proclaim the rights of the commonplace and to impose them wherever it will' (Ortega y Gasset 1932: 14; the passage was originally emphasised). The 'commonplace mind' had managed to achieve this coup of sovereignty because the Philosopher Rulers had slipped into decadence (here, of course, Ortega y Gasset was in many ways mirroring Pareto and Mosca). The inattentiveness of the legitimate legislators had meant that the masses (which should have done only what they were told, because they should have been capable of stimulation only from the outside), were carrying out 'functions in social life which coincide with those which hitherto seemed reserved to minorities'. Moreover, Ortega y Gasset suggested that the rule of the mass was a product of the refusal to accept the legitimate and naturalized superiority of the minority (his minority can be seen as synonymous to the double strangers): 'these masses have ... shown themselves indocile to the minorities – they do not obey them, follow them, or respect them; on the contrary, they push them aside and supplant them' (Ortega y Gasset 1932: 17).

In other words, Ortega y Gasset was fundamentally asserting that the Western European conditions of modernity were not at all mute. The existing social relationships could not be treated as if they were a garden. Rather, in Ortega y Gasset's scheme, the zone which should have been as nothing responded to the assumptions of the legislators with attempts to destroy any and all imputations of magic. Thanks to the activity of the masses, the double strangers became either filth to be extirpated or elitists to be ignored. For Ortega y Gasset, the situation represented nothing other than a retreat from freedom. According to him, the rise of the masses to the positions of authority which did not rightly belong to them meant that modernity itself was threatened with destruction. The sovereignty of the commonplace was not a proper sovereignty at all because, for Ortega y Gasset, modern sovereignty involved reflexive, purposive leadership towards the improved social relationships of the future. Yet it was precisely the future which the masses were said to hold as an irrelevance. The authority of the masses was a return to reification: 'it lives without any vital programme, any plan of existence. It does not know where it is going, because, strictly speaking, it has no fixed road, no predetermined trajectory before it' (Ortega y Gasset 1932: 37). That is, the authority of the masses was not acceptable to the narratives and self-images of modernity because it had no

purpose. It possessed no project. It involved an abandonment
of history.

According to Ortega y Gasset, only the privileged and coherent minorities could generate and impose the projects and
the new beginnings, and only they could prevent the decay
of modernity into barbarism. For him, modernity could be
defended, and its promises could be achieved, only if the
contemporary Philosopher Rulers were able to recreate their
vitality and impose it in the name of freedom:

> There is no hope for Europe unless its destiny is placed in
> the hands of men really 'contemporaneous', men who feel
> palpitating beneath them the whole subsoil of history, who
> realize the present level of existence, and abhor every
> archaic and primitive attitude. We have need of history in
> its entirety, not to fall back into it, but to see if we can
> escape from it.
>
> (Ortega y Gasset 1932: 73)

It would rather seem that in Western Europe at least, all the
escape routes were found to be dead ends. It rather seems that
the efforts of the pretenders to the mantle of sovereignty to
associate themselves and their projects to the body of that which
needed to be remade, were largely unsuccessful. Consequently,
Ortega y Gasset mirrored Plato and Stockmann and complained
about the tragedy of the stupid ruling the intelligent, whilst
Adorno identified a tragedy of mass cretinization.

The double strangers read their utter marginalization as so
much proof of their necessity. Ortega y Gasset saw the answer to
all contemporary problems in a relentless and resolute restatement of the most ambitious aims of modernity. The tendency
towards restatement was a typical feature of modernity. Modernity certainly involved the practice of a profound reflexivity in
social relationships, but the *targets* of reflexivity were always
some *other* groups which were said to be indulging in false and
ambivalent practices. The *agents* of reflexivity never interrogated their own social position or suitability as potential legislators. The double strangers simply assumed their own right to
domination, and they naturalized it through ritualization and
repetition. As such, the failure of Western European social
relationships to approximate to the garden ideals was taken as
proof of the failure of nerve, if not the intrinsic stupidity, of

those in need of freedom. Everything was the fault of the ambivalent sites or practices which could not be accommodated within the designs of order. The double strangers at no time doubted themselves publicly, or, at least, if they did, the doubt was soon externalized and directed elsewhere.

In Western Europe, then, the Soviet-type system was a virtual impossibility. The impossibility was not due to any inherent qualities prevalent in the West but absent in Central and Eastern Europe. Rather, the Soviet-type system could not be practised in any universal, and universalizing, manner simply because of the absence of the social preconditions of that system. The legislators of modernity found Western European social relationships as already active, already viable, and already able to reproduce themselves through indigenous resources. Certainly, many of those relationships might have been considered outrageous and absurdly parochial from the point of view of the narratives and the projects of modernity, but it could not be doubted that they claimed and commanded legitimacy and authority. The old allegiances made sure that the social terrain was able to speak for itself, without a specialist translator, and even less a ventriloquist. That was precisely the point which Edmund Burke tried to bring to wide realization. As such, the question of sovereignty was made immensely complex. In the ideal relationships of modernity, sovereignty was seen in collective terms, with the *agent* of sovereignty defined as a small and a privileged, a magical, circle. But Western Europe did not permit the realization of ideals.

The universalizing interpretation of the road to freedom could not be established and maintained in the typical conditions of Western Europe. The double strangers could not be the indubitable sovereigns of modernity. Through professionalization they had lost all the contact and involvement which the practical activity of makeability presupposes. The turn to a proxy sovereign (such as the 'proletariat'; Gouldner's shopping for an agent) failed because the selected groups either refused or were unable to be bought. Either the particular exchange offered by the double strangers had not been constructed as widely meaningful (outside of fundamentalist ghettos), or the plaintive cries of the too weak and yet totally committed legislators could not penetrate the 'vigorously repetitive though objectless cultic ritual' of the existence of the masses (Adorno

1989: 203). Alternatively, the mass was held to be too barbaric to be capable of accepting the authority of the Philosopher Rulers of modernity. In sum, the only possible leadership of the collectivity had lost all contact with its erstwhile followers, and the potential replacement leaders of the way to freedom were held to be beyond all help.

As such, Western European modernity could rely only on one other sovereign; the individual. Because of the multiplication and intersection of legitimate authority, and the pluralization of social constructions of order, any notions of a universal and universalized collectivity were unsustainable. Too many groups or too many people seemed to escape the categories of any one collectivity (as Burke again realized very clearly). From the point of view of any single project or hermeneutic system, there always seemed to be a plurality of ambivalence. So much escaped firm classification and ordering that the possibility of order itself was thrown into doubt. That potential abyss, which was endemic to non-garden situations, could only be avoided by a relocation of sovereignty, and of the ordering principle of social relationships, away from any collectivity or mass, and to the individual.

There were a number of more mundane pressures which also tended towards the construction of the individual as the sovereign of Western European modernity. Importantly, the professionalization of the double strangers caused practical and intellectual closure between one magical circle and another. There could be only one result. It became increasingly impossible for double strangers to know precisely where the constituency of the culture of reflexive discourse started, and where it finished. Inevitably, that blurring between the acceptable and the unacceptable statement could only be avoided by a turn towards the importance of the social location from which the statement had been made. The inclusion of an individual within any realm of potential legislators was determined *not by what was said*, but the *position from which* the utterance was made. Ultimately, and highly ironically, the cognitive commitments which created the double strangers in and for themselves were turned on their heads.

The investment of individuals with certain qualities and capabilities represented a response to the possibility of the disruption of all order. It represented an acceptance of the impossibility of all collective or vanguardist claims to sovereignty, and yet the turn to the individual was a means by which the plurality of competing social arrangements and institutions could be all tied together. The individualization of freedom made sovereignty a very diverse matter, indeed a personal and a private matter, but it also connected any one individual with all other individuals (what is best for me is best for you, what is best for you is best for me). With the stress on the individual, freedom, and therefore modernity itself, was simultaneously personalized and yet totalized. Invariably, the double strangers responded with attempts to develop institutional arrangements which connected their own exclusivity to a multiplicity of individuals, through a rhetoric which stressed anthropological alibis (i.e. economic rationality as an expression of human nature, cooperation as a reflection and ethic of reciprocity). That is, the double strangers were instrumental in the formation and encouragement of a system of a diversity of political parties. The party system of Western Europe was a means by which the double strangers could overcome their potential irrelevance and filthiness and, perhaps just as importantly, connect themselves once again to sovereign agents.

Indeed, Thomas Stockmann responded to his own fall with the construction of what was essentially a party institution. Stockmann's dilemma was that although he had been crushed by the townspeople, and although his magic had been redefined as reprehensible self-interest, he was still confident in his own mind that he was right. Right about the pollution of the baths, right about the petty narrow-mindedness of the existing authorities, right about what had to be done. Typically, this self-acclaimed legislator was prepared to extend reflexivity to all social sites except that occupied by himself. Consequently, Thomas Stockmann did not see his decline as a purely personal problem (inevitably, Ibsen left personal, private worries to Stockmann's wife). Rather, 'the worst thing is this: I don't know of anybody with enough independence of mind to feel like taking on my work after me' (Ibsen 1988: 104). Stockmann saw his difficulty as, at heart, one of a lack of ability to reproduce magic and as an exhaustibility of the resources of sovereignty. He resolved to overcome all those problems through the deliberate formation of a new social institution.

Stockmann's answer was to establish a new school for, 'the street-corner lads ... the real guttersnipes' (Ibsen 1988: 105).

The school would embark upon the enterprise of showing another group of social outsiders that they shared common interests with a dispossessed intellectual, and that if they turned their basically shared experiences into an institutionalized project, they could transform all social relationships. Thomas Stockmann indeed went shopping for an agent, and he was able to participate in a meaningful exchange relationship because he went shopping, not with a promissory note which could be cashed in the future, but with ready money which could be used in the here and now. Garden relationships invariably inclined towards some kind of utopian anthropology simply because there was nothing which could cast legitimate doubt on the wildest aspirations and assumptions (the tendency towards utopianism was expressed especially clearly in the Soviet literature of the Stalin years: see Clark 1977; for discussion of another kind of utopian anthropology in garden situations, see Bauman 1989). But where the garden conditions did not prevail, anthropological arguments had to be rooted in mundane reality and, moreover, they became little more than justifications and excuses for institutions which re-established some kind of practical linkage between the professionalized double strangers and the world which they thought they had a right to reconstruct. This was precisely what Thomas Stockmann realized at the end of his turbulent career as a frustrated legislator.

But the response of the Western European double strangers to their social conditions of existence, their enthusiasm to indulge in a formalized system of marginality called the political party, did not mean that they wholly and graciously abandoned the old gardening pretensions. Quite the contrary. It only needed the slightest glimmer of an opportunity for the garden sensibility to reappear. For example, Thomas Stockmann at least in part conceived of his school as little more than a training ground for a Praetorian Guard. The members of the school (that is, the party members) were seen with little more than unabashed contempt. The point was that although Stockmann established some kind of anthropologically justified exchange relationship between himself and them, he never doubted their passivity and purchasability. 'Just for once, I'm going to try an experiment on these mongrels. You never know what you might find amongst them' (Ibsen 1988: 105). Stockmann was fated to

operate in an active and indigenously reproducible environment, but that did not mean that he entirely renounced all
gardening ambitions. Rather, those ambitions became immensely
attractive and compelling if a mute social group could be found
and their practical makeability bought.

The same inclination can also be found in the work of John
Stuart Mill. Of course, Mill was deeply committed to institutional
arrangements which stressed the formal equality of all participants. Mill was normally unable to treat equals as if they were
mute, but as soon as any arrangements were encountered which
could be treated as if they were indeed silent, Mill's attitude
changed quite radically. Whilst discussing the equal immutable
sovereignty of all individuals, Mill stated that, 'It is, perhaps,
hardly necessary to say that this doctrine is meant to apply only
to human beings in the maturity of their faculties' (Mill 1910:
73). That position had important implications. The recognition
of the sovereignty of individuals only on the basis of an anthropological egalitarianism was turned by Mill into a justification
for special treatment of those groups of individuals who did not
need to be treated as equal. 'Despotism is a legitimate mode of
government in dealing with barbarians, provided the end be
their improvement, and the means justified by actually effecting
that end' (Mill 1910: 73).

Mill was unable to practise the relationships of the garden in
some circumstances, and he elevated that incapacity to the status
of institutional arrangements which emphasized the idea that,
'Over himself, over his own body and mind, the individual is
sovereign' (Mill 1910: 73). But when he was dealing with groups
or arrangements which were not able to speak for themselves,
Mill was perfectly prepared to resort to typically garden-type
activities. Indeed, he was happy to restate utopian anthropological arguments and turn the indigenous resources into nothing more than a raw material out of which an improved future
could and should be constructed. 'Liberty, as a principle, has no
application to any state of things anterior to the time when
mankind have become capable of being improved by free and
equal devotion' (Mill 1910: 73).

Consequently, Mill was operating something of a dual-track
strategy. In the domestic environment, he was only able to
reconnect his legislative ambitions to the ability to put those
ideas into action through a resort to anthropological alibis (the

free individual; utilitarianism). This strand of his work can be interpreted as a recognition and a prime illustration of the inability of the Western European double strangers to treat social relationships as immutably passive and from a position of exclusive activity. However, the other strand of Mill's legislative programme was rather different. Mill was prepared to treat those relationships which could not reproduce their own legitimacy as an affront to human improvement. As such, he defined them as nature, as simple anathema. Mill denied their ability to speak for themselves, and treated them as if they were mere means towards a far more important end.

Barbarians were simply means to the end of universal improvement, but the sovereign individual was an end in him- or herself. The possibility of the identification of barbarism made the double strangers once again aware of their obligations to history and to freedom. Barbarism was the external site of a filthy heterogeneity which reconfirmed to the double strangers the importance of the projects of homogenization. What Mill repudiated as barbarism was the Other *par excellence*, and thus the measure by which was judged the need for the creation and enforcement of a universalizing order called civilization. In other words, the garden ambitions were never entirely submerged. The common purpose of the intellectuals of modernity was never wholly forgotten, despite the fracturing of the possibility of the double strangers struggling both in and for themselves. At the risk of sounding exceedingly trite, it might be said that Mill's velvet glove which protected and nurtured the sovereign individual, contained an iron fist.

In sum, then, the Western European double strangers experienced modernity as an immense difficulty. In Central and Eastern Europe modernity was difficult as well, but 'there' the main problem was one of knowing how to go on (the paradigmatic question of Central and Eastern European modernity was indeed, 'What is to be done?'). But in Western Europe, the double strangers were forced to acknowledge that the indigenous and time-honoured social arrangements themselves constituted so many more-or-less viable ways of going on. Consequently, the garden ambitions were confronted with a situation which denied the possibility of gardening activities. It is, then, necessary to distinguish between the *achieved* universal garden of Central and Eastern Europe, and the *aspired* universal garden of Western Europe. Perhaps the easiest and most useful way of making that distinction is to refer to the relationships of Western European modernity as being analogous to an *allotment*.

An allotment is a portion of land which is let out for cultivation. In particular, an allotment is a small plot of land, which is surrounded by other allotments; each plot is rented out by some legitimate local authority to whoever wants to grow her or his own plants. It is up to the *rentier* of each plot to decide what will grow on each individual plot, but the designs for the fine allotment have to be compatible with local by-laws and restrictions. Each *rentier* can do whatever she or he pleases so long as the traditional authorities tacitly agree, and so long as each does not transgress beyond the boundaries of their own plot. The allotment system is an exercise in boundary drawing in the name of a permissible heterogeneity. Certainly, within each single allotment the struggle is for homogeneity and total compatibility with the blueprints of order. But immediately beyond the confines of the single patch is the practical expression of another project, of an alternative mode of improvement.

Each allotment is made susceptible to gardening ambitions, but each *rentier* knows that the ambitions cannot be universalized. Each *rentier* is aware of nothing so much as the silly or excellent projects of neighbours and, in any case, the land can only be cultivated so long as the rent is paid to the local authority. The allotment holder has no necessary association with the land; any linkages are purely contractual. The *rentiers* can only establish firm links with the land, links which will enable practices of makeability, to the extent that certain exchange relationships are maintained, and to the extent that intimations of identity can be achieved through ritualized behaviour (wellington boots) or the usurpation of the connections of others (quiet readings of *Gardening for Beginners*). The allotment *rentier* does not cease to want to control the other plots, but she or he knows that the control will always be lacking whilst the other plots have their own authoritative speakers. Each *rentier* has to struggle to achieve some relevance over the allotted terrain, but she or he has no relationship, and therefore no connection of makeability, with the plots of the neighbours.

The implication of the allotment situation for the question of sovereignty is extremely serious. Quite simply, it is impossible to identify the ultimate sovereign with any degree of certainty.

Instead, the case for sovereignty over any single plot, let alone the whole system of allotments taken in total, is claimed by a plurality of authorities each of which can claim some legitimacy. There is no single meaning of the allotment; its order cannot be said to reside in any single design. Instead the meaning of the allotment resides in a complex multiplicity of individual designs which can themselves only be reconciled through an emphasis upon some central, common, theme. The meaning and the practice of sovereignty is individualized to the extent that the interests of each individual is seen as simultaneously an expression of the interests of all. Allotment cultivation is, so to speak, a form of gardening which is structurally incapable of universalization. Both garden and allotment relationships are typified by an abhorrence towards ambivalence; they are both projects of the extirpation of illicit, filthy, difference. The only difference between them revolves around the largely contingent matter of the vistas over which that abhorrence is allowed to spread.

I propose that the metaphor of the allotment summarizes the position of double strangers in the conditions of Western European modernity. The metaphor is also a means of illustrating the multiple meanings of sovereignty in Western European modernity, meanings which were themselves all ordered by an emphasis upon the evidently ontological and anthropological individual.

The metaphor can also explain why the social arrangements of Western European modernity ostensibly demonstrated such a profound stability and popular allegiance (notwithstanding a number of brief episodes). Quite simply, the pluralization of authority which was the result, and the condition, of the inability of the legislators of modernity to treat the social terrain as if it were a mute garden, and the subsequent individualization of sovereignty, meant that no single interpretation of freedom could be elevated to a position of all-inclusive domination. No single blueprint for the improvement of social relationships could be upheld to the complete exclusion of all others.

There was no single standard of the truth or of the ultimate meaning of freedom, and, by extension, no definite site which could be challenged. A spatial metaphor might explain. If it is fair to say that the Soviet-type system was spatially represented by Red Square or Wenceslas Square, then it was in principle possible to darken the heart of the system by simply taking over or redefining that symbolic space (for example, Josef Koudelka's famous photograph of Wenceslas Square on 22 August, 1968). But it was quite impossible to draw such a spatial analogy for liberal democratic arrangements where the meanings of freedom were individualized and where hermeneutic systems were pluralized. If there had been a popular march to Trafalgar Square, say, no universal freedom would have been challenged (although *some* ideas of freedom would have indeed been thrown open to doubt), whilst in Paris it would have been difficult to decide what the destination of any protest should be. The point is that Paris possesses a number of symbolic spaces, each of which claims to be *the* site of freedom, but each of which has to exist within the shadow of other, competing sites. The Paris of the discourses of modernity was a massive allotment, and each separate plot had its own enthusiasts, its own legislators. Moreover, in an effort to maintain their own exclusivity, the double strangers were increasingly forced into professionalization to maintain claims of magical abilities. Each group of professionals expressed itself through an allegiance to its own symbolic spaces and practices, and by attacks on those defended by others. Consequently, the lack of identity became a problem rather than an opportunity.

In Western Europe, then, there was no generally agreed-upon standard of the success of any given blueprint (instead the standards, self-referentially, could only come from within the blueprint itself). There was no single meaning of the flight of the angel of history, no one joke which could force a smile on the angel's face. And since there could be no universal success, because there was no consensus as to what success actually meant or involved, neither, of course, could there be any universal failure. The allotment situation was immune from any complete new beginning; its slate could never be wiped entirely clean because no would-be wiper had a long enough reach.

According to Hannah Arendt, one of the meanings of revolution is that, 'Not thought, only the practice, only the application would be new' (Arendt 1963: 50). Arendt's statement might be applicable to *some* entrances into modernity, but the aphorism certainly does not hold good for Western Europe. In the West, not the practice, only the thought was new.

5

SEWAGE

The narrative and hermeneutic systems of European modernity tended to talk of *social relationships* only very rarely. Indeed, where those relationships were forced to be open to some reflexivity, they were more often than not identified as quite mundane and virtually beneath the dignity of the exercise of freedom. Instead, social relationships were pulled together and elevated to a great height by the concept and the image of *society*. In the conditions of European modernity, the routine daily life of women and men was fairly dismissively given less importance than the grand sweep of a more fundamental and a more significant entity called *society*. It was society itself which became quickly associated with all positive values (because society was intrinsically reflexive) as opposed to what was consequently held to be the atavism, or just plain badness, of the natural and of nature. Indeed, the conditions and the practices of both the garden and the allotment situations of modernity were quite impossible without the assumption of a distinctive milieu called society.

However, and despite how it might have seemed in the conditions of modernity, since society is essentially a *concept* and an *image*, it cannot be considered as a reality out there. On the contrary, society is a socially and a historically specific way of coming to terms with social relationships which could not be understood or brought together through a turn to any other referent, such as God or what Agnes Heller calls the 'naturalistic artifice' (Heller 1990; it was largely the naturalistic artifice, where social arrangements were interpreted as, simply, pre-ordained by nature, which caused Thomas Stockmann so many difficulties). Put more assertively, *the concept of society was a product of the peculiarly modern consciousness.* Perhaps that is the explanation of why sociology, the self-proclaimed scientific study of society, emerged only at the time, and in the places, of the appearance of the double strangers and of modernity. Perhaps it explains why the modern sociological project was frequently so closely associated with various legislative enterprises, or, alternatively, why sociology was so often identified as a study in the service of freedom.

The concept and the image of a society, represents the creation of an order and involves a most fundamental act of boundary-drawing between the free world of the social and the reified world of the natural. The phrase *social relationships*, implies some relatively open-ended, and not necessarily institutionalized, network of reciprocity (however unequal the power relationships of that reciprocity might be). But a *society* is a very distinctive closed system. A society is a bounded community, which definitely includes some practices or people (us), and definitely excludes others (them). As such, the modern awareness of society involved the marginalization and the treatment of any other collections of practices or people, as either utterly horrible or as a source of fraternal assistance (in a restatement of the basic problem posed by the stranger: friend or foe?). Of course, whether that ambivalence and marginality was at all surmountable tended to be a most difficult question to answer.

Society, and the associated birth of sociology (and it might be said that in modernity, the existence of sociology actually was something like the sign of the practical reflexivity of social relationships, an idea implicit to Anthony Giddens' idea of the *double hermeneutic*, see Giddens 1990) was not concerned too much with the Hobbesian problem of the preconditions of social order. Rather, the central issue was one of the imposition of an intelligible order on a social landscape which, thanks to the processes of Enlightenment and urbanization, was experienced as a realm subject to tendencies towards absolute chaos. As Alain Touraine has put it: 'The idea of society ... was an image of order' (Touraine 1989: 11).

Georg Simmel recognized the status of the concept of society with special clarity. In one of his more obviously neo-Kantian moments, Simmel made the point, which to him was perhaps largely axiomatic, that whilst only individuals *really* exist, the concept of society had the status of an intellectual abstraction, a

119

classification, which enabled some grasp of the precise relationships which were the habitat and the building site of all the individual and collective interpretations of the question of sovereignty. 'The stubborn assertion that ... there exist nothing but individuals ... cannot prevent us from speaking of ... thousands of ... synthetic events and collective phenomena – and, therefore, of society in general' (Simmel 1950: 6). Simmel was suggesting that whilst it was certainly true to say that only individuals can be observed, it was also crucially the case that individuals were created through non-observable classifications. Moreover, those non-observable categories, 'constantly supersede individual existences. If we were to rob our cognition of all such intellectual syntheses because only individuals are "real", we would deprive human knowledge of its least dubious and most legitimate contents' (Simmel 1950: 7).

For Simmel, the denial of the concept of society and, by extension, the denial of the modern *uses* of sociology, involved also a denial of the possibility of knowing anything at all significant about social life (Simmel 1950: 7). That was tantamount to saying that modernity was impossible without abstraction. That was hardly a new idea. Immanuel Kant, of course, in his 'What is Enlightenment?' essay, had established that the free use of the intellect, the ability to think in abstraction which went beyond the world of given appearances, was one of the measures of the sufficient and mature modern age (Kant 1970). Perhaps, even, Georg Simmel was hinting that modernity was impossible without sociology.

Simmel was virtually declaring that without the abstract and synthetic, but nevertheless quite indispensable, image of an order called society, it would be quite impossible to practise any reflexivity in the realm of the relationships of women and men. That is, without the concept of society, social relationships might fail to come up to the high standards which had been set for them by the self-proclaimed courageous intellectuals and would-be legislators like Immanuel Kant. Consequently, the relationships would have been bereft of any meaning and worth. When Simmel elevated social relationships to the status of society, he was assuming a place in one of the main spheres of European modernity; the attempt to construct and treat social relationships as an intelligible, reflexive, potentially free terrain clearly separated from nature.

But whilst the concept of society centrally played a part in the creation of order out of practices which were susceptible to interpretation as otherwise meaningless and chaotic, natural and reified, the concept had other important implications. One of the key features of the image of society was the sense that it had definite boundaries which were relatively easy to identify. A society was not just a synthetic classification which allowed reflexivity and freedom or what was established in the programmatic projects to be improvement. A society was conceived also as a spatial device which played a fundamental part in the division of the world into a plurality of intelligible units. The nation-state was the institutional expression of that cognitive and practical classification of sets of social relationships into a number of separate and identifiable societies, each of which possessed its own indigenous resources of reproduction, and each of which was able to treat competing nation-states as either indubitably other (and therefore beyond involvement) or as ambivalent and consequently in need of assimilation or annihilation.

Benedict Anderson calls the nation-state an *imagined community*. The phrase is also a useful way of coming to terms with the basis of the concept of a society. As Anderson says of the nation-state: 'It is *imagined* because the members of even the smallest nation will never know most of their fellow-members, meet them, or even hear of them, yet in the minds of each lives the image of their communion' (Anderson 1983: 15). However, the point that the nation and, by extension, the society, was an *image* which put the things, and especially the strangers, of the world into an orderly system of classifications, did not therefore mean that it was fictitious and a grotesque mask over some more fundamental universality. On the contrary, it was through these interpretive classifications (which Anderson (1983) correctly links to modernity, albeit by implication rather than clear statement, with his stress on the printed word as a means of communication) that the world was made to speak and actually *mean* something. The concepts and the images of society and the nation-state ensured that the coming and staying of unknown people or practices could be explained, and that some symbols of order and belonging might be constructed. Modernity involved the creation of cognitive systems which tried to overcome the potentially infinite plenitude of strangers by emphasizing opposed communities of a fraternal 'us' and a difficult 'them'. The strength of the hold of those imaginations over the women and men of modernity should not be underestimated. To quote Benedict Anderson once more: 'Ultimately it is this fraternity that makes it possible, over the past two centuries, for so many millions of people, not so much to kill, as willingly to die for such limited imaginings' (Anderson 1983: 16).

The identification of social relationships as a distinct entity called a society, which was organized by and through an institutional arrangement called the nation-state, reached a highpoint in the nineteenth century with the development of organic interpretations of order. Indeed, the organic interpretation tended to be pushed to the most ambitious and universalistic lengths. This was particularly true of how the idea was taken up and used by Herbert Spencer. In the *Principles of Sociology*, Spencer almost anticipated Simmel when he, too, made it plain that for him, the use of the concept and the image of society represented the imposition of some standards of order upon mundane practices. Spencer took that creation of order, and the identification of clear boundary lines, to such lengths that in his hands society became not simply an abstraction but also a reification. Herbert Spencer implicitly saw the world as nothing other than a plurality of internally coherent (or at least homogeneous and solidary) entities which dealt with the existence of the other entities with varying degrees of attraction or repulsion.

Herbert Spencer admitted that any given society was made up by 'discrete units', but went on to suggest that, 'a certain concreteness in the aggregate of them is implied by the general persistence of the arrangements among them throughout the area occupied. And it is this trait which yields our idea of a society' (Spencer 1969: 8). In other words, he classified sets of social relationships as possessing a high level of continuity. It was that continuity which made it possible to lump relationships together within the imagination of a single and independent societal body. However, he also believed that the traces of continuity could be found only over restricted geographical areas. Consequently, he spoke of a society, conflated it with the nation-state, and saw it as comparable to a biological organism. After all, 'the permanent relations among the parts of a society, are analogous to the permanent relations among the parts of a living body' (Spencer 1969: 8). More than that, and as a further proof of Spencer's tendency to unthinkingly conflate concepts which perhaps should have been kept rather more distinct, he thought that to the extent that, 'an ordinary living organism may be regarded as a nation of units which live individually, and have many of them considerable degrees of independence, we shall have less difficulty in regarding a nation of human beings as an organism' (Spencer 1969: 14–15).

The analogy between society and a biological organism had a number of important strands. They all revolved around the assumption that because the essential traits, and indeed the developmental laws, of living bodies had been discovered by advanced science, it was in principle possible to say something equally scientific and incontrovertible about the fundamental features of social life. At least in part, the organic analogies for the interpretation of societal existence served to naturalize the claims to magic which the double strangers tried to make with greater or lesser degrees of success. To a large extent, the very line of argument which Herbert Spencer adopted meant that the identification of correlations was virtually inevitable. In these connections, an evidently objective statement about natural organisms was meant to provide the basis for an equally true comment about the normal developmental tendencies of societal relationships.

Firstly, a living body was understood as tending towards a condition of *equilibrium*, that is to say, towards a situation where all was as it should be, and where nothing would normally escape the most rigid and the most orderly classification. Secondly, a living body was said to *grow* in terms of a definite and fairly easily intelligible series of stages, from youth to maturity, from simplicity to complexity, from smallness to largeness. Societies were understood in much the same way. As Herbert Spencer put it: 'living bodies and societies so conspicuously exhibit augmentation of mass, that we may fairly regard this as characterizing them both' (Spencer 1969: 9). Thirdly, a living body is clearly *identifiable* as something which is apart from other bodies and yet only self-aware, and indeed, knowable, to the extent that it relates with other autonomous bodies. Similarly, societies were understood as clearly bounded and yet knowable by the degrees of difference or similarity which they had to other societies (witness Spencer's emphasis on cross-cultural comparison). Fourthly, and so typically for the narratives of modernity, a living body was subordinated to the *interventionist* and the legislative practices of experts who promised that they were able to make things better. Of course, the experts were quite happy to make such promises. In other words, in the system of the organic analogy, a society was understood as a definite entity which was inherently orderly and possessed of its own, indigenous resources of reproduction. But that same body was also, however, passively compliant to the practices and the projects of that select band of intellectuals which was able to treat it with some detachment as an item of scientific interest.

It is quite noticeable that in Spencer's analogy, the societal organism under investigation is *out there*. It was at no time encountered or interpreted as a direct experience for the magical double strangers. Spencer simply and perhaps inevitably assumed between sociology and society precisely the same relationship as that which pertains between surgical medicine and a physical body. Just as the skilful surgeon is able to indulge in the makeability of some living organisms, or at least in their reconstruction (and as the intimation of exclusivity surrounding the surgeon's position is enhanced, the meaning of makeability becomes ever more extravagant), so Spencer implicitly assumed that the modern legislators, the surgeons of social ills, could remake the societal body on the grounds that they would bring only improvement.

That might seem a curious thing to say about Herbert Spencer. It might seem to be plain wrong to put Herbert Spencer into the same group as most of the other nineteenth-century social engineers. After all, Spencer is more typically held out as a prime example of a social Darwinist who believed that we can do as much about the laws of social evolution as a tadpole can do about the laws of natural evolution. Certainly, that kind of resignation in the face of an overwhelming law does rather seem to be the ethical implication of Herbert Spencer's sociological enterprise (an implication which was, however, thoroughly typical of modernity since it removed all mystery from the affairs of women and men; Spencer's point was that this law was entirely transparent to reason). There does indeed seem to be little in common between Spencer's faith in a perfectly knowable law of development which went on through its own motor of fitness for survival, and the more usual hyperactivism of the nineteenth-century reforming intellectual, who retained some belief in the ability to practise sovereignty for him- or herself, or who thought that it was a relatively simple task to buy a proxy sovereign.

However, it is quite plausible to argue that if consideration is given to some of the wider implications of Herbert Spencer's position, it can be seen that he was a quite typical nineteenth-century intellectual and, like most others, he was thoroughly inspired by legislative, interventionist interests. In a sentence, all the improving projects of modernity shared the assumption that improvement was achieved to the extent that waste and filth (nature, habit, tradition), were expelled from the societal 'body', leaving only a pure and perfect core. The legislators took upon themselves the ability to help expel any waste products which society could not properly expel itself (hence, and as an example, Lenin's attacks on Russian backwardness). One of Spencer's main arguments as a kind of evolutionist was, of course, that society was an organism which could successfully evacuate its own filth just so long as its normal functioning was not hampered by the activities of women and men. Herbert Spencer believed that societies worked well so long as individuals did not meddle with their intrinsic tendencies. This position was implicit to his connection between natural and societal organisms as both possessing tendencies towards equilibrium. But, and here Spencer rather keenly moved into the camp of the modern legislators, only intellectuals like the sociologists, who had carried out vast and ambitious comparative studies of different societies, could possibly know what meddling might actually be. Only the sociologists could know what activities of women and men might harm the normal and, inevitably, the ethically beneficial process of societal development.

In other words, the apparently resigned attitude of Herbert Spencer masks only inadequately the assumption that those possessed of free knowledge could actually do things for the best. For example, it took a special kind of person, for whom social life was an objective *out there*, and not some overbearing reality, to know that, when correctly understood, social welfare would cause only difficulties. Of course, Spencer was not brutal enough to want to, 'exclude or condemn aid given to the inferior by the superior in their individual capacities', but he felt it had to be acknowledged that, 'when given so indiscriminately as to enable the inferior to multiply, such aid entails mischief' (Spencer

1940: 80–81). Behind the mask, Herbert Spencer was simply seeking to naturalize legislation and the domination of certain social groups by linking it to what was said to be the inevitable operation of an evolutionary law. Clearly, a lapse into a naturalistic fallacy in ethical thought, which would suggest that what is must be (such as the continuation of poverty), was not without a number of useful social and political implications.

But the direct superimposition of the image of a single organic society in any given context was vastly complicated in the allotment-type situations which invariably prevailed in the conditions of Western European modernity. Certainly, the modern commitment to the annihilation of filth was never renounced in the allotment situations, but the precise identification of the dirty was an extremely difficult task. On the one hand, the double strangers who believed that they should have been the practical legislators had very little ability of their own to indulge in relationships of makeability, whilst, on the other hand, no single blueprint of the improved future was able to gain a widespread and a general legitimacy. Consequently, social relationships in Western Europe could not necessarily be subordinated to any *one* vision of order. It was impossible to say with any great certainty where the imagined community of the societal organism started or finished (perhaps the only exceptions were Britain and Spain, where societal boundaries could be relatively easily superimposed upon definite geographical areas. Of course, however, the relationship between modernity and the Iberian peninsular is itself not a straightforward matter.). Moreover, the Western European tendency to understand sovereignty as an affair of individuals and individuality contributed towards making it difficult to locate or name the exact groups which might be entirely bounded by the embrace of the societal body.

The creation of *individual* roads to freedom in principle denied, or at least opened up the possibility of the denial, of the creation of any order whatsoever. Since sovereignty was a matter for individuals and individuality, there was absolutely no necessary reason to think that the imagined communities of sovereign individuals would display the tendencies towards equilibrium and distinctiveness which they evidently ought to have displayed. As such, the cognitive and the practical search for a universal standard of order which could encompass all individuals was immensely and increasingly pressing, and the imposition of that standard needed to be ever more rigorous. Had it not been, the promises of freedom in Western European allotment-type situations would have foundered on the the reefs of perpetual ambivalence. There would have been only margins, and little or nothing by way of a heart to the social relationships which were conceived in terms of the societal body. In particular, any and every group of strangers would have been threatened with the definition of itself as filth. And everyone would have been a stranger to one degree or another.

In other words, and simply in order to make sense of the order of things, the allotment-type situations maintained an intellectual commitment to the image of society. Allotment contexts never lost the emphasis on boundary-drawing. They differed from garden situations only in terms of the geographical extent of the inclusionary pretensions, and in terms of the treatment of whatever was found on the other side or on the margins of firm classification. Yet it was still difficult to establish who or what should be seen as one of the legitimate and benign parts of the organic society.

In the hermeneutic and moral narratives of modernity, that particular circle was squared through story lines which created standards of inclusion and exclusion, and yet which saw the precise location of the boundary line between order and ambivalence or outright filth as open to historical movement (with the history being interpreted as an almost necessary process of *development*). Two of the dominant stories, which reflected the idea that anything inside the societal body was intrinsically orderly and reciprocal whilst anything outside was rather more doubtful, involved the identification of an 'expanding circle' of moral significance, and the identification of an evidently increasingly inclusive social status of citizenship. Each of these schemes told a story of an increasingly humanitarian and logical assimilation of previously ambivalent groups within the societal body.

Behind the surface differences, and perhaps the stories of moral significance and citizenship were not too different at all, the stories were examples of how the experience of an increasingly large, and an increasingly diverse, range of strangers was invariably dealt with in the allotment situation of modernity. The two approaches were indebted to themes derived from the organic analogy and, in particular, that part of the analogy which stressed developmental growth and the 'augmentation of mass' (in Spencer's fairly heavy-handed phrase) (Spencer 1969: 9). Herbert Spencer was especially aware that the process of the growth of the societal organism inevitably entailed the assimilation of increasing heterogeneity (that is, strangeness) *within* the body of the otherwise thoroughly homogeneous (else it would have been impossible to imagine society as a definite and a distinctive body). As Spencer said of the process of growth in a society: 'At first the unlikenesses among its groups of units are inconspicuous in number and degree; but as population augments, divisions and sub-divisions become more numerous and more decided' (Spencer 1969: 9). The problem was one of explaining how it could be possible to talk, at one and the same time, of increasing divisions and yet also of the increasing relevance of the concept of society. The narratives of moral significance and citizenship, which essentially put the criteria of inclusion and homogeneity on wheels, could explain both processes.

The idea of the expanding circle of moral relevance was expressed with a great deal of clarity, and just as much enthusiasm, by William Lecky in his ambitious, and, with its universalistic pretensions, very nineteenth century *History of European Morals*. He thought that he had discovered the truth of the 'natural history of morality'. Lecky suggested that throughout history, the essential motives behind moral ideas had remained largely the same; the only changes had involved the extent to which women and men upheld the ideals and the areas over which the ideals could be extended. Lecky saw his history of morality as an intrinsically orderly process which in many ways demanded direct comparison to the growth of a living organism. According to Lecky, a history of morality reveals, 'an orderly and necessary change, as society advances, both in the proportionate value attached to different virtues in theory, and in the perfection in which they are realised in practice' (Lecky 1911: 147). The foundations of the apparently natural history of morality which Lecky excavated rather seem to reflect the expression of circumstances and assumptions intrinsic to allotment situations. Lecky assumed that whilst freedom and sovereignty were individual concerns, it was nevertheless still possible to construct some general and universal order, some homogeneity, out of the diversity, out of the heterogeneity, of social arrangements.

William Lecky thought that it was not only possible but also necessary, for any given individual to come to terms with the plurality of strangers in the urban spaces of the towns or the cosmopolitan spaces of the Enlightened intellect. This could be achieved by means of a careful classification of strange individuals, not as resolutely and always intrinsically ambivalent and intrinsically filthy, but as actual or potential examples of homogeneity. He was stating that whilst people might certainly seem to be different and strange, they should be treated as if they are the same. For Lecky, it was the expansion of the recognition of homogeneity which constituted the developmental logic of the natural history of morality. It is worth quoting Lecky at some length on this point, which clearly involves the recital of a tale of liberal humanitarianism and increasing civilization. He wrote:

> Men come into the world with their benevolent affections very inferior in power to their selfish ones, and the function of morals is to invert this order. The extinction of all selfish feeling is impossible for an individual, and if it were general, it would result in the dissolution of society. The question of morals must always be a question of proportion or of degree. At one time the benevolent affections embrace merely the family, soon the circle expanding includes first a class, then a nation, then a coalition of nations, then all humanity, and finally, its influence is felt in the dealings of man with the animal world. In each of these stages a standard is formed, different from that of the preceding stage, but in each case the same tendency is recognized as virtue.
>
> (Lecky 1911: 100–101)

As Herbert Spencer might have said of it, this passage indicates the identification of a most profound process of the augmentation of the societal mass.

Of course, it would be tremendously easy to sneer at Lecky and mock his fairly ridiculous tale. Undoubtedly, much of what Lecky says is fairly silly. But his work does demand attention, not so much because of its intrinsic merits, but because of what it reveals about attempts which the would-be legislators of modernity typically made to try to construct order and improvement out of plurality and potential chaos. The point is that

Lecky was telling a tale which coincided very sharply with the modern emphasis on the benefits of freedom from any kind of reification and any kind of unreflexive behaviour. Lecky's expanding circle of moral significance was simultaneously an expanding circle of reflexivity. It represents a profound faith in the development of the possibilities of modernity.

The passage from Lecky (1911: 100–101) contains a number of important dimensions. Essentially, Lecky was saying that individuals are born natural and selfish, and that they can be turned into moral beings only through the work of society. Lecky was clearly working in terms of an intrinsically modern perspective that it was only social life and, undoubtedly more significantly, societal regulation, which could guarantee an avoidance of the pit of the Hobbesian state of nature. However, once Lecky's individual had been turned into a proper unit of the societal body (that is, presumably, once the wild natural being had been fully subordinated to the demands of the greater organism), she or he was able to see beyond personal motives, identify the same motives in all others, and, consequently, recognize an increasing number of sites of homogeneity (or at least, of quite secondary heterogeneity within a more fundamental realm of homogeneity). With the expansion of the orbit of the moral sensibilities, the places of invidious strangeness and filthiness were to be pulled within the comforting embrace of societal reciprocity and benevolently assimilated.

Through this kind of story, William Lecky was able to turn the fractured terrain of allotment situations into the condition of a most all-encompassing legislative enterprise. He was also able to come to terms with his lack of ability to indulge in practices of makeability by turning modernity into its own myth, and by saying that improvement would happen anyway. Lecky was aware that not all the groups which might augment the societal organism could be treated in exactly the same way (for instance, animals really do need to be treated differently than members of one's own family, regardless of any moral arguments to the contrary), and he was prepared to accept a plurality of sovereignty. But Lecky's concept of the expanding circle of moral significance meant that he always remained able to emphasize the relevance of universal, and universalizing, interpretations of freedom, order, and sovereignty. For Lecky, precisely because we are all different, we are all the same. Given the viability of the concept of society, Lecky rather seems to have assumed that we *must* all be the same; and be made to be so.

The concept of citizenship had much the same hermeneutic and practical impact. It, too, attempted to avoid the collapse of all order into ambivalence by the creation of a system which was able to turn individual heterogeneity into the stuff of an interpretation and understanding of the world which stressed total homogeneity. The idea of citizenship also involved a tale of the assimilation of the formerly ambivalent through a perfectly clear and intelligible (and therefore modern) process which was held to occur much of its own accord. Again, modernity created its own myths. The best-known sociological treatment of the question of citizenship was that developed by T.H. Marshall. He understood the growth of citizenship as the ever greater permeation of equal reciprocity throughout the relationships between 'insider' social groups and groups of strangers (see especially Marshall 1973). In essence, the narrative of citizenship copied the method of the notion of the expanding circle of moral significance, and repeated the idea that heterogeneity can be reconstituted in terms of the statement of a most emphatic and orderly homogeneity. Quite simply, as soon as someone is called a citizen, she or he is also being assimilated into the body of societal equilibrium, and being called the *same* as the caller.

To recall the argument briefly, Marshall identified a societal and a historical process of the recognition of three different kinds of citizenship, each of which was embodied in a distinctive conception of rights. Firstly, Marshall identified *civil rights*, which revolved around the recognition of the equality of all citizens in the face of the law, regardless of other characteristics. Secondly, Marshall spoke of *political rights*, which emphasized the right of all citizens to participate in elections and to stand for public office. Finally, Marshall identified *social rights*, which concerned the equal claim of each and every citizen to a minimum level of economic welfare and security. Marshall's main point was that these three areas of citizenship had been gradually extended, either thanks to benevolence or struggle, to include groups which had previously been excluded from the societal body on the grounds that they were too different. In other words, Marshall was telling a quite up-lifting tale of the decline of strangeness and the final overcoming of ambivalence through the increasing hold and inclusiveness of the single identity of citizenship (for a guide to some of the wider debates around the concept of citizenship, see Barbalet 1988).

Much like the concept of the expanding circle of moral significance, Marshall's theory and account of citizenship should be understood as an attempt by a putative legislator (steeped in the culture of reflexivity) to create universality and a single explanation of order from out of the plurality and potential chaos of the allotment-type situation. Both narratives were based on the fundamental assumption that despite visible differences, it was still possible to treat all individuals and societal groups as identical in all *important* respects. But, of course, it needed a special type of awareness to actually unravel what those important respects might actually be.

Ultimately, the consequence of these attempts to create an order based on homogeneity was a failure to accept the legitimacy or significance of surface differences. In the last instance, the responses to the allotment situation were as intolerant of heterogeneity as the projects which were imposed in the garden situations. The difference was that in allotment situations, the annihilation of diversity could only be intellectual. In the garden-type situations, the annihilation could frequently be physical as well.

Despite the narrative logic which implied the contrary, the universalization of the experience and activity of sovereign individuality through stories like citizenship or expanding moral significance, did not mean that all citizens or morally significant beings were treated equally. Rather, the allotment-type situations continued to identify certain groups as problematic and unpleasant to the extent that they were unable to maintain their inclusion through an inability to reproduce claims to legitimate exclusivity (magic), or if they lacked the resources of professionalization. The working of the idea of citizenship was especially interesting in this respect. The point was that the idea of citizenship assumed that all individuals could be treated the same because they made much the same demands of the societal body, possessed more or less the same interests, made fairly equal claims to their putative rights. The difficulty was that some groups of citizens did in fact tend to possess different interests than others, and were forced to make greater claims than the other groups.

The groups which demanded more were marginalized, constructed as a problem, and treated as only ambivalently included within the boundaries of society. Certainly, they were not subjected to the stronger exclamations of the rhetoric of dirt and filth, but they were nevertheless identified as *inadequate citizens*. Their citizenship was undeniable, but their adequacy for citizenship could be made somewhat questionable. That is, the problem was turned against itself. The issue of inadequate citizens did not reflect badly on the concept and the image of society. On the contrary it reflected badly on those individuals or groups which aspired to be included within the society. As such, those groups became a site and a cause of fears and anxieties about the maintenance of societal life. Many examples of such groups of inadequate citizens could be given. To give just a few illustrations, from a European perspective it would be possible to identify cases of the construction of the inadequacy of gypsies, Jews, guest workers, ethnic minorities, homosexuals, and, of course, the poor.

A fine example of this line of thinking was provided by George Orwell's treatment of the poor and, more specifically, by his obsession with the smells of poverty. One of the more horrible episodes in Orwell's loathing of smells and dirt can be found at the beginning of *The Road to Wigan Pier*. There, Orwell spoke about his time at the boarding house run by Mr and Mrs Brooker. 'Mr Brooker was a dark, small-boned, sour, Irish-looking man, and astonishingly dirty ... If he gave you a slice of bread-and-butter there was always a black thumb-print on it' (Orwell 1962: 7–8). A little later, George Orwell remarked that, 'at any hour of the day you were liable to meet Mr Brooker on the stairs, carrying a full chamber-pot which he gripped with his thumb well over the rim' (Orwell 1962: 11). We are left to make our own connections between the thumb in the chamber pot and the thumb mark on the slice of bread.

Now, Orwell was not saying that Mr Brooker could be identified as the personal embodiment of all filth and treated accordingly. Rather, Orwell's point was that Mr Brooker was fully enclosed within the circle of moral significance, and fully included within the rights of citizenship, but that nevertheless he was astonishingly dirty. The assumption was, of course, that to the extent that Mr Brooker was a member of the societal body, he should have revealed a clean pair of hands (society as clean and pure, nature and the state of nature as dirty and dangerous).

Consequently, Mr Brooker was presented simultaneously as an *equal* but as *inadequate*. Orwell's wider message seemed to be that dirty individuals treat their fellow citizens badly, and that, therefore, those dirty individuals are nothing other than inadequate members of the societal body. As such, they become the sites of ambivalence within society itself. The logical implication of this argument was that Orwell felt that something had to be done either to clean up the Brookers, or to make sure that the victims of poverty (upon whom the Brookers preyed), would not have to come into contact with such dirt.

The demand for cleanliness and purity, the demand for *decency* (an important word for Orwell), to some extent constituted the heart of George Orwell's socialism. The tragedy of Orwell's socialism was precisely that he lived in social and political circumstances which made it impossible for him to put that essentially moral conviction into practice. Orwell accepted the inclusion of the Brookers within society, but he created them as a site of the most profound ambivalence. Indeed, Orwell's description of the repulsive habits of the Brookers is telling exactly because he felt that he *should* have treated them empathetically as equals, because the universalizing narratives of morality and citizenship embraced them, but he felt quite unable to treat the Brookers as adequate to the demands of citizenship. Consequently, he could speak of them only to the extent that they were disgustingly inadequate, only to the extent that they were in need of either education (you *ought* not touch excrement and immediately afterwards butter bread) or surveillance (you *must* not touch excrement and butter bread). As such, George Orwell was able to construct an image of the adequate and fully significant citizen by means of a concentration on a group of strangers within. To misquote a phrase of Orwell's which is now little more than a banal motto: in allotment-type situations, all individuals might have been equal, but some were more equal than others.

Orwell managed to marginalize people like the Brookers, who might have well been repugnant but do rather seem to have been victims of poverty themselves (and, therefore, to some extent demanding of Orwell's sympathy rather than horror). The side effect of this kind of argument, which was not, of course, peculiar to Orwell, was that groups like the poor were identified as in some way of less relevance as sites of moral significance or as citizens, than those groups or individuals which did not betray signs of inadequacy. Consequently, groups like the poor became dirty strangers. And, of course, people like the Brookers did not possess the resources which would have enabled them to speak for themselves or resist their identification by others as ambivalent. Ultimately, there was nothing whatsoever that the Brookers could do about George Orwell's act of their secular excommunication.

In other words, despite the inability of any collective definition of sovereignty to gain general legitimacy in allotment-type situations, and despite the individualization of sovereignty, it was still typically the case that totalizing narratives emerged which in principle equally included all citizens. Had such narratives not appeared, the social construction of order would have been at best difficult, at worst, quite impossible. But allotment situations were always characterized by a commitment to the concept and the image of society as a bounded community. Consequently, they were the context for processes by which various sites of ambivalence were identified, various groups of dirty strangers marginalized, and various constructions of order and of the extent of the bounded society imposed. That is, and as George Orwell implied, *the devices which ostensibly upheld the sovereignty of individuality, and which apparently accepted heterogeneity, were, in fact, intimately involved in the social construction of homogeneity.*

Those groups of inadequate citizens, those groups which seemed to have fallen out of the magic circle of moral significance and citizenship (perhaps rather like Milan Kundera in Prague) became morally and societally *insignificant*. In this vein, John Berger has commented that, 'Twentieth century consumer economy has produced the first culture for which a beggar is a reminder of nothing' (*Guardian* 22 March 1990: 23). Berger was using rhetoric which was more than a little over-inflated. It is not the case that the beggar is a reminder of nothing. On the contrary, the beggar is a visible reminder of the extent of societal boundaries, and a practical reminder of what inadequacy looks like. But Berger's point was well made. It is important to explain how it could be that in Western European societies, which ostensibly treat all individuals as equal citizens and as equally moral claimants, some individuals are totally ignored and left to fall outside of the definite boundaries of that distinctive entity called society. Arguably, the beggars are consigned to live on or beyond the margins because they are societally constructed as morally insignificant, and, just like the Brookers, because they lack the resources to be able to do anything themselves about that invidious construction.

If Zygmunt Bauman's analysis of the Nazi treatment of Jews is applied (with due variation) to the treatment of beggars, it would perhaps lead to the conclusion that beggars are ignored because they are morally invisible (Bauman 1989). Bauman makes the point that one of the reasons why the Nazi system was able to indulge in mass murder was because the Jews were constructed as beyond the 'universe of obligation'. This 'universe of obligation', which perhaps bears direct comparison to what I have been calling the circle of moral significance, 'designates the outer limits of the social territory inside which moral questions may be asked at all with any sense'. Bauman continues: 'On the other side of the boundary, moral precepts do not bind, and moral evaluations are meaningless. To render the humanity of victims invisible, one needs merely to evict them from the universe of obligation' (Bauman 1989: 27). This is a profound point which arguably can go a long way towards explaining the situation which John Berger identified. Indeed, mild, relatively benign, hints of the process of eviction can almost certainly be seen in George Orwell's description of the Brookers.

However, it is perhaps wrong to talk about the *invisibility* of those who fall outside of the 'universe of obligation'. It is more useful to talk instead of their *insignificance*. The point is that I *do* notice the face of the beggar, her plight actually does mean something to me, but *I do absolutely nothing about it*. The beggar is not invisible, she is a very real feature of my life in an urban environment, but I do nothing because, to me, she is quite *insignificant*. To me, as someone who is included within the boundaries of society, who worries about my obligations towards other individuals who live within the margins, the beggar is *beyond*; beyond my universe, beyond my obligations, beyond my help. I reduce her to the signs of her inadequacy, I make myself see only the dirty clothes and the torn and tattered carrier bags. I take those things to be signs of her insignificance to me. That is, if I see anything. More often than not I confirm the beggar's situation beyond my universe, and indeed reconfirm those boundaries, by the physical act of averting my gaze from her. In looking away, I am pushing her away and, of course, also trying to avoid the uneasiness (perhaps the Sartrean sense of *nausea*) which she inspires. Similarly, George Orwell reduced the Brookers to a dirty thumb print and a pile of soiled paper. The beggar and the Brookers are visibly and culturally outside of the social and moral world which I inhabit, and consequently they are of little or no significance to me (but modern communication systems can ensure that the victims of, say, the Ethiopian famine are placed at the heart of my cognitive and moral universe).

The Jews were in much the same situation in relationship to the Nazis. Had the Jews been morally *invisible* rather than plain *insignificant* it might have been the case that the effort of the Final Solution would have never been made. The Holocaust was possible primarily because nobody cared (or at least, because not enough people cared), not because nobody noticed (or at least, they did not notice because in the first place they did not care). But, of course, annihilating Final Solutions are not practised against the modern beggars of Western Europe, and it is quite reasonable to assume that even in the future they never will be. That is because, notwithstanding the lack of a desire to pursue such policies, the allotment conditions disallowed that option. Final Solutions or, with due variation, gulag practices, were only possible in certain garden conditions of modernity, where the meanings of freedom and sovereignty had been put under a single banner, and where it was relatively easy to make sure that the groups constructed as dirty strangers would be unable to speak for themselves, or find any one prepared to speak on their behalf (I am not directly nor practically conflating the Holocaust with the gulag; I am simply seeking to make an analytical point). In those garden situations, which arose only very occasionally, insignificance led to physical obliteration, whereas in the allotment situations, groups like the poor can be obliterated only at a citizen level, or geographically by their concentration in high-density housing estates (high density because inadequate citizens by definition do not warrant adequate space).

In the allotment-type conditions of European modernity, the image of order implicit to the concept of society, and the totalization of individuality through citizenship and moral significance, was constructed and confirmed at the expense of the utter insignificance of those groups which were unable to resist

being constructed as dirty strangers and which were unable to
prevent themselves being placed beyond the margins of the
universalized and reciprocal community of free and sovereign
strangers. It was precisely the construction of moral insignificance on the grounds of inadequacy which informed also the
boundary-drawing measures of the garden situation of the
Soviet-type system. As a *method of the hermeneutic construction
of order*, there was little or no difference between the classification of marginality and ambivalence in either the garden or
allotment conditions of modernity.

One of the key concepts for understanding the strategies of
inclusion (the ordering of strangeness) and ambivalence (the
danger of strangeness) in the Soviet-type system was the notion
of the 'Comrade'. The notion was usefully discussed by Anatoli
Rybakov in his weighty, but fairly predictable, novel, *Children of
the Arbat* (Rybakov 1988). The book tells the story of a circle of
young friends who live in the Arbat, the intellectual and artistic
centre of Moscow, and who fall foul of Stalin's purges. One of
the more interesting episodes in the novel concerns the interrogation of Sasha Pankratov, a tragic hero of the story, by
an officer named Dyakov. At one point in the interrogation,
Dyakov mentions two well-placed officials known by Pankratov.
The significant thing was that Dyakov had not used the title
'Comrade' when talking of them. 'Dyakov hadn't said "*comrades*
in high office", but "*people* in high office", and he'd said it
intentionally' (Rybakov 1988: 171). Rybakov's point is that in the
Soviet-type system, the application or denial of the title of
Comrade could be a matter of the most profound importance.

Quite simply, to call someone by the name Comrade was to
include them within the circle of moral significance and within
the orderly boundaries of the society. It was, of course, also to
subordinate their individuality to the interests and reciprocity of
the collectivity. A person who was called Comrade was being
named and identified as a friend, and any strangeness was being
ignored or made relatively unimportant. After all, one Comrade
was in all relevant respects exactly the same as any other
Comrade. Each was included within the boundaries of the
community, each was involved in entirely reciprocal relationships with the other, and each was constructed as entirely
homogenous with any other.

As such, to deny or to remove the application of the title of

Comrade was deliberately to exclude an individual from the bounded collectivity. It was to marginalize that person, it was to make them a stranger, and, by extension, it was to construct them as morally insignificant. This was what Rybakov's Sasha Pankratov saw very clearly. Pankratov realized that the denial of the label of Comrade to any individual, and even more so to any member of the Party, could mean only that the individual had been identified as some kind of danger, and was being subjected to a process of deliberate extirpation (Rybakov 1988: 172). The denial of Comrade implied a refusal of comrade*ship*. It went rather further than simply involving the identification of a woman or man as inadequate. To refuse to call someone a Comrade was implicitly to construct them as an *enemy*. Since the title of Comrade suggests an individual who shares interests and activities in common with others, the denial of the title suggests a deep lack of affinity and, perhaps more importantly, a *destruction* of reciprocity. That destruction was a two way process. On the one hand the once-but-no-more Comrade was being identified as someone who threatened to demolish societal bonds. On the other hand, the defender of society (and in the Soviet-type system that meant the Party), had to forcefully remove the dangerous individual from the bounded community. And, more or less by definition, non-Comrades were thoroughly insignificant and worthless. They were treated as such through their cognitive and physical removal to places beyond the margins of 'normal' order.

Lenin was always quite sure about the treatment which was appropriate to the groups which lived on or beyond the margins of society. For Lenin, it was perfectly obvious that the maintenance of the society and of the collectivity involved reciprocity on the part of the adequate:

> Only the voluntary and conscientious co-operation of the *mass* of the workers and peasants in accounting and controlling *the rich, the rogues, the idlers and the rowdies,* ... can conquer these survivals of accursed capitalist society, these dregs of humanity, these hopelessly decayed and atrophied limbs, this contagion, this plague, this ulcer that socialism has inherited from capitalism.
>
> (Lenin 1964: 410)

A veritable thesaurus of complaints against the societal body.

Lenin was quite clear that this hermeneutic identification of filthy strangers had certain practical and strategic implications. 'These enemies must be placed under the special surveillance of the entire people; they must be ruthlessly punished for the slightest violation of the laws and regulations of socialist society' (Lenin 1964: 411).

Lenin thought that various methods were needed, 'in achieving the single common aim – to *clean* the land of Russia of all vermin, of fleas – the rogues, the bugs – the rich, and so on and so forth' (Lenin 1964: 414). He proposed that a number of 'shirkers' should be imprisoned and made to clean toilets (an interesting conflation of the filthy with filth which to some extent anticipated Orwell). Lenin also thought that it would be a tremendously good idea if the shirkers, 'be provided with "yellow tickets" after they have served their time, so that everyone shall keep an eye on them, as *harmful* persons, until they reform' (Lenin 1964: 414). Release on probation was seen as particularly useful. But a more aggressive proposal was made in passing in Lenin's typically dry, matter-of-fact prose: 'one out of every ten idlers will be shot on the spot' (Lenin 1964: 414). The point was, of course, that beyond the punitive example which they offered, these idlers were in all other respects quite insignificant and, because they did not possess their own resources which might provide the basis of some opposition to Lenin's plans, there was absolutely no reason *not* to shoot them.

In this context, Alexander Solzhenitsyn's remarks about the gulag archipelago as a sewage disposal system take on a further dimension. As a victim of the gulag, Solzhenitsyn rather seemed to have internalized the societal construction of his own insignificance. By implication, he was able to talk of his own experience of the gulag to the extent that it was not so much the social, human individual called Alexander Solzhenitsyn who was made to suffer, but rather a piece of filth which was cleansed from the pure societal body. This particular person who went through the gulag could see himself only as a mute and organic thing, as something which, had it been adequate to the measure of Soviet utopian anthropology, would not have been forced into the sewage disposal system in the first place. It was almost Kafkaesque; Solzhenitsyn virtually implied that he could only come to terms with his presence in the gulag by assuming that had he been an adequate Comrade, he would not have been pulled into the sewer. Yet Solzhenitsyn also knew that, 'the prison sewers were never empty. The blood, the sweat, and the urine into which we were pulped pulsed through them continuously' (Solzhenitsyn 1974: 25). Solzhenitsyn reduced himself to the status of a droplet of muck in a wave of scum. Moreover: 'The waves flowed underground through the pipes; they provided sewage disposal for the life flowering on the surface' (Solzhenitsyn 1974: 47). That is, in the garden conditions which nourished the Soviet-type system, the possibility of the success of socialist society, indeed the very awareness and self-identity of that society, was only reproducible to the extent that increasing quantities of fertilizer could be processed, used, and held up as an illustration of the impurity beyond the boundaries of society.

Indeed, Solzhenitsyn goes so far as to imply that the sustained reciprocity of the Comrades was only created and maintained to the extent that all the adequate citizens could be made to have a stake in the marginalization of the inadequate (that is, those who were not Comrades). He also stressed how the identification and creation of the insignificance of marginal groups was a continuing process, rather than the result of a single act of boundary-drawing. 'Those who had not yet been swept bodily down the sewer hatches, who had not yet been carried through the pipes to the Archipelago, had to march up above, carrying banners praising the trials, and rejoicing at the judicial reprisals' (Solzhenitsyn 1974: 47).

Perhaps inevitably, given his astonishing sourness and self-conviction, Solzhenitsyn understood all the marching around as part of the universalization of guilt, presumably as yet one more instance in the terrible movement of Holy Russia away from Orthodoxy. But there was rather more to the marches than that. They were certainly orchestrated, and they were indeed playing a role in the collectivization of responsibility for the purges. But, more importantly, they were practical demonstrations of social order. To put the matter rather more anthropologically, the marches can be interpreted as rituals of the confirmation and consolidation of reciprocity and of the reproduction of society within its new, more restricted boundaries. The marches, and indeed the gulag, were products of the modern hermeneutic of conceiving of social relationships in terms of a closed and definitely bounded entity called *society*.

Indeed, the production and reproduction of marginal, ambivalent groups, on the basis of their illicit strangeness represented one of the main ways in which modernity proceeded in its processes of reflexivity and the march towards freedom. The relentless identification of sites which were seen as little more than outcrops of a heterogeneity which needed to be uprooted or assimilated, was a central component of both the garden and the allotment conditions of modernity.

The reduction of individuals like Alexander Solzhenitsyn to the level of a set of bodily fluids and odours, or the reduction of the Brookers to a pile of grubby papers and a thumb in a chamber pot, meant that criteria of inclusion and of adequacy could be imposed with some force and some viability. Modernity was able to last as long as it did only because the quest for homogeneity was able to create its own places of the terribly heterogeneous. It lasted only to the extent that the struggle against the filthy strangers never ran out of steam, either because of a lack of strangers without their own resources of reproduction, or because of a lack of the awareness of homogeneity.

It was only on that basis that the aims of modernity were pursued with such relentless enthusiasm. It was only through the perpetual recreation of things outside of the societal organism, which were variously identified as nature, or inadequacy, or as treachery towards the reciprocity of Comradeship, that freedom remained such a vital and an important goal.

6

FREEDOM

It must be said that Alexander Solzhenitsyn's depiction of Soviet society, with circles dancing on the surface above the most effective subterranean sewage disposal system, is chilling. But, beyond some comments about the collectivization of guilt, Solzhenitsyn failed to realize that the dancing and the disposal were two aspects of the same process of the creation of the bounded community of the Soviet society (Solzhenitsyn 1974). Put another way, it was only through these two different and yet the same acts of the construction of inclusion, that Soviet society was able to become a meaningful and accepted milieu for the interpretation of the world. When they ran through Red Square, or when they were pushed into the gulag, the women and men who were to be, or who had failed to be, Soviet Comrades, were engaged in the creation of a memory of society as something distinct from all reification. As Paul Connerton has usefully put it: 'If habit-memory is inherently performative, then social habit-memory must be distinctively social-performative' (Connerton 1989: 35).

It is worthwhile, then, considering precisely how that 'social performance' of 'social-habit memory' was carried out. In the characteristic rituals of the Soviet-type system, each individual was restrained and constrained by the patterns which were created by the massive collective units, and by the leadership of the experts. After all, it needed a detached, God's-eye view, to be able to see the beauty of the patterns at all. The leaders became, in a very real and also a very double sense, Guardians of the Totality. Indeed, it is quite reasonable to say of the ritual patterns, like the Czechoslovakian Spartakiade, that, 'The regularity of their patterns is acclaimed by the masses, who themselves are arranged in row upon ordered row' (Kracauer 1989: 145). More than that, the participants in the demonstrations of the 'social habit-memory', 'can no longer be reassembled as human beings. Their mass gymnastics are never performed by whole, autonomous bodies whose contortions would deny rational understanding. Arms, thighs, and other segments are the smallest components of the composition' (Kracauer 1989: 147).

Those short passages are taken from Siegfried Kracauer's attempt to use the Tiller Girls as a microcosm of the relationships of modern capitalist production. However, he was also making comments which might explain why the representative rituals of the creation of the boundaries of Soviet society took the mass, organized, form they did. The rituals were the performative expressions of the ideal blueprint of the perfect society. Consequently, whilst Siegfried Kracauer was able to express only a melancholy disgust on account of the rise of the 'mass ornament', it was importantly the case that in the context of the Soviet-type system, the marshalled rituals were *aesthetically perfect* precisely to the extent that they reflected the image of the *perfect society*. (Kracauer spoke of the aesthetic qualities of the Tiller Girls only by way of a backhanded compliment: 'the *aesthetic* pleasure gained from the ornamental mass movements is *legitimate*. They belong in fact to the isolated configurations of the time, configurations which imbue a given material with form' (Kracauer 1989: 148).)

The rituals did not emphasize rational regimentation simply because a regimented individual subjectivity was required by rapid industrialization (to say the least, such an argument would be rather reductionist). Rather, the rituals took the mass, collectivized, but nevertheless aesthetic, form they did precisely because they were held to be significant signposts on the road to freedom, 'where every man is a note in a magnificent Bach fugue and anyone who refuses his note is a mere black dot, useless and meaningless, easily caught between the fingers like an insect' (Kundera 1982: 8).

Of course, in the garden situation which was fundamentally the condition of possibility of the Soviet-type system, it was in principle not too difficult to go about the creation of a society in accordance with a variation on a theme by Bach. On the one hand, the social terrain was treated as empty, and held to put no obstacles in the way of the ambitious blueprints. On the other hand, any potential obstacles or sites of recalcitrance were either coerced into their *proper place* in the grand fugue (and thus deliberately denied their own expressions), or they were easily uprooted and thrown into the pull of the sewage disposal system. Quite simply, the arms and thighs could be firmly ordered as 'the smallest components of the composition' because few other compositions could be produced, and even that handful of alternatives which did appear possessed entirely inadequate resources of reproduction.

All the time the garden situation could be maintained, the Soviet-type system was more or less impregnable. Or, at least, there were few reasons for its collapse. Very clear, albeit changing, criteria of societal inclusion and societal exclusion, could be imposed and readily understood by all. There was no significant debate over who was within the boundaries of society and who was outside, simply because there were not two parties who could possibly participate in the dialogue of a debate. One side of the debating chamber was too busy *performing* rituals of the creation of a memory of society, whilst the other side was too busy with the *planning* of new rituals, or with the shovelling up of more filth.

However, and with a special blend of success, benevolence, structural and systemic ossification, negligence, and, simply, crass stupidity, the Soviet-type system moved out of the unique and historically privileged garden situation. The system was more or less viable all the time it allowed the expression of just *one* definition of freedom (that is, a collective definition), and all the time it had the resources and the energy to maintain and defend that single interpretation. It began to fall apart as soon as the resources and the energy which went into events of the ritual construction and reconstruction of society were exhausted, and as soon as alternative definitions of freedom were accorded some, however grudging or accidental, credibility. The alternatives became imaginable as soon as different social arrangements and projects were accepted as historically viable (the other side of 'Socialism in One Nation'), and as soon as previously disallowed principles of sovereignty were expressed through the signing of things like human rights conventions. Through both of those means, the Soviet-type system pluralized the meanings of freedom and sovereignty and, in so doing, sowed the seeds of its own decay.

The pluralization of the meanings of the promises of the future was significant because it logically implied the complete redundancy of any single and putatively universal blueprint and, indeed, of any single highway to the planned destination. The meaning of the flight of the angel of history became inherently controversial. Not least, the idea that really existing socialism was the definitely right road to somewhere (Communism) could be repudiated on the grounds that really existing socialism actually was on the road to nowhere. As such, the Soviet-type system created spaces in which the alternative definitions of freedom could *to some extent* flourish. Moreover, and crucially, it allowed for the creation in practical, legal codes of a yardstick of ideal practices and arrangements which could be the measure of a kind of immanent critique of actual relationships.

The beauty of the Communist blueprint was that, despite the claims to scientificity, it was so vague in particular details, and yet so very eloquent on grand generalizations, that very little *substantive* could be said of it (as an early example, witness Marx's flailing efforts to talk about the *details* of the future in the *Critique of the Gotha Programme*). The other side of that particular coin was, of course, that very little could be said against that future. However, when the formal codifications of human rights were enshrined in the different (and yet remarkably similar) national legal codes, the Soviet-type system was expressing details which evidently withstood little comparison with actual, day to day, relationships and procedures.

Thus, the *real* (that is, the experienced world), was made susceptible to a critique from the perspective of *ideal* forms to which the everyday was said, and indeed perhaps even meant, to approximate. This is, of course, what the signatories of the Czechoslovakian Charter 77 realized extremely clearly. Similarly, the ratification by the Polish government of the United Nations International Pacts on Human Rights in 1977 meant that it was possible to offer alternative blueprints for Poland on the grounds that, 'human and civil rights are inviolable and inalienable; they can not be relinquished' (Andrzejewski *et al.* 1978: 275). Against this ontological and anthropological legitimation of ethics and alternative projects, the incantations of the legislators of the existing institutional arrangements that human rights consists in low unemployment, a better use of technology,

146

and the state support of family life, could be only boring if not simply irrelevant. It was certainly very tame stuff indeed (see, for example, Gierek 1978). Increasingly, in the nations of the Soviet-type system, what might be called the *institutionally legitimated and consolidated social habit-memory*, was quite bereft of any performative content except of the most facile kind.

So, it is nothing more than Panglossian to suggest that the system collapsed thanks to the 'Heroic Efforts of the Great Oppressed Masses'. Rather, the collapse was ironically due to its very success in animating previously mute sites. But the collapse was also due to the system's own multiple failures: the failure to maintain garden circumstances; the failure to reproduce the ideals of the blueprint as something more than hollow rhetoric; the failure to create a reproducible and self-sustaining society; the failure of the leaders of the collective to move outside the warm certainties of the sealed train. Ultimately, the collapse was largely attributable to *the failure of the closest approximation to the ideal institutional and social arrangements of modernity to prevent itself solidifying into a quasi-naturalized myth.*

Of course, however, the Soviet-type system in Central and Eastern Europe did need a little final push before it finally collapsed. But the push, indeed, only needed to be slight. It would be enervating to believe in the world historical impact of the 'Heroic Efforts of the Great Oppressed Masses', and thus to also believe in the achievement of a unitary emancipation, in a Great Revolution. But it would be naive.

However, the perfectly justifiable caution over a faith in the heroic masses, quickly runs against a serious empirical difficulty. Quite simply, if the collapse of the Soviet-type system was due to the internal failures of that system, rather than attributable to any major outside intervention, it is difficult to explain how and why so many people so quickly took to the streets of Prague and Leipzig some little time *before* the system's admission of defeat. Whilst it would indeed be rather simplistic to say that really existing socialism was overthrown by a popular and a populist uprising, it was nevertheless typically the case that the last push against the institutional arrangements of the system was made by a sizeable opposition which was *aware of itself as* an opposition (although it would be misguided to see the opposition as a homogeneous constituency with entirely common interests; see, for example, Lash 1990). However weak internally the

Soviet-type system might have been, it still had to be given a final nudge by some outside force. In the last days of the system, an opposition took to the streets as a *self-conscious and self-identifying* group, as a group both in itself and for itself, which tried to achieve something more ambitious and more difficult than to simply turn around and appropriate for itself the labels which were meant to identify it (and its individual members) as dangerously ambivalent from the point of view of society.

Obviously, it would be easiest to propose that the opposition groups emerged around the alternative definitions of freedom which had been allowed to enter the former garden. Certainly, concepts like human rights were at the very heart of the opposition's position, but there was absolutely no *necessary* connection between a statement of inalienable rights and an opposition to existing institutional arrangements. For example, Andrei Sakharov felt able to assume a significant place in the apparently reformed apparatus of the Soviet Union, whilst the Charter 77 movement scrupulously avoided any overt hint that it wished to overthrow the state, or for that matter even challenge it. On the contrary, according to all its statements, Charter 77 merely wished to force the institutional apparatus to practice its own, self-proclaimed, ideals. Consequently, the desire to radically *transform* arrangements rather than simply *reform* them, must have drawn its impetus from elsewhere. It would have been otherwise improbable that the leaders of the opposition could have so easily stepped into the command positions of the system's wreckage.

The important area to explore is how and why a radical opposition was sustained which, in the moment of its proclaimed victory, did not just dissipate but, instead, was able to coherently establish the networks to support and maintain a new and already legitimate leadership elite. The interesting thing was that the new leaderships, the old oppositions, fundamentally consisted in a group of double strangers, just like the old and discredited legislators of modernity.

Certainly, the obstacles to opposition were great, most obviously during the Leninist and the Stalinist years of the creation of societal boundaries (both hermeneutically and through practical performance). The few, the very few, sites of actual or potential opposition to the demands of the blueprint were subjected to processes of the most difficult assimilation which left their inclusion within the body of the Comrades perpetually in the balance. These sites were quite isolated and entirely unable to overtly resist any identities which might have been imposed upon them from outside. Undoubtedly, one of the most poignant illustrations of this kind of psychological warfare against opposition is provided by the career and the experiences of Dmitri Shostakovich. Shostakovich occupied a deeply unsettling position, somewhere between the performance of functions of the creation and memory of society, and the name always at the top of the *next* list of enemies of the people. Any opposition which Shostakovich might have wanted to offer was reduced to a poignant musical code which, in the Tenth Symphony at least, involved a solitary piping against the overwhelming forces of the massed orchestra.

Indeed, the oscillating career of Dmitri Shostakovich provides fine illustrations of the two dominant means for dealing with illicit alternatives which emerged in the Soviet-type system after the performance of the gulag option had been exhausted, after the rituals of societal inclusion and exclusion had become rather empty. The basic problem confronting the system after its creation was one of dealing with the new cohorts of would-be legislators; on the one hand the system needed new intellectuals if it were to maintain its commitment to the project of the perfect future, but on the other hand, the young legislators had to be disciplined in the ways of the programme, and any excess numbers had to be carved off. The very success of really existing socialism in creating its own generations of double strangers faced it with the very real difficulty that new interpretations of freedom might also have been in the making. Firstly, attempts were made to assimilate or 'buy-off' alternative definitions of freedom and sovereignty through the firm incorporation of the rising generations of the double strangers. This strategy also involved the deliberate incorporation of all cultural products by the institutional arrangements of the project. Secondly, a more orthodox strategy of the conditions of modernity was employed which involved identifying as a dirty stranger any individual or group which refused assimilation into the societal body and the treatment of them accordingly.

Shostakovich experienced the weight of these two strategies during the years of the ossification of the Soviet-type system, and before that historical moment, of course, he knew the threat of the gulag. But the post-boundary drawing (that is, the post-gulag) attempts to deal with versions of freedom which diverged from the version sanctioned by the legislators, were not applied to Dmitri Shostakovich alone. The strategies were of far greater social, historical, and cultural significance than they otherwise could have been, had they merely been incidents in an individual biography. Indeed, if Miklos Haraszti is right, the two strategies, of a preferred assimilation or a modest annihilation, constituted the central components in the cultural policies of the arrangements of really existing socialism (Haraszti 1987).

It must be said that with the retrospective wisdom bequeathed by the events of 1989, Haraszti's analysis seems more than a little dated, but his book remains extremely valuable to the extent that it is a reflection on the relationship between the tradition of art as the free creation of the individual (sovereign) artist, and a society conceived as an expression of the free collective will (Haraszti clearly believed that his analysis had a wide currency, but Ferenc Feher has suggested that it is only relevant to Hungary during the period of Kadar; see Feher 1990).

Haraszti's account of the position of 'artists under state socialism', to quote the subtitle of his book, seems to be fundamentally predicated upon the neo-Frankfurt School thesis that artistic products should possess some quality of *aura*. The problem is that Haraszti never makes his assumption of the aura at all explicit. Rather it operates as something like the never said, and presumably therefore almost metaphysically free, counterpoint to the status and position of artistic creation and cultural production in the conditions of really existing socialism. Simply put, the aura of the work of art is that strangeness which surrounds and permeates the original painting or text because it is perceived as removed from specific and determining social and historical conditions of existence. For Adorno, of course, the aura was to some extent the vindication of the validity of art and, more broadly and significantly, the context of ideal aesthetic experience. Meanwhile, in his late work, Walter Benjamin forcefully argued that the modern possibility of technological reproduction robbed art of its aura and, thus, democratized access to it. As Benjamin enthusiastically put the matter in his famous essay, 'The Work of Art in the Age of Mechanical Reproduction': 'For the first time in world history, mechanical reproduction emancipates the work of art from its parasitical dependency on ritual ... Instead of ritual, it begins to be based on another practice: politics' (for a discussion of the debates between Adorno and Benjamin, see Buck-Morss 1977). According to Miklos Haraszti, it was precisely this close connection between art and politics which explained why in the Soviet-type system art possessed little or nothing of an oppositional potential. Haraszti was in no doubt that art should possess the qualities ascribed to it by Theodor Adorno. Yet, in Central and Eastern Europe prior to 1989, art manifestly *did not* possess the qualities of aura. Given this line of thinking, Haraszti's perfectly reasonable question to art was: Why not?

Haraszti approached an answer to the problem of art's missing aura through an analysis which seems to be more than a little indebted to Weber's diagnosis of bureaucracy. Haraszti stressed that in the post-Stalinist period, each branch of artistic enterprise was overseen by a distinct ministerial department which drew very clear boundary lines between the art form which it was competent to administer, and the art forms of other responsible ministries. Those distinctions were traced by Haraszti throughout the educational system (Haraszti 1987: 110). The meanings and interpretations of what *should have been* a profoundly auratic activity were thus thoroughly embedded in everyday life and turned into affairs for rational management.

More than that, the artist could only function as an artist to the extent that she or he produced work which umambiguously fell within the classifications and areas of competence of the responsible ministries. 'Transgressing genre boundaries is considered improper. The artist who is between genres or who mixes them is being provocative' (Haraszti 1987: 110). According to Haraszti, the direct linkage between artistic activity and spheres of bureaucratic competence meant that artists had to practise a diligent self-censorship so that none of their products fell outside of the institutionally codified realm of legitimate art and into the difficult, and intrinsically oppositional, realm of the illegitimate. According to this analysis, 'Artists do not produce for an independent public that spends its money according to taste; they still create for the state' (Haraszti 1987: 113).

To this extent, then, the Soviet-type system was able to destroy, or at the very least domesticate, the oppositional qualities which art possesses according to Adorno and Haraszti, through the expedient of a rigid and rational bureaucratic apparatus which claimed to foster art rather than diminish it. Without bureaucratic support, which was forthcoming only when a work was within the boundaries of ministerial responsibility, it was even likely that the artistic status of a cultural practice or product could be denied. Haraszti highlights a paradox: in really existing socialism, art could approach the mere *possibility* of aura only if it were bureaucratically defined as art. Yet that very act of definition inserted the work of art into daily life and, consequently, utterly robbed it of any chance of an ideal and an oppositional aura. But there was more to the matter again than even this exceptionally tidy piece of aesthetic surgery.

Max Weber was keenly aware that one of the main explanations for what he saw as the inevitability and permanence of bureaucracy once it had been established, was the deep interest of the employees in the maintenance of the system which otherwise trapped them. 'The individual bureaucrat cannot squirm out of the apparatus in which he is harnessed ... the professional bureaucrat is chained to his activity by his entire material and ideal existence' (Weber 1948: 228). That sentence can also be read as a rather fine summary of how Miklos Haraszti understood the social and economic position of the artist in the Soviet-type system. Haraszti was quite explicit that the potentially oppositional qualities of art were bought off by the simple expedient of the institutional apparatus incorporating artists by paying them salaries and providing them with resources which stretched far beyond what any free market might offer. The artists became functionaries of the state, with a direct and powerful 'material and ideal' commitment to its continued well-being. After all, 'the intelligentsia had nothing to lose but its independence; in return, it gained half a world, and possesses it on condition that it protects the unity of this world and interprets its own power as service' (Haraszti 1987: 18).

The implication of all of this should be clear. Miklos Haraszti was saying that a cultural practice which should be the site of a most profound challenge to the mundane realities of daily life had, instead, been tamed and domesticated through a mixture of bureaucratic paternalism and, simply, by what amounted to the bribery of the artist (bribery, that is, if it is assumed after Adorno and Haraszti that artists should be individual producers of opposition). In these social and aesthetic circumstances, art was entirely assimilated to a safe place within the societal body, and the artist entered into a Faustian bargain which, it was supposed, would never have to be settled, and which would never expire. If the artists had any doubts before signing the contract, the doubts soon evaporated at the summer schools, the prize givings, and with the stream of commissions from the paymasters of the culture industries. Any individuals who refused the rewards were isolated and condemned as either fools in need of help or threats in need of surveillance and coercion. That is, the refusal of the blandishments of the system's glittering prizes was taken to be an indication of individual inadequacy for inclusion within society.

According to Haraszti, the system of bureaucratic aesthetics produced two paradigmatic kinds of oppositional figures; the 'naive heroes' and the 'maverick artists'. Evidently, however, 'Both are doomed to irrelevance' (Haraszti 1987: 150). The naive hero was destined to become an irrelevant ghost from the past because she or he refused to accept the right of the state to take a stake in her or his work. But, in denying the legitimacy of the state and the censors, the naive hero was, from the point of view of the system, simultaneously denying that what she or he produced was, in fact, art. The heroes who refused the role of the ministries 'are exiled from the world of aesthetics. Their work cannot be produced, published, or displayed' (Haraszti 1987: 151). The naive hero indeed ceased to be an artist. As such, this possible site of opposition was simply pushed way beyond the boundaries of art and of society.

Now, whilst the naive hero upset only the firm classifications of bureaucratic aesthetics, the challenge offered by the maverick artist was rather more considerable, 'for he rejects state culture at its foundations. He disrupts the smooth operation of the machinery of monopoly and provokes independent activity' (Haraszti 1987: 152). All of that was achieved through the establishment of independent distribution networks for cultural practices (*samizdat*). The creation of social networks outside of the institutional arrangements of the state was the basis of the threat posed by the maverick artist, but it was also the basis of her or his impending irrelevance. '[T]he maverick artist transgresses by willingly sacrificing the privileges of the assimilated. He aims to be a poor artist in order to remain a free one' (Haraszti 1987: 153). But the maverick artist succeeded in becoming only the dangerous stranger, a resolute outsider. Freedom was found in complete irrelevance.

Certainly, Miklos Haraszti's analysis of the incorporation of art and the artist is extremely useful. But there is perhaps cause to question whether the alternatives on offer were as stark as Haraszti suggests, a choice between assimilation or annihilation (in one way or another). Quite simply, if that dichotomy exhausted all the options, then no self-conscious opposition, however small and optimistic it might have been, would have been at all possible. Rather, it is more useful to move away from the terrain of the choice between inclusion within *society* or exclusion from *society* and, instead, to try to explore the situations of different institutional arrangements and *social relationships*. If that shift in perspective is carried out then, it seems to me, it would be slightly absurd to juxtapose an intelligible society to an oblivion or a 'nature' which constitutes the milieu of opposition (in any case, to operate on the basis of that kind of dichotomy would be to simply repeat one of the key self-images of the narratives of modernity). Instead, it is more useful to try to understand the nature of the social relationships and hermeneutic enterprises which were practised by the groups and individuals which were evacuated from the societal body but without falling into the ultimate fate of the sewage disposal system.

In these terms, it is clear to see that important and vociferous fragments of the groups and individuals which were meant to have been consigned to nothing in the post-Stalinist situation did not in fact socially evaporate or disappear into thin air. The problem which confronted the Soviet-type system had two dimensions. Firstly, the system had to find effective means of buying-off any potential sites of the generation of alternative definitions of freedom. Here, the variously hard and soft treatment dealt out to Dmitri Shostakovich, and the Faustian bargain with art and the artist, would be the exemplary solutions. The second problem was one of how to deal with that small but nevertheless significant rising generation of double strangers which could make hermeneutic and moral appeals for leadership and exclusivity, but which could not be found places within the institutions (simply because there were not enough jobs to go round).

The system attempted to deal with the members of the rising

cohorts who could not be bought or employed through a method which was in principle brilliantly straightforward. But in practice the strategy was one of the main reasons why opposition groupings were ready and waiting to step into the spaces vacated by the old leaderships. The strategy was predicated on the notion that the challenge of the rising generations could be countered if their status in the magic circles of power and exclusivity could be diluted and if, instead, these potential subjects of new freedoms were turned into entirely mundane components of the 'substantialized nothing' of daily life.

It was assumed, perhaps not entirely unreasonably, that the would-be leaders needed intellectual stimulation if they were to flourish. The answer to the unwanted cohorts was, therefore, perfectly simple; deprive them of access to cosmopolitan cognitive systems, and insert them in overwhelming daily relationships, and their claims to exclusivity will dissolve. The challenges could, in theory, be cretinized. The policy was practised most judiciously by the Czechoslovakian authorities after the Prague Spring. As such, 'Philosophers, lawyers, journalists became bricklayers, waiters, clerks' (Garton Ash 1989: 56). Undoubtedly, this kind of approach was the preferred method of dealing with the problem of the rising generations of potential double strangers (generations rather than individuals who could be, and of course were, thrown into prison) in the era after the societal boundaries had been etched into the system's collective memory, and after the exhaustion of the enthusiasm for the rituals of boundary drawing.

But there was a profound futility as the heart of this Czechoslovakian solution. The point was that the exclusion of certain groups and individuals from the orthodox and legitimate communication channels of the system, led to, not their cretinization, but, rather, to the development of an awareness of frustrated career ambitions and to the creation of an experiential disjuncture between the demands of free knowledge and the demands of societal inclusion. That is, the attempts of the Soviet-type system to destroy the possibility of any alternative ideas of freedom emerging from within the societal body ironically led to the unintended creation of the most fertile ground for the culture of reflexive discourse.

Moreover, the lack of identification with the system which had tried to remove the exclusivity of the rising generation by embedding them in the mundane, the lack of involvement in the system which had tried to alter their social consciousness by altering their social conditions of existence (in a policy initiative derived from a comment by Marx), meant that the frustrated rising generation defined the system and the embrace of incorporation as something *over there* which *happened to* individuals. That is, they identified the societal body as a reified, quasi-natural system which admitted of no alternative and was, therefore, an affront to the promises and possibilities of modernity. Consequently, the philosopher window cleaners were able to develop universalizing and universalistic interpretations of the reasons for their exclusion from the sites of legislation. They could also explain why the system's freedom was actually no freedom at all.

Thanks to the accidental creation of the social conditions of existence of a reflexive culture, the interpretations of exclusion became understandings of oppression and the basis of new meanings of freedom. Ideas of human rights represented one particularly useful handle around which those meanings could take an especially firm hold. For the rising generation which had been subjected to forcible exclusion from the sealed train, the source of all social oppression was elsewhere and, therefore, it could be effectively challenged by its mirror opposite; the identification of a universal oppression led to the identification of a universal freedom. *The withering garden situation generated counterfactual universal interpretations of the meanings and the practices of freedom.*

Indeed, in modernity freedom was conventionally thought of and imagined as an objective situation, as some definite condition which was the goal and the achievement of the project. But the history of modernity was characterized by the fact that nobody, and even less any institutional arrangement, ever felt able to relax efforts towards the attainment of freedom. The efforts demanded in the name of freedom were unremitting, and the individual or society which was trying to achieve freedom had to be virtually inexhaustible and, most certainly, quite unflinching in its commitment. From the point of view of the demands of freedom, it would rather seem that all the efforts to reach the goal were never good enough.

The explanation is rather simple to find. It is illustrated by the fact that whilst the Soviet-type system was intended to be one arrangement which would ensure steady progress along the road to freedom, it was opposed in the name of another interpretation of freedom which was able to present itself as the solution to all the internal contradictions and all the waste products of the system (again, I am not saying that it was this alternative freedom which inspired the 'Great Oppressed Masses' to throw off their shackles; I am more modestly saying that the alternative interpretation constituted an axis around which opposition could gravitate and, thus, be ready to take over once the system collapsed). The history of modernity seems to suggest that despite the declarations of the legislators, freedom was not at all some transcendent, and only temporarily extra-societal, condition against which existing failings could be measured. Quite the contrary, *freedom was an imagination peculiar to those groups or individuals which were in conditions where alternative social and cultural arrangements could be thought.* Freedom was a universal ideal to the extent that it was the product of a group which retained a commitment to reflexive discourse despite its more or less total exclusion from the institutionalized circles of magic.

Since the freedom of modernity was derived from the practice and the possibility of reflexivity, freedom could never be achieved. Freedom could never be achieved because the category of freedom was itself empty of all intrinsic or essential meaning. Freedom had meaning only in so far as it was a desirable counter-factual to the prevailing conditions and experiences of existence. That is, freedom was nothing other than that way of life which was better than this way of life. It was simply the future, the projected, utopia, in contradistinction to the present which was thus rendered oppressive, flawed, and unsatisfactory. But freedom turned out to be utopian in rather another sense.

This was where the Soviet-type system created its own opposition (indeed perhaps every vision and performance of society generated the opposition it deserved). To the extent that it inadvertently placed the rising generation of aspiring double strangers in a limbo between societal normality (nothing is more ordinary than a window cleaner) and intellectual exclusivity (philosophers are not terribly typical), it created the conditions in which the reflexive discourse could only take the form of an enthusiastic and urgent search for alternative arrangements and meanings. Since the rising generation had been deprived of its putative birth right (leadership of society) by *this* system, the condition of freedom inevitably had to be like *that*. The political demand was one of bringing *those* arrangements *here*. The opposition to really existing socialism consequently coalesced around a valorization of all that was officially denigrated. More or less schematically, wherever the Soviet-type system put a minus sign, the opposition put a plus sign.

The precise practical implications of this kind of societal and ontological mirror gazing can be seen especially clearly in the essays which Vaclav Havel wrote whilst being subjected to temptation and normalization by the societal body. Throughout his oppositional works, which are very deeply embedded in a reflexive discourse, Havel comes across as a profoundly manichean kind of thinker. It would, of course, be easy to dismiss Havel's essays on the grounds that they are prime examples of what can happen when a playwright of variable literary merit starts dabbling in social and political philosophy. However, such a rejection would not be too useful. It would not only be astonishingly condescending to reject the work because it was not produced by a professional social or political philosopher, but Havel's essays are significant because they clearly link in to themes expressed by other frustrated double strangers whose credentials as political thinkers are very rarely questioned. Moreover, Havel did fairly self-consciously betray a profound debt to an intellectually credible phenomenological position which seems to have come from Edmund Husserl via Jan Patocka (for the similarities between Havel and other strands of pre-1989 Central European oppositional thought, see Garton Ash 1989: 161–191. A very different interpretation of the similarities can be found in Scruton 1988, 1988a).

It is worth discussing aspects of Havel's more theoretical work in some detail for two reasons. Firstly, his oppositional essays can be read as suitable illustrations of dominant strands in the tradition of Central and Eastern European 'dissent' (that is, Havel can be taken as a *representative* thinker. I am by no means seeking to suggest that he was the best thinker or the only one worth bothering with). Secondly, and perhaps more pragmatically (or tritely), Vaclav Havel must have been expressing some important and attractive themes else it is improbable that he could have been elevated to the position of President, and to the status of the moral and existential conscience of a society as quickly as he was.

What Paul Ricoeur has said of Patocka might also be taken as a suitable summary of Havel's thought. Undoubtedly, it is fair to say that Havel's essays can be read in terms of, 'an urgent plea to cultured men to rediscover the principle of their personal responsibility by a return to critical reason.' Like Jan Patocka, Vaclav Havel constructed his oppositional essays around the thesis that, 'in the event of a people's extreme abjection, philosophical pleading for subjectivity is becoming the citizen's only recourse against the tyrant' (Ricoeur 1977: 153, 155).

That pleading for subjectivity was especially vivid in Havel's open letter to Gustav Husak of 1975 (Havel 1975). Certainly, the letter was primarily concerned with the social and political situation in Czechoslovakia during the period of 'normalization' after the events of 1968, but it is clear from the tone of Havel's argument, and indeed, from the drift of the rest of his political writing, that the argument was meant to be of something greater than a purely local significance.

Havel's main problem in the letter was one of explaining how social order was possible and how it was being maintained. His analysis essentially revolves around an identification of the modern problem of creating a clearly bounded entity called society, and then of ensuring that all individuals are incorporated within the boundaries. Quite simply, Havel suggested that the incorporation of individuals, which met with at least tacit support, was achieved through a carrot-and-stick strategy of fear and rewards. As Havel presents it, the Soviet-type system had been able to make all individuals internalize and fear the awareness that those who fall outside of the boundaries of the societal body are put into a deeply invidious position. That fear permeated everywhere: 'For fear of losing his job, the schoolteacher teaches things he does not believe; fearing for his future, the pupil repeats them after him' (Havel 1975: 4). Indeed, fear was also identified as the core of the ritual performance of society and its memory. According to Vaclav Havel, 'Fear of the consequences of refusal leads people to take part in elections, to vote for the proposed candidates and to pretend that they regard such ceremonies as genuine elections' (Havel 1975: 5).

Moreover, this deep involvement of all individuals in the

operation and maintenance of the system, however grudging that involvement might have been, meant that everyone was made to fear the possibility of exclusion. 'Everyone has something to lose and so everyone has reason to be afraid' (Havel 1975: 6). The Soviet-type system had, indeed, evidently made sure that everyone had something to lose because it implicated everyone in one way or another in a highly effective network of prizes. Havel proposed that within the system, within the societal body, 'in a way, we are all being publicly bribed' (Havel 1975: 9). The bribery worked because it made sure that all individuals were aware of nothing so much as the Golden Gate which would open if only they did the next small thing that was asked of them: 'If you accept this or that office in your place of work ... you will be rewarded with such and such privileges. If you join the Youth League, you will be given ... access to such and such forms of entertainment' (Havel 1975: 9).

The central imperative of the system was, then, quite obvious. The combination of the fear of exclusion and rewards for inclusion and incorporation resulted in the ethical position: 'Think what you like in private, as long as you agree in public, refrain from making difficulties ... and the doors will be wide open to you' (Havel 1975: 9). Now, Havel uses the words public and private in a totally conventional sense, where the former pertains to relationships involving the society and its members at large, and where the latter refers to relationships involving individuals or, at most, very small groups. The interesting thing is, however, that Havel's interpretation of the ethical grounding of really existing socialism bears comparison with Immanuel Kant's description of the requirements of Enlightenment. Havel emphasized a distinction between the private and the public domains and so did Kant.

In the 1784 essay Kant placed a great stress on the private and the public requirements which the free use of reason made of individuals (Kant 1970). In these terms, Havel's thesis that the Soviet-type system asked all individuals to agree in public represents a direct overturning of Kant's position. Kant spelt out his views on the public and the private demands upon the individual whilst discussing the case of a clergyman. Kant wrote:

the use which someone employed as a teacher makes of his reason in the presence of his congregation is purely *private*, since a congregation, however large it is, is never any more than a domestic gathering. In view of this, he is not and cannot be free as a priest, since he is acting on a commission imposed from outside. Conversely, as a scholar addressing the real public (i.e. the world at large) through his writings, the clergyman making *public use* of his reason enjoys unlimited freedom to use his own freedom and to speak in his own person. For to maintain that the guardians of the people in spiritual matters should themselves be immature, is an absurdity which amounts to making absurdities permanent.

(Kant 1970: 57)

But for Havel, the collective definition of freedom and sovereignty was indeed attempting to make absurdities permanent. Of course, Immanuel Kant and Vaclav Havel were using the concepts of the private and the public in rather different ways, but the profound distance between their diagnoses of the ethical situation and responsibilities of the individual is perfectly clear. Havel was describing a system in which a clergyman could say much as he wanted to the congregation so long as it would be sanctioned by the institutional arrangements of the state, whereas Kant was imagining a future where the clergyman upheld God to the congregation and cared not at all about the demands of the state.

Perhaps the implication is obvious. To the extent that Havel's own social consciousness was a product of the conditions of European modernity, *inevitably he was forced to identify the existing social and institutional arrangements of freedom as a direct affront to freedom*. For Havel, the Soviet-type system could be nothing other than a contradiction of the true foundations and expressions of human creativity and freedom. He did not, perhaps even could not, doubt that the prevailing conditions of existence amounted to little more than a *lie*. The proof and the measure of that lie was provided by the activities of the apparatus of state surveillance. Indeed, the ability of the police to involve themselves in all the individual's public affairs, 'without his having any chance of resisting, suffices to rob his life of some of its naturalness and authenticity and to turn it into a kind of endless dissimulation' (Havel 1975: 8). Freedom and truth, then, logically were all of those things which were repudiated and

161

denigrated by the operations of the institutional arrangements and by the performance and memory of the societal boundaries.

Certainly, Havel did not doubt that the Soviet-type system represented an attack on all that is good and true about humanity. He took that argument to such lengths that the system became not simply a problem for Czechoslovakia, or for Hungary. or Poland, or wherever. More than that, in Havel's hands, the Soviet-type system became tantamount to an *ontological offence*. It had robbed human life and human being of its authenticity, it had disallowed, to recall Paul Ricoeur's nice phrase, *philosophical pleading for subjectivity*, and, so, the system had infringed the real meanings of freedom. It had destroyed the marks of human being and the practices of being human. Thanks to the institutional operation of the system, 'Life must needs sink to a biological, vegetable level amidst a demoralization "in depth", stemming from the loss of hope and the loss of the belief that life has a meaning' (Havel 1975: 15).

It is at this point that it becomes immensely clear that for Havel any analysis of Husak's Czechoslovakia is also, at least in part, an analysis of a universal human predicament. The ontological abyss identified by Havel is held to be endemic to modernity, and of something greater than local interest. After all, the Soviet-type system, 'can but confront us once more with that tragic aspect of man's status in modern technological civilization marked by a declining awareness of the absolute'. Vaclav Havel was in no doubt that the diminishing recognition of the challenge of the absolute, of the universal, involved nothing less than 'a *crisis of human identity*' (Havel 1975: 15, original emphasis). It is noticeable that just as Miklos Haraszti bewailed the incorporation of art's aura as a consequence of a process of bureaucratization, Havel bewails an intrinsically and peculiarly modern dilemma of the banalization of the more profound qualities of Humanity (Humanity with a very big 'H'). Havel saw only, 'a bureaucratic order of grey monotony that stifles all individuality; of mechanical precision that suppresses everything of unique quality; of musty inertia that excludes the transcendent' (Havel 1975: 25). That is, Havel was moaning about the achievement of the perfectly clear world which the conditions of modernity, and the legislators of modernity like Thomas Stockmann, had so wanted. Perhaps Max Weber indeed wrote the most prescient description of the operation and implications of the institutional arrangements of really existing socialism.

But Havel was able to see a way out of absolute pessimism, an exit from the inevitability of 'vegetablization'. His point was that whilst the system sought to totally administer life, and totally force it into clear and orderly categories, life is an eruptive force which ultimately resists any efforts to discipline it. Havel saw the force of life as a profound and fundamental power which rips through all the false attempts to contain it; he saw life as a kind of benign ambivalence which reasserts the possibility of the transcendent, as a natural energy which ruins fusty society. As Havel put it in a passage which is rather edging into pomposity: 'Life rebels against all uniformity and levelling; its aim is not sameness, but variety, the restlessness of transcendence, the adventure of novelty and rebellion against the status quo. An essential condition for its enhancement is the secret constantly made manifest' (Havel 1975: 23–24). Presumably the events of 1989 would, for Havel, be a vindication of life; the collapse of the Soviet-type system would be interpreted as nothing other than the moment when the forces of life finally shattered the bureaucratic attempts to regulate and order them.

Havel's method of argument in the letter to Husak was, then, quite interesting. It began with a reflection on the position of the individual and the demands which are made upon the individual if she or he is not to fall outside of the boundaries of society. The analysis then proposed that the requirements of inclusion are based on a combination of fear and false, tarnished idols and, consequently, the practices of inclusion were inevitably identified as a contradiction of the true and real basis of individuality. Havel finally proposed that an existence which approximates to those real requirements of being human will be one lived in the awareness of the transcendent. It will be an existence which always strives to achieve something rather than an existence which wallows in the inertia of the given.

In other words, Vaclav Havel's social and political philosophy moves from a critique of the temporary to a description of the basis of a universal human condition and, thereby, to an appreciation of a universal individuality. The crisis of human identity can, for Havel, be overcome if the embeddedness in the present of human existence which bureaucracy presupposes and exacerbates, can be transcended by the forces of life. In so doing, the achievement of freedom would once again become a viable project. Havel vested all hope in the possibility that individuals who are forced to live in highly specific social, historical, and geographical conditions, might be able to grasp that universal condition and circumstance of individuality which always resides behind and beneath the deliberate mechanisms of systemic social existence.

On the one hand, this meant that Havel applauded cosmopolitan hermeneutic systems as a means of access to the universal and, just like some latter-day Thomas Stockmann, utterly decried, 'the sentimental philosophy of kitchen-sink country-bumpkin earthiness, and the provincial *Weltanschauung* based on the belief in its general good naturedness' (Havel 1975: 18). On the other hand, it meant that Havel emphasized the intrinsic ethical and existential goodness of a universal pre-reflexive life-world which was juxtaposed to what was thus seen as the badness of anything particular which tried to move beyond the terrain of that life-world. That is, Havel carried out a kind of radical phenomenological bracketing away of the local which enabled him to come up with an ideal of the universal human condition which is the true basis of all that we are *as opposed* to a societal life which was thus identified as rather terrible. Havel turned an exercise in Husserlian methodology to the interests of a neo-Rousseauian Romanticism.

This turn to the universal, pre-societal, essence of human being was especially clear in the 1984 lecture 'Politics and Conscience', which Havel was to have delivered when the University of Toulouse conferred an honorary doctorate upon him (Havel 1984). It is worth quoting the lecture at some length since it shows how Havel's method enabled him to shift more or less at will from statements about the individual man or women, living in one nation at one particular time, to very wide-ranging statements about a universal humanity which takes the form of declarations and practices of an individual responsibility irrespective of local circumstances. Havel was in little doubt that properly understood, all humans experience the world as a milieu of two parts; on the one part we know the world which is familiar to us, and, on the other side, we should 'bow down humbly because of the mystery of it', in the face of that world which lies beyond our personal horizons. Havel continued in a profoundly grand, ontological, way:

Our 'I' primordially attests to that world and personally certifies it; that is the world of our lived experience, a world not yet indifferent since we are personally bound to it in our love, hatred, respect, contempt, tradition, in our interests and in that pre-reflective meaningfulness from which culture is born ... At the basis of this world are values which are simply there, perennially, before we ever speak of them, before we reflect upon them and inquire about them.

(Havel 1984: 137)

So, in these universal terms, any society is bad enough because it represents some fundamental kind of qualification of the pre-reflexive life-world which all individuals simply *know*, presumably in some sublime or beautiful way. But the Soviet-type system would be utterly terrible because it represented nothing more than the complete disqualification of the primordial 'I' (Havel's term; not mine) in the interests of the beauty and freedom of a societal equivalent to a Bach fugue.

In other words, Havel was simply using a cosmopolitan hermeneutic category of free human being as a mirror opposite to the perceived requirements of societal existence and saying that the former is freedom. And, arguably, this ostensible universal condition was freedom *simply because* it could be identified as something like the mirror opposite to the prevailing social relationships and institutional arrangements.

Havel's method is, in important respects, similar to the strategy which Edmund Husserl proposed as the only certain way of grasping the transcendental individual behind the local social, historical, and cultural circumstances of individuality. After all, the very interest in making a plea for subjectivity is a *universal* interest. Havel tried to carry out nothing other than a most profound act of bracketing which would peel away the circumstances of societal existence in order to reveal the fundamental truth, the pre-societal but nevertheless social, essence of all that we are.

Moreover, in the precise situation in which it was developed, Havel's analysis meant that individuals *like him*, who had been forced out of the societal body, or who had refused a place in it, or who had been subjected to the policy of cretinization, became something like the living representations of the possibility of grasping the essence of human being. Consequently, the individuals like Vaclav Havel, who had indeed been subjected to processes of a kind of benign annihilation (if that is not a contradiction in terms) could claim to be *the new and the true* leaders of modernity. Their leading role was accepted in so far as they were able to form communication systems and social networks which could constitute the context for the identification of new sorts of magic. The very attempts at exclusion practised by the Soviet-type system went quite a long way towards helping create the possibility of those new identifications. After all, since the system was wrong and a lie, then anyone vilified by the system was, more or less by definition, worth defending and listening to. Indeed, it could almost be said that the remarkable eloquence of the original leaders of the events of 1989 was some sort of backhanded compliment to the ability of the regimes of really existing socialism to foster and radicalize philosophical reflection on rather abstract questions of individuality and freedom.

There was one other implication to this way of thinking. Certainly, Havel never made the point explicit in his own work, but a number of other oppositional thinkers were not slow to point out that the Soviet-type system had to a large extent been *imposed* upon the silent and wasted remnants of what were previously indigenously self-reproducible national communities. Indeed, the very concept of the Soviet-type system, along with its identical category of really existing socialism, fundamentally involves the subordination of national features to a transnational and abstract institutional arrangement. Inevitably, then, freedom became associated with ideals of national self-determination, or, at the very least, with the absence in the affairs of Central and Eastern Europe of interference from the Soviet Union. It was not too large a step to move from a notion like Havel's pre-reflexive givens to the practical identification of this life-world with national belonging (a step which Havel, however, never made despite the drift of a number of themes in the 'Politics and Conscience' essay; Havel 1984).

The opposition to really existing socialism was able to be aware of itself as a self-conscious opposition to the extent that it coalesced around precisely those principles and interpretations which had been denied by the established institutional arrangements. The opposition groupings were able to reproduce themselves, firstly, to the extent that their number was supplemented by more and more cohorts of disgruntled double strangers who were superfluous to the existing institutions and, secondly, to the extent that they were able to identify concrete examples of the practice of freedom. Inevitably, given that freedom in modernity was nothing other than that way of life which was imagined as better than this way of life, freedom for Central and Eastern Europe was, with due reservations, imagined as looking something like a domestic variation on the arrangements and practices prevailing in Western Europe. As such, the transcendental individuality generated through a critique of the arrangements of really existing socialism, tended to find a practical referent and a mundane justification in the ideal of individuality upheld in the allotment-type situations of Western Europe.

Indeed, it was the entrenchment of commitments to individuality in Western Europe which explains why those allotment situations tended to display a remarkable resilience to single moments of collapse and, more generally, why they rarely, if ever, proved to be the environment for the development of universal and universalizing ideals of freedom. The point was that in allotment situations, the criteria of other social arrangements, the sources of the imagination and the practice of freedom, were already contained within the societal boundaries. That is, allotment situations did not breed universal ideals of freedom, and were rarely subjected to frontal assault, simply because they generated their own places of opposition which for the most part disagreed with existing arrangements at a purely managerial, rather than an ethical, level. Moreover, the double strangers of those arrangements of modernity were too detached, too irrelevant to be able to impose or justify any grand programmes of improvement.

Allotment situations gave rise to interpretations of freedom as the practice of *other forms of individuality* as opposed to freedom as the establishment of an entirely *new arrangement of social relationships*. The Western practice of individuality was deeply embedded in daily demonstrations of inclusion and exclusion in relation to the boundaries of society. In particular, individuality revolved around what might be called *consumerist decisionism*. Freedom was understood to involve nothing other than more consumption and more decisions. Alternative social arrangements, and therefore freedom itself, was imagined on the basis of alternative arrangements and practical demonstrations of consumerism. Individuals became free and avoided the fate of exclusion from the societal body to the extent that they could demonstrate adequacy for inclusion through the possession of things. Hence, again, the insignificance of the beggar.

The idea of consumerist decisionism needs a little explanation. It does indeed imply a profound individuality, but it was an individuality of a highly specific sort. It was not cut of the philosophical cloth used by someone like Vaclav Havel (and not just Havel; his thought might be idiosyncratic but it was by no means untypical of dominant themes in opposition literature; for example compare Havel with Haraszti 1987; Konrad 1984). For Havel, of course, true individuality, and indeed the universality of individuality, was embedded in the pre-reflexive life-world which exists independently of any moment of *doing* and is, instead, an essential facticity of *being*. The form of individuality practised in Western European modernity was rather different and, indeed, entirely indebted to contingencies of time and place. It was *consumerist* because it emphasized the purchase and use of goods by the individual person, who was thus rendered the ostensible sovereign in the market place. But it was *decisionist* because it referred to no essential ethical or ontological condition. It was a sovereignty of *doing* rather than a sovereignty of *being*. Indeed, consumerist decisionism had the effect of denying the place of overriding ethical considerations in the practice of individual subjectivity. All that mattered was the signification of inclusion.

According to Jurgen Habermas, '*Decisionism* as a worldview today no longer is ashamed to reduce norms to decisions ... As soon as certain fundamental value judgments are posited as axioms ... their acceptance is based solely on a decision, a commitment' (Habermas 1974: 266). Consequently, and as Carl Schmitt clearly saw, 'The decision becomes instantly independent of argumentative substantiation and receives an autonomous value ... But what is inherent in the idea of the decision is that there can never be absolutely declaratory decisions' (Schmitt 1985: 31). In the specific conditions of Western Europe, then, this meant that individuality revolved around a simple *act of consumption* which possessed nothing at all by way of an ethical commitment or content. Certainly any assumption of the life-world as the essential core of the universal human condition could be given no importance whatsoever in a context where societal inclusion and exclusion was established on the basis of the active possession of various temporary things. (Orwell would have probably treated the Brookers more kindly had they used handkerchiefs or tissues to wipe their noses instead of old newspapers.) Indeed, the very boundaries of the societal body were constituted around the evidence of the ability to practise sovereign individuality through decision-making in the market-place (such that it could be argued in these terms that I am a better person than a beggar because I wear nice shoes; she is less significant than me because she wears grubby sandals).

Hence, once again, the difficult and ambivalent position of the poor in the societal systems of Western European allotments. The point was, of course, that poor people were *by definition* unable to practise a limitless decisionism in the market place. Their sovereignty was restricted by material circumstances (that is, by the lack of the financial resources to reproduce sovereignty). Consequently, they could only be inadequate to the require-ments and the measure of inclusion within society. The poor became dirty strangers; they were the embodiments of the fear about what societal annihilation and nature might involve (and dirt, of course, is nature). It was precisely the evidence of their poverty which made the glittering prizes of the market all the more attractive. To recall the phrase of Paul Connerton, it might be said that in Western European modernity, societal habit-memory was socially performed through purchasing. Free-dom, then, could only be found and imagined through a relentless involvement in decision-making and in the relentless consumption of the marks of societal adequacy.

The allotment situations were incapable of producing uni-versal and collective interpretations of freedom, or for that matter of individuality, which would have been able to capture any wide and reproducible legitimacy. And there was nothing at all that the intellectuals, the would-be legislators, could do about it. Quite simply, given the practice of individuality through a normless decisionism, and given the identification of freedom with the demonstration of adequacy as a consumer, there was absolutely no ontological or anthropological basis upon which universal systems could be established. As such, the Western European interpretations of society were fairly immune to any of the kinds of juxtaposition of freedoms which were possible in Central and Eastern Europe. The allotment situations already contained the space for a plurality of freedom and, so, it was quite impossible to finally and irreversibly knock down one meaning of freedom in the name of an alternative meaning. The social conditions of existence were not right for the production and reproduction of transcendental categories, or of a more-or-less self-conscious opposition which derived credibility and purpose from the culture of reflexive discourse. Indeed, in the West the possibility of the reflexive discourse was either institutionally marginalized or, inevitably, bought off by diversion into a different act of consumption and a different moment of decisionism.

There is, then, a most profound paradox which is highlighted if the oppositional social and political philosophy of someone like Vaclav Havel is considered against some of the arrangements and practices which were held to be so desirable, so free. Havel in particular wanted to make the case for the ability and right of all individuals to practise a responsible subjectivity. At least in part, the self-conscious opposition to the Soviet-type system, of which Havel was of course a leading speaker, thought that many of the freedoms it wanted and desired could be found in the institutional arrangements and the societal practices prevailing in Western European modernity. But where the Central and Eastern European interpretations of freedom and individuality invariably took a turn towards the transcendental and the universal, the Western European practices of individuality and its criterion of freedom, were completely embedded in an ethically empty contingency of time and place. That is, the self-conscious opposition to the Soviet-type system, which was able to step into the power vacuums so quickly and so legitimately after the collapse of really existing socialism, was founded upon a mixture of philosophical speculation and misunderstandings.

The post Soviet-type institutions of Central and Eastern Europe were founded upon the assumption that, at least in part, freedom looked something like that which happened in the West. But they only discovered that within the promises and the myths of modernity, freedom cannot be identified with any achieved arrangements and relationships at all.

7

DIVERGENCE

Now, it seems quite acceptable in the light of the history of the question of sovereignty in the conditions of European modernity, to understand freedom, that great incitement and that great destiny, as, simply, the possibility of difference. Such a position can go quite a considerable distance towards explaining why freedom proved to be so elusive and, indeed, why freedom was so desirable. After all, and essentially, freedom involved little or nothing more than the projection into the future of idealized images of alternative social arrangements. As such, freedom could never be achieved (there is always a different set of arrangements of one kind or another) and neither could its meaning and attraction be exhausted. Rather the opposite. The only exhaustion was experienced by those who were attempting to reach what they took to be some objective condition.

Specific hermeneutic commitments coincided with specific social sites to make freedom (the possibility of it, the practice of it, the imagination of it) the unique preserve of the *double strangers*. That is part of the importance of Ibsen's tale of Thomas Stockmann. Ibsen's play anticipated and prefigured many of the complex relationships, struggles and debates, of European modernity. Not least, Ibsen implicitly operated on the terrain of the central dilemma of modernity. The problem was whether the road to freedom was travelled by some collective and homogeneous group under the leadership of a heterogeneous vanguard which was ostensibly seeking to clear the ground of obstacles in order to make the world suitable for freedom, or whether the destination was arrived at through a plurality of individual paths, each of which existed within a broader movement towards freedom, but each of which was more or less left to its own devices so long as it did not display tendencies towards inadequacy for inclusion in the societal body (essentially, that was the drift of the stories told by Lecky and Marshall).

Indeed, the implication of this two-sided problem was that social relationships, conceived as a solidary entity called a society which inclined towards a final equilibrium, became at one and the same time the context, the measure, and the problem, of the struggle for freedom. Quite simply, to the extent that freedom was the reflexive imagination of the possibility of alternatives, the alternative was in important part, and by definition, displayed by the social relationships and the societal practices pertaining *over there* rather than *here*. Consequently, whilst the struggle for freedom was to some extent waged through attempts to expel from the societal body all those groups or individuals who might have been handicaps on the great march to perfection, it was also always the case that one more group was in need of annihilation since the practical measures of freedom were *always* in some way *different*. In other words, and as the case of the Soviet-type system demonstrated particularly vividly, the attempt to create a transparent homogeneity resulted only in the process of the identification and the difficulty of one last site of illicit heterogeneity. The beauty and the horror at the heart of European modernity was exactly the ultimate impossibility of the aims of modernity.

The experiential and the existential difficulty of modernity, which runs like a thread through its cultural practices and products, was precisely the fear that the individual man or woman might belong to the next group of strangers which had to be jettisoned and wiped from the slate in the name of freedom. And, since urbanization and the development of the cosmopolitan communication systems of the Enlightenment meant that everyone was a stranger to some degree (unless the individual totally accorded with the demands of order and of homogeneity) everyone felt the threat of potential annihilation in one way or another.

The history of European modernity was one of the juxtaposition of a perfect future with an inadequate and a flawed present. It involved nothing other than a complete division of the social from the natural. The projects of modernity were so many attempts to close the gap between the awful *is* and the attractive *ought*. As such, freedom was simply the imagination and the putatively practical promotion of the ideal. It was a critical reflexive rejection of the real. However, to the extent that the real, existing, relationships and arrangements were the condition of possibility of the imagination of the alternative arrangements, the existing forms inevitably had a considerable influence on the projections of what the perfect, the free, future could and should be like. That is, freedom was imagined only from the point of view of the identification of existing reification. The individual or the societal body could only be free in the future to the extent that the individual or the society imagined itself as bound in the present.

The embeddedness of the future in the present, of the ideal in the real, was clearly illustrated by Vaclav Havel. Perhaps the embeddedness would inevitably be demonstrated in his work, given his tendency to perform a kind of radical phenomenological reductionism. But it is quite clear that, for Havel, the free future was the product of the flawed present (and then, in a cycle of self-legitimation, that imagined future fed back into the interpretation of the present to render it *yet more* flawed). Certainly, Havel tended to implicitly conflate some of the institutional arrangements of the West with freedom. But the precise social situation of his imaginations meant that other features of life in the West were identified as versions of entrapment. In particular, Havel frequently identified a general practice of a repellent consumerism, which was, for him, prevalent throughout Europe. As such, the identification of consumerism in the present had a definite impact on the imagination of the future and, so, consumerism was denied a place in Havel's version of freedom.

Of course, in Vaclav Havel's scheme of things, consumerism would be a most terrible kind of oppression. On the one hand, consumer goods would simply be so many bribes by which individual pleas for subjectivity would be bought off by the demands of bureaucratic administration in industrialized and urbanized societies. On the other hand, the decisionistic practice of consumerism would have been interpreted as an ontological offence against the qualities of true humanity. Consumerist decisionism would have been a temporalization, a particularization, of what should have been universal. Put another way, Havel implicitly understood consumerism as a false heterogeneity of the truly and the properly homogeneous.

In the 1975 letter to Gustav Husak, Havel made the comment that women and men had increasingly turned to the possession of consumer goods, and the practice of consumerism, to express their innermost sentiments. It is hard to know whether Havel was writing with concern or contempt when he said of his fellows that, 'They fill their homes with all kinds of equipment and pretty things, ... they make life agreeable for themselves, building cottages, looking after their cars, taking more interest in their food and clothing and domestic comfort' (Havel 1975: 11). To some extent, this passage is typical of the intellectual legislators of modernity, who lived by the myth that material goods were either beneath their interest or simply a means by which the fools could be deluded. In a more or less similar vein, when Thomas Stockmann discovered that his trousers had been torn when the mob attacked his house, his reaction was an uneasy combination of bourgeois virtue and intellectual disdain for possessions. As Thomas Stockmann said: 'You should never have your best trousers on when you turn out to fight for freedom and truth. Well, it's not that I care all that much about the trousers – you can always put a stitch in them for me.' What Stockmann did care about was, 'the idea of that mob going for me as though they were my equals' (Ibsen 1988: 87). Stockmann was indeed an updated member of Plato's class of the Philosopher Rulers. Arguably, so was Havel.

But Havel was, of course, trying to do something more than simply express the conventional lack of interest of the intellectuals in material comforts. Havel was making the point that the profound temporality and particularity implied by the care of cars or the ownership of 'pretty things' involved nothing other than a dilution of the essence of human being. Havel was performing a critique of the flawed present in the name of the perfect future, and since consumerism was evidently a feature of the present in the Soviet-type system, it had to be rejected wherever it might appear. As such, Havel saw, 'on the one side, bombastic slogans about the unprecedented increase in every sort of freedom and the unique structural variety of life; on the other side, unprecedented drabness and the squalor of life reduced to a hunt for consumer goods' (Havel 1975: 13). For Havel, then, freedom meant also a release from the imprisonment of universal human being by the particular being of consumerism. In Havel's system, the choice was one between material comfort and intellectual honesty. Given that the whole justification for Vaclav Havel's existence was precisely the commitment to a 'philosophical pleading for subjectivity' that was not too much of a choice at all.

But for those groups and individuals which had not been pushed beyond the societal boundaries and which had, instead, been fully implicated in its institutional arrangements and its understanding of order, the choice was rather different. For these groups and individuals, freedom was indeed to a large extent identifiable with the practices of consumerism. The point was that, for those groups which did not nominate to opt for philosophical security instead of material comfort, it was the case that consumerism was a measure of freedom in Western Europe which was entirely absent within the confines of the Soviet-type system. For the individuals and groups which bore no profound allegiance to the practical and the hermeneutic demands of a reflexive culture, the marks of freedom were indeed readily evident in a consumerist decisionism.

The practice and the appeal of consumerism took a hold in Central and Eastern Europe on two levels. Firstly, the attraction of the imagination of consumerism was promoted and consolidated by the reception of Western television which was *already* legitimate simply because it came from outside, and the messages of which were desirable merely because they came from *over there*. Certainly, the significance of television in facilitating imaginations of freedom should not be underestimated, but perhaps it is necessary to express a degree of caution over how significant an impact this particular form of cosmopolitan communication might have had. Secondly, and undoubtedly more importantly, to the extent that the Soviet-type system was characterized by a *dictatorship over needs* (Feher, *et al.* 1983), the free individual expression and satisfaction of needs which ostensibly occurred in the West was by definition highly attractive.

Scott Lash has provided an anecdotal illustration of the important point that the Soviet-type system attempted to satisfy consumer demands through the practice of something like a dictatorship over needs. He has written of the East Germans who visited West Berlin shortly after the breaching of the Berlin

Wall. They were, 'seemingly identically dressed in their mass-produced stone-washed jeans and jean jackets' (Lash 1990: 157). So, for these groups and individuals, certain kinds of clothing were demonstrations of their lack of freedom, and indeed, from the point of view of a consumerist observer, one of the most noticeable features of the East Germans was, presumably, the correlation which could be drawn between their lack of political and civil freedoms and their inability to practise a free, individualistic and individualizing, decisionism over the issue of the clothes they wore.

Evidently, one of the most attractive features of West Berlin for the individuals from the East was a cinema marquee which was showing the then popular American film, *Sex, Lies and Videotape*. As Scott Lash saw it, 'The *Sex, Lies and Videotape* marquee for them had extraordinary symbolic charge as an embodiment of Western consumerism and permissiveness' (Lash 1990: 157). The charge was essentially contained in the East Germans' interpretation of their existing social arrangements as lacking or deliberately denying the space for sex and voyeuristic high technology combined with a wanton disregard of any kind of personal or existential responsibility. Much of the success of the film in North America and Western Europe was almost certainly due to exactly the same reasons.

As such, behind the more obvious moves of Central and Eastern Europe in the post really-existing-socialism period, obvious moves which took the form of the self-conscious establishment of self-consciously democratic institutional arrangements, perhaps it is reasonable to identify fundamental processes which vindicate the old social scientific convergence theory.

According to the leading protagonists of convergence theory, such as Clark Kerr, it is possible to identify certain 'exigencies of industrialization' which ultimately mean that all industrialized societies will produce and exhibit the same values, belief systems, and institutional arrangements irrespective of present differences. In particular, Kerr suggested that all industrialized societies eventually display the arrangements of a *pluralistic industrialism* in which the market is identified as the most effective means of resource allocation, although the hard edges of the operation of the market are softened by a strong state apparatus. Clark Kerr and his collaborators asserted (with rather questionable empirical justification) that the success of any process of industrialization ultimately entails that, 'the more reliance has to be placed on localized decisions and markets instead of centralized decisions and plans; and markets bring the middle class approach in their wake' (Kerr 1973: 86; see also Kerr 1983). In other words, for Kerr, the logic of industrialism would inevitably lead to social and economic arrangements which looked much like those which *ideally* prevailed in the capitalist system of Western Europe and North America.

At this general level, the events of 1989 might indeed be read as a justification for dusting down the convergence theory which had earlier been demolished to the satisfaction of most social scientists (for a discussion of some of the debates surrounding the theory, see Rojek 1986). The events can indeed be said to reveal to some extent a certain set of exigencies in the organization and operation of modern industrialized societies which mean that, eventually, they all look much the same in all significant respects.

However, it is perhaps necessary to express a great deal of caution about this application of an old and difficult theory. On the one hand, the 'text-book' problems of convergence remain; the theory really is determinist; it really does overstate the similarities of industrial societies; it really does posit a single explanatory device which leaves out as much as it contains. But, in the specific case of the history and relationships of European modernity, and especially in the specific case of the collapse of the Soviet-type system, there are other reasons to doubt the usefulness of identifying tendencies towards convergence thanks to industrialization. Not least, Galbraith has pointed out that any convergence with some unified and unitary world called capitalism was quite impossible. Indeed, Galbraith feels that, 'changes in the structure of capitalism rendered obsolescent even the term capitalism itself'. Galbraith continues: 'Capitalism in its original or pristine form could not have survived. But under pressure it did adapt' (*Guardian* 26 January 1990: 23). For example, and to put the matter rather simplistically, Britain and Germany could both be called 'capitalist', but any similarities between them are of less economic and institutional importance and interest than the very real differences they display.

But Galbraith was perhaps merely making a point of classification. The reasons for the dubious usefulness of talking about determining 'exigencies of industrialization' in Central and

Eastern Europe go rather further than semantics. The point is that in Central and Eastern Europe by the final years of the Soviet-type system, industrialism had been discredited as an apparatus of oppression and, therefore, it was to one degree or another excluded from the visions of freedom. Certainly, the individuals who lived the experience of really existing socialism identified their freedom with, to some extent, the possession and the provision of things in an *industrialized* way (depersonalized sex, video technology, for example), but whilst the products of industrial production might have been highly desirable, industrialism itself was more or less rejected.

It was rejected as a key component of the most popular designs of the new, improved, post-Soviet social arrangements, precisely because it was so closely associated with the institutions and the projects of really existing socialism. After all, the material resources which underpinned that particular definition of the future were to have been provided by massive and rapid modernization. Except in Czechoslovakia and East Germany, the nation-states of Central and Eastern Europe had no memory of large-scale industrialization and industrialism which was not at the same time a memory of the imposition of the collective road to freedom. For those societies, industrialism was synonymous with *this way of life* and, as such, it could only be excluded from freedom. Meanwhile, Czechoslovakia was indeed possessed of a popular and indigenous memory of an industrialism which was highly advanced and successful. As such, in Czechoslovakia, the Soviet-type management of industrial production was, perhaps perfectly reasonably, identified with fossilization and irrationality. The case of East Germany was, of course, based on a series of utterly unique memories and events.

So, in Central and Eastern Europe, the existing arrangements of industrialism, and the historical memories of industrialization, were collapsed into a mythological story of the destruction of the indigenous resources of production and reproduction and, indeed, of the devastation of the organic life-world. This kind of interpretation of industrial production was a recurring theme in Vaclav Havel's work. For Havel, there was a direct linkage between what industry had done to the environment and to human being, and what the Soviet-type system had done to society and to individuals. The 'Politics and Conscience' essay begins with the memory of a massive factory chimney, which, 'spewed dense brown smoke and scattered it across the sky' (Havel 1984: 136). Havel's objections to the brown smoke were more than aesthetic and more than ecological; Havel saw in the smoke an awful signification of what happens when humans who are embedded in the particularities and the specificities of time and place arrogantly assume that they can take the place of God.

Havel saw the smoke as an indication of the fact that, 'people in the age of science and technology live in the conviction that they can improve their lives because they are able to grasp and exploit the complexity of nature and the general laws of its functioning' (Havel 1984: 141). But all the attempts to free social and human life from the demands of nature, and that essentially means the entire hopes and ambitions of modernity were, for Havel, doomed to failure: 'People thought they could explain and conquer nature – yet the outcome is that they destroyed it and disinherited themselves from it' (Havel 1984: 141). To some extent, then, Havel's *philosophical and ontological* solution to the problems and the difficult promises of modernity was to turn away from them and, instead, return to some kind of natural artifice. Vaclav Havel's *political* problem was precisely the impossibility and the popular unattractiveness of such an abstract and possibly even atavistic argument.

It is rather hard to know whether Havel's repudiation of industrialism was an act of the most profound bad faith or an act of the most profound honesty. It is hard to know whether Havel's theme owed much to Horkheimer and Adorno or whether it owed much to Tolkien (there are amazing narrative similarities between Havel's description of life within and without the arrangements of really existing socialism, and Tolkien's description of life in Mordor, under the shadow of Mount Doom, and life in the happy and organic community of The Shire).

But, regardless of the doubts which might be caused by the line of argument, Havel clearly felt that it was of great power and depth. He used it again in the first speech which he delivered as President of Czechoslovakia. In that speech, Havel mentioned the impact which had been made upon him by the aerial view of a chemical plant next to which was a giant housing estate. Clearly, the sight impinged upon Havel's understanding of the life-world in a very real and a very direct way. The experience went beyond purely intellectual capacities: 'No study of statistics available to me would enable me to understand faster and better the situation into which we had got ourselves' (Havel 1990: 11).

Havel repeatedly made the point that some direct correlation existed between the devastation of humanity and the devastation of the landscape. For him, there was a connection between imposition upon the environment and imposition upon memories and meanings of the organic, and by definition good and free, community. 'We have polluted our soil, our rivers and forests, bequeathed to us by our ancestors, and we have today the most contaminated environment in Europe' (Havel 1990: 11). The reference to a 'contaminated environment' was clearly meant to be susceptible to more than a single reading. After all, 'The worst thing is that we live in a contaminated moral environment. We felt morally ill because we became used to saying something different from what we thought' (Havel 1990: 11). So, just as the dark smoke of the factory chimney worked as something like a cancer for the natural world, so the lies required by the arrangements of the Soviet-type system, were something like cancers of the moral and societal body.

All of this is by way of saying that, despite first impressions, it is perhaps not too useful to see the movements of modernity in terms of a convergence caused by some logic of industrialism. Quite simply, industrialism in Central and Eastern Europe took place in a highly specific (garden) situation. And, once the context had collapsed, so did much of the justification and support (but not the practice) of industrialism itself. However, the general theme of convergence should not be rejected out of hand. Certainly, *there is little or no reason to identify in European modernity tendencies towards convergence attributable to industrialization and industrialism, but there is reason to identify certain tendencies towards convergence which are attributable to the concept and the practice of the market.*

Of course, and at the most basic level, the market was identified as desirable by some sections of the societies of Central and Eastern Europe (although not by other sections) after the intermezzo of really existing socialism purely because it was said to be the mechanism which maintained societal production and reproduction in Western Europe. As such, the practice and the ideal of the market was to some extent much the same as the

meaning of freedom. But the market system was also deliberately *made to seem* highly desirable. From the point of view of
the definitions and interpretations of freedom which were
generated in Central and Eastern Europe during the period of
the Soviet-type system, the market was highly attractive on at
least two main counts.

Firstly, the market was made to seem like the final arrangement of freedom simply because the economic systems of
Western Europe, which formally operated in a post-scarcity
context, possessed the social, moral, communicative, and economic resources which enabled them to produce and reproduce
their legitimacy and well-being. Indeed, in view of the means at
the disposal of the Western European resolutions of sovereignty
and freedom, it was perhaps not too surprising that the Soviet-
type system was quite unable to reproduce popular active or
even tacit support for state-ordained welfare and consumer
provisions. Inevitably, those *provided* services were frequently
identified as one more example of oppression simply because
they had been provided in the context of the existing, real,
meanings of society rather than in the context of the imagination of ideal arrangements (hence the claims of many of the old
oppositional, now legislative, double strangers, that individuals
possess no *rights* but do possess *obligations*; see Scruton 1988,
1988a).

Secondly, the market was identified as an attractive kind of
arrangement of society because it was able to generate around its
commodities what Wolfgang Fritz Haug has called an *aesthetic
illusion* (Haug 1986). The Soviet-type system produced goods on
the basis of their use-values and their ability to satisfy needs
(needs, that is, which had been sanctioned and accommodated
by the plan). But in the capitalist market system, commodities
are bought and sold to the extent that they not only are useful,
but importantly to the extent that they *appear* to be useful. The
commodities of the market seemed to possess qualities and uses
which were entirely absent from the commodities of the planned
system.

As Haug sees it, in modern capitalism (in so far as that general
umbrella terms retains any meaning), the *appearance* of the
commodity, which is produced by advertising techniques and
the like, has become more important than the commodity itself.
'Something that is simply useful but does not appear to be so,

will not sell, while something that seems to be useful will sell ... [T]he aesthetic illusion – the commodity's promise of use-value – enters the arena as an independent function' (Haug 1986: 17). By an extension of Haug's point, it might be said that the arrangements and the institutions of the market could be 'sold' in Central and Eastern Europe because they appeared to be useful and independently valid. And, of course, they were supported by powerful economic and symbolic resources which could make sure that the mask of the beautiful appearance never slipped. Meanwhile, the Soviet-type system was never, or at least was very rarely, able to make itself *seem* useful, and so its messages and its ideals could not be easily sold. Arguably, the identification of the profound seductiveness of this kind of aesthetic illusion can make a large contribution to an explanation of why the collective versions of freedom which were upheld by the Soviet-type system never took much of a hold in the allotment situations of Western Europe.

The practical implication of all this was that market arrangements and institutions were identified as possessing a legitimacy and a value in themselves. The market was identified as the institutional shell for freedom, and, as such, it became the form in which the states which had emerged out of the Soviet-type system invested many of their hopes. The market became something more than the shining, neon-lit, home of sovereign individual consumers, able to demonstrate existential being and responsibility through the choice of toilet paper. The ideal of the market became instead an absolutely fundamental *ethical imperative*.

The evident necessity of the market and its institutions had, of course, long been recognized in some of the central narratives of modernity. The theme was perhaps expressed with particular clarity by Friedrich Hayek. For Hayek, the exigencies and the practices of market pressures are a certain guarantee that the plurality of individual sovereigns can be turned into an intrinsically ordered and orderly society. It is worth quoting Hayek's questionable masterpiece, *The Road to Serfdom*, at some considerable length on this point. As Hayek said, whilst commending his own position:

> The liberal argument is in favour of making the best possible use of the forces of competition as a means of

co-ordinating human efforts ... It is based on the conviction that where effective competition can be created, it is a better way of guiding individual efforts than any other. It does not deny, but even emphasises, that, in order that competition should work beneficially, a carefully thought-out legal framework is required, and that neither the existing nor the legal rules are free from grave defects. Nor does it deny that where it is impossible to create the conditions necessary to make competition effective, we must resort to other methods of guiding economic activity. Economic liberalism is opposed, however, to competition being supplanted by inferior methods of co-ordinating individual efforts, and it regards competition as superior not only because it is in most circumstances the most efficient method known, but even more because it is the only method by which our activities can be adjusted to each other without coercive or arbitrary intervention of authority.

(Hayek 1944: 27)

This long passage uses the ideal image of the market, which Hayek thought had been destroyed by the early-to-middle twentieth century, or at least thought was in the process of destruction, to develop a very grand notion of the unitary and orderly society tending towards equilibrium.

Hayek was happy to accept the sovereignty of individuals. He interpreted the plurality and diversity of sovereignty as, in its most significant respects, the basis of a recognition of homogeneity. Hayek's point was that individuals might be sovereign in the market place, but importantly, the possibility of heterogeneity and fundamental disorder was overcome by the demands of 'effective competition'. Competition in the market place was interpreted as binding all individuals together in thoroughly mutual relationships of reciprocity. Consequently, the diverse potential roads to freedom were all placed within the embrace of a single explanatory device and a single institutional arrangement (compare Hayek's story with those of Lecky and Marshall). As such, order could be created out of the reciprocal and relational flux of economic competition. The market was identified as an ordering principle which could draw together different kinds of activity into a general system of equal exchange.

More even than all that, Hayek understood the arrangements of the free and open market to be the only sure guarantee that social order and the equilibrium of the societal body could be maintained and reproduced. As soon as the operation of competition was subject to interference, the possibility would arise of the most disastrous oppression. In many and mysterious ways, then, did Friedrich Hayek see the market as the shell and the practice of freedom. A moral imperative indeed.

Now it would be fairly easy to dismiss this argument were it not that Friedrich Hayek's commitments clearly express, and indeed glory in, an allotment-type definition of sovereignty and social order. In a series of moves which were typical of intellectuals' reflections on allotment environments in the middle of the twentieth century, Hayek accepted the pluralization of the meanings and the practices of freedom, but he was able to interpret that plurality as an essential form of order. Moreover, Hayek's caution against interference in the *indigenous reproducibility of market arrangements* might be read as one version of the irrelevance of the double strangers in allotment situations. Of course, someone like Theodor Adorno responded to his inability to indulge in effective practices of makeability with a mixture of deep melancholy and a degree of utter contempt. But Friedrich Hayek responded to his complete detachment from the practices of women and men with an attempt to make some constructive use of his societal irrelevance. Instead of finding fault with existing social, cultural, and institutional arrangements, Hayek simply said that his inability to make and remake the world was positively advantageous. For Hayek, anything which he might have been able to do to change or impinge upon the ways of the market and of competition, could have only meant the imposition of ethically and practically *inferior* forms of organization.

It seems to be perfectly reasonable to suggest that Friedrich Hayek attempted to make sense of his hermeneutic and biographical marginality by interpreting it as a cautionary tale for European modernity. After all, and as he asked rhetorically in the first pages of *The Road to Serfdom*, 'Is there a greater tragedy imaginable than that in our endeavour consciously to shape our future in accordance with high ideals, we should in fact unwittingly produce the very opposite of what we have been striving for?' (Hayek 1944: 4).

However, Friedrich Hayek's work possesses something rather greater than purely theoretical significance. Indeed, for the nation-states which emerged out of the ruins of the Soviet-type system, the Hayekian identification of the market and competition with freedom and, moreover, with an ethical imperative, was more or less self-evident. In other words, arguments which looked very much like those of Friedrich Hayek were frequently taken up in Central and Eastern Europe as something like the new blueprint which would truly establish freedom after the awful diversion of really existing socialism.

The point was expressed particularly clearly by Leszek Balcerowicz, who was the Minister of Finance of Poland who drew up, and attempted to implement, the transition from central planning to a market economy. Balcerowicz's replacement blueprint was perhaps inevitably ambitious: he attempted to balance the state budget; provide credit, incentive, and development funds for new businesses; revise taxation; reduce state subsidies; and, importantly, he initiated the massive privatization of state concerns. Balcerowicz sold his proposals on the grounds that they represented the 'best way forward' for Poland because they were (apparently) already tried and trusted in the West (and, therefore, they could be identified with the practices of freedom. Balcerowicz was trying to import *there* to *here*). But interestingly, Balcerowicz went beyond the question of problem solving to suggest that the institutional arrangements which he envisaged, and which the market required, were *ethically necessary*.

According to Leszek Balcerowicz, the *project* behind the reforms would lead Poland, 'to a situation that is regarded as normal in developed countries of the world and in our country has hitherto been regarded as an inaccessible ideal' (Balcerowicz 1990: 225). Balcerowicz continued to sketch that previously unattained ideal:

> Such a situation occurs when people are rewarded for their hard work, enterprising spirit, and abilities to put their talents to good use, when their work is used in such a way that it brings profit and satisfaction, when the results of this work are not wasted but allocated, according to the will of the country's citizens, for the development of the country's civilization, for its cultural achievements, and for the protection of life and the natural environment.
>
> (Balcerowicz 1990: 225–226)

Indeed, the active or tacit support of the 'citizens' (a by no means neutral category) for the economic restructuring was taken to be a measure of the ethical acceptability of the proposals. The support 'is proof of the enormous possibilities of our society, which in conditions of freedom and sovereignty is capable of achieving even the most difficult goals' (Balcerowicz 1990: 238).

Those remarks are much richer than Leszek Balcerowicz probably intended when he uttered them. The reference to 'difficult goals' implies that the collapse of really existing socialism in Poland meant that a new project was needed. The failure of the collective blueprint of sovereignty and freedom was not at all taken to mean the failure of blueprints *as such*. Moreover, it was precisely the difficulty of the achievement of those new goals which Balcerowicz read as an indication of their importance and goodness (presumably, he would have used the argument that 'the medicine is not working if it is not hurting').

But, just as significantly, Leszek Balcerowicz was also hinting at the emergence of new practices and criteria of boundary-drawing around Polish society. To the extent that the restructuring measures were supported, society was demonstrating its desire to realize its potentialities. But, to the extent that any demonstrations of opposition occurred they were immediately identified as examples not of the failure of the reforms themselves, but, instead, of the weakness and inadequacy of certain groups which thus demonstrated their ambivalent incorporation within society. As such, those groups would need to be fully assimilated by society and thereafter watched vigilantly, or they would need to be subjected to a benign annihilation. Of course, this is in no way to imply that Balcerowicz was presaging a new gulag. He could not be proposing such a strategy of physical annihilation because he was operating in an emergent allotment situation and, moreover, he certainly had no desire to practise that kind of boundary-drawing option. Rather, the necessarily more subtle expulsion would have involved things like a lack of representation and a lack of material resources.

But the short sentence about the support of the society for economic restructuring contains one more extremely important dimension. At the end of the sentence, Balcerowicz said, probably in a fairly off-the-cuff or rhetorical way, that through unflinching support and hard work, Polish society would be able to achieve the most difficult goals. In itself that was, perhaps, not much to say, and was probably intended to simply secure a measure of enthusiasm for the new plans. But, given the history of European modernity, it is very important that Leszek Balcerowicz was able to tell his fellow citizens that difficult goals could be reached. Quite simply, in the moment of saying that, Balcerowicz was implicitly implying that he already knew what those goals were, and what their achievement would look like.

Yet, and perhaps by definition, that realization of the new goals was not currently indigenous to Polish society. If the appearance of the goals was already known, they must have been realized already, in which case any project would have been more than a little redundant. For Leszek Balcerowicz to know already of the forms and the arrangements which would be achieved at the end of the project, he must have been in some way detached from the society which was embarking upon the project. That is, Balcerowicz was attempting to establish his credentials as a typical double stranger and, thus, struggling to react to the failure of one version of modernity by establishing the ideal arrangements of the other form of modernity. Unfortunately, he failed to realize that in the one form of modernity the double strangers historically became the fairly dictatorial leaders of a collective societal body, whilst in the other historical arrangement of modernity, the double strangers became simply irrelevant.

Consequently, it is certainly reasonable to interpret the processes and relationships in Central and Eastern Europe after the collapse of really existing socialism in terms of a more-or-less deliberate convergence with the market arrangements and institutions which *ideally* existed in Western Europe. After the events of 1989, countries like Poland, Czechoslovakia, Hungary, and perhaps, possibly, even Bulgaria and Romania, did indeed attempt to turn images of what happened in the West into the ethical and practical justification for new projects and new hopes. Much of the impetus for that convergence came from the multifaceted ability of the market economies of the West to present themselves as infinitely attractive, highly aesthetic, and indigenously reproducible. Additionally, of course, the appeal of market arrangements and institutions was derived from the recognition practised by the opposition groups of the Soviet-type system that since the market was said the be the principle of the free and orderly society *over there*, it must have been freedom *per se.* This is not to ignore the important point that for the oppositional strands which owed a very deep allegiance to the reflexive discourse, consumerism was not at all a good thing to import. But, given the paths they had chosen, consumerism could not be kept out.

However, all those fairly voluntary movements towards putatively identical arrangements throughout Europe, in no way meant that with the collapse of the Soviet-type system Europe entered a period either of repose or of decadence. The widespread acceptance of the market as the ordering principle of society, the virtual universalization throughout Europe of the individual interpretation of sovereignty and freedom by no means implied that the European continent moved into a milieu of *post-history* or of an *end of ideology.* Exactly the opposite. The establishment of the market as the ethical legitimation for the new projects in Central and Eastern Europe released a set of unforeseen, dangerous, and extremely disturbing, antagonisms.

Quite simply, the ability of the old opposition groupings to step into the positions of legislation in Central and Eastern Europe after the Communist appointees moved out, entailed the disintegration of the single, universal, meaning of freedom into a multiplicity of irreconcilable meanings. The opposition groupings and individuals gained great strength and support from their ability to generate and uphold universal definitions of their situation. But as soon as the opposition became the new legislators, it entered into new social relationships, new social conditions of existence and, as such, the previously unitary and generally legitimated meaning of freedom utterly fell apart. As such, the problem of freedom was again stimulated, and Central and Eastern Europe was forced to confront a whole series of conflicts over what freedom was and what it involved. That is, behind the assured tone of someone like Leszek Balcerowicz, behind his rhetoric of appeals to a bounded and coherent society, there lurked deep gulfs of interpretation, deep reservoirs of distrust and disagreement.

The Soviet-type system's attempts to maintain exclusivity and to deal with the rising generations of would-be legislators more or less by accident transformed the superfluous double strangers *in themselves* into the double strangers *for themselves.* The oppositional intelligentsia was confident and, in its own terms, able, to indulge in radical practices of makeability to the extent that it retained a commitment to the self-images of the narratives of modernity. Its cognitive and hermeneutic cosmopolitanism enabled it to initiate alternative projects by appealing to the 'experts', wherever they might have come from (hence the speed with which the post-Communist Polish authorities, for example, sought advice and aid from the International Monetary Fund and Western academics).

Moreover, the oppositional intelligentsia did not have to go to too much trouble 'shopping for an agent' (to use Gouldner's excellent phrase) which could carry out the demands of freedom, unlike the double strangers in the allotment situations of modernity. The agent of the new projects was to be the intelligentsia itself, and its message was one of a free national society made up of a plurality of free and sovereign individuals. This was to some extent the appeal which Leszek Balcerowicz was trying to express, and it was certainly a significant theme in the work of the likes of Havel.

But the success of the intelligentsia in recognizing its welding into a group *for itself*, a success which was demonstrated by the speed with which these particular double strangers stepped into the positions of legislation, was the cause of a profound existential crisis for the group once it achieved what it had always said it had desired. It was also the basis of the conflicts and struggles which characterized Central and Eastern Europe after the collapse of really existing socialism.

Quite simply, an oppositional intelligentsia can only survive *for itself* in conditions where, firstly, it can reproduce a single, coherent, message in contradistinction to the officially sanctioned message and, secondly, where it can be reproduced in its magical strangeness by the exclusionary tactics of the existing societal institutions. The culture of reflexive discourse was a fine prism through which the intelligentsia was able to construct its own magic and its own definitions of freedom. But its existential and hermeneutic power dissipated as soon as it moved from a position of opposition and into one of leadership. The very point of the reflexive culture was that it was *critical* of existing relationships and arrangements, but in 1989 the agents of that critique entered positions where it could have no place or little pragmatic worth. That is, the protagonists of *that way of life* became the legislators of *this way of life*.

The very ability of the oppositional intelligentsia to assume responsibility for the new projects by which society lived and created itself, had extremely serious consequences for the group itself. It not only ceased to be entrenched in reflexivity, but it also became increasingly anachronistic at all to talk about a homogeneous and yet heterogeneous intelligentsia of double strangers *in itself* and *for itself*. The tense relationship of internal homogeneity and external heterogeneity was shattered through success. The putative universality of the *intelligentsia*, the community and coherence of the old oppositional double strangers, was torn apart and instead there appeared various small and particular groupings of *intellectuals*.

One group assumed control of the legislative functions and occupations, whilst another was forced into a position of struggling from outside to gain some influence. To some extent, the establishment of democratic institutions can be interpreted as at least in part a rapid attempt to domesticate the struggle between insider and outsider intellectuals in Central and Eastern Europe. The commitments to democracy were signs of attempts to pull the disagreements between the intellectuals firmly within the boundaries of the societal body. But each group tried to legitimate its continued existence, and, indeed, produce and reproduce that existence, through the announcement of particular meanings of freedom.

The implication was that the attempts of Leszek Balcerowicz, and the others like him, to create new projects after 1989, could not possibly be based on universal tacit or active support. Despite the rhetoric of universality and despite the pretensions towards the status of an archetypal double stranger, projects like that associated with Balcerowicz were destined to become little more than highly specific party-political platforms. The double strangers were domesticated; their magic dissipated and they became little more than decisionistic problem solvers. Balcerowicz and the others were not in the social and the societal contexts which would have enabled them to be the great hero legislators of modernity which they so desperately longed to be.

But that was not all. Despite the cosmopolitanism to which it was committed in the years of opposition, it was the case that the intelligentsia took over the positions of legislation on a series of national stages and, at least in part, through the eruption of national sentiments which had been suppressed by the old restricted internationalism. Vaclav Havel made the point quite eloquently when he said that the Soviet-type system, 'harshly suppressed whatever authenticity – or if you like 'otherness' – the subject nations had. From the structure of the state administration to the red stars on the roof-tops, everything was the same, that is, imported from the Soviet Union' (*Guardian* 7 September 1990: 27). A powerful proportion of the intellectuals who had been unable to secure for themselves positions in the post-Soviet administration, and for that matter a considerable number who had secured such roles, turned their definitions of freedom towards an imagination of the nation, with its ideational expression in nationalism. These intellectuals, of whom Alexander Solzhenitsyn would be an especially vivid if not absurd example, revived populist memories of the allegedly organic and happy, pure, national community as it had ideally existed before the Red Army, before Socialist Internationalism, and before difficulty. They propagated ideas of the national societal body which had no place for strange groups and ideas (and that invariably and inevitably meant the rise of anti-semitism).

Consequently, behind the institutional moves towards convergence between Central and Eastern Europe on the one hand and Western Europe on the other, a series of new and dangerous conflicts emerged. As soon as the old oppositional intelligentsia moved into positions of control and authority and tried to mobilize its own projects for improvement, it was torn along three main lines of rupture. It was fractured into a legislative, governing, elite, a counter-elite, and a national elite. Certainly, there was a degree of overlap linking the national elite to either or both of the other two, but the differences between them were of far greater significance than any similarities. Each fragment of the once coherent intelligentsia was pushed into situations where it pursued its own aims and interests in the name of a freedom which was essentially nothing more than the mirror-opposite of its own specific conditions of existence. But in every case, and despite the rhetorical and ontological statements to the contrary, each group of the intellectuals had traded a however tenuous grip on some kind of universality for an embeddedness in particularity. They had therefore sown the seeds of their own potential irrelevance.

Of course, there was also the serious gap in expectations between the intellectuals and the people. The intellectuals developed visions of the improved future which were frequently extremely abstract or quickly tarnished by practical problems and opportunities. Yet the people equated their new-found freedom with the ability to buy more and better commodities. That is, the freedom which the people upheld and wanted so keenly was treated with disdain or incredulity by their new leaders. Ultimately, that could only cause major conflicts.

Freedom itself became an intrinsically contested concept in Central and Eastern Europe when it had earlier been possible simply to juxtapose one universal definition with another. After 1989, the ideal and the projects of freedom were upheld by a plurality of social groups from a plurality of societal, hermeneutic, and cultural positions. As such, the nation-states which emerged after the Soviet-type system were haunted by as many definitions and projects as there were social groups able to claim the resources and the legitimacy to be able to speak for, and in the name of, *true* freedom. Again, the turn to the ideal arrangements and institutions of the market became particularly attractive since the market provided a way of making sense of this collapse of the universal into a plurality of largely decisionistic particularities. But perhaps more usefully than even that, the market offered a principle by which some ethical and beneficial order could be made out of the potential chaos.

Yet it was precisely the turn to the arrangements and the institutions of the market which made sure that the fracture of freedom could never be overcome. The emphasis upon the sovereign individual, making decisions about what to buy and what to possess, meant that freedom was transformed from an abstract, ideal principle contained within the project and instead it became an entirely mundane part of day-to-day reality. The dissipation of the once-coherent intelligentsia of double strangers around various institutionalized political platforms meant also that there was no sufficiently detached group which could remove all hopes from the present and push them forwards into the future. After all, if everyone agreed about the meaning and requirements of freedom, there would have been no point indulging in political debate, and, indeed, there would have been a return to the prime garden terrain of modernity. But once lost, garden situations could never be recovered.

An even more serious problem arose. Certainly, attempts were made to draw new societal boundaries around participation in national markets, but markets were also understood to be inherently open-ended, and allowing of the activity of strangers. That is, whilst the market was an immensely useful and valuable ordering principle of one sort, in the precise situation of Central and Eastern Europe after 1989, it was at the same time a woefully inadequate tool. It was quite incapable of establishing what was, or what was not, legitimate intervention from outside. The societal boundaries which it established were fundamentally porous. Invariably illegitimate intervention, and therefore the place of the dirty strangers who were held responsible for all problems, was identified as coming from those groups which lacked the economic resources to be able loudly to speak for themselves, or which lacked the ability to look like adequate citizens. Consequently, the hardy perennials of the Gypsies and the Jews became capable of only an ambivalent inclusion, whilst the activities of multinational hamburger enterprises posed no problems whatsoever. Moreover, because decisionist versions of freedom possess no content outside of the act of the decision, no universally legitimate boundaries between the sweep of one national market and the sweep of another could possibly emerge.

If some groups of double strangers, some members of the old oppositional intelligentsia, had been able to make legitimate and reproducible claims to speak on behalf of the entire societal body, perhaps those problems of freedom would not have appeared. The point was, however, that no double strangers after the collapse of really existing socialism were able to speak with such a loud, clear, and unchallenged voice. The very convergence of institutional arrangements in Central and Eastern Europe with the arrangements which were said to exist in the West meant that the projects of economic regeneration associated with names like Leszek Balcerowicz, or the projects of spiritual and ontological regeneration associated with names like Vaclav Havel, could never become the basis of universal meanings of freedom. They were consigned to particularity.

The nation-states which emerged from the rubble of the Soviet-type system were forced to recognize that, in chasing the great goal of freedom, they were chasing nothing other than a chimera. The commitment to freedom which constituted the reason why modernity went on could never be achieved because freedom was always *like that*. But when *like that* became *like this*, it ceased to be freedom. And no group was in a position to be able to provide new meanings or new interpretations which could be the stuff and the justification of new projects. Instead, and perhaps inevitably, freedom was mundanely individualized. As such, in 1989, Europe itself entered into a social and a historical condition in which hermeneutic or practical universality was an impossibility, in which homogeneity could neither be achieved nor known. A condition in which there was only heterogeneity. A condition in which the strangers finally swamped any and all attempts to decisively order them. A condition in which the problem of strangers became quite irreconcilable except to the extent that the strangers bought the same things as the known friends.

The ontological heroes who strode across the pages of the great texts of European modernity – the proletariat, the vanguard, the transcendental subject, the Superman – left the stage to be replaced by a plurality of individuals, all attempting to create and practise an identity out of the transient and contingent material and resources of time and place. Indeed, they lacked the ability, the faith, or the interest to see beyond the moment of the decision, and the erstwhile double strangers lacked the ability to *make them see.*

Essentially, this was, or perhaps it is more honest to say that this *is*, a condition in which the attempts of modernity to exclude the dirty and ambivalent strangers from the perfect society of the future, were forced to come to terms with the fact that instead of rendering the world more perfect they had by their own standards created just more filth. Ultimately, the projects, the hopes, and the efforts, associated with European modernity were incapable of stopping, or of even halting for a brief moment, the terrible flight of the angel of history. His smile was really a smirk.

8

CONCLUSION

In the wake of the collapse of the Soviet-type system of really existing socialism, all Europe – 'their' part as well as 'our' part – struggled to live by the ideals of much the same stories, much the same institutional arrangements, and much the same interpretations and practices of sovereignty. In practical terms, this tended to involve two things. On the one hand, the social marginality of the divided double strangers, and the frequent incommensurality of the interpretations of freedom which they upheld, was domesticated through formal commitments to broadly liberal-democratic political practices. On the other hand, the disrepute and failure of the collective definitions of freedom more or less schematically resulted in a positive evaluation of individual sovereignty and, more specifically, its market-oriented, consumer, decisionist variant.

Indeed, the idealization of the ideals of the market was perhaps inevitable. The market was able to resolve political and societal difficulties without avoiding the hermeneutic and existential requirement to construct some meaningful symbolic order out of the things of the world. Quite simply, the beauty of the market, and the source of its longevity in comparison to collectivist positions, was its ability to throw all sovereignty firmly into the laps of however many individuals and, yet, interpret that profound pluralization as inherently stable. The market could be seen as a classification of order because, firstly, it could be identified as the place where certain anthropological truths of human being could be practised and seen particularly clearly (such as avarice and selfishness dignified to the status of 'human nature') and, secondly, because the very idea of the market involved the identification of some essentially orderly and

195

reciprocal forms of individual activity. This second strand was, of course, very strong in the work of Friedrich Hayek, a double stranger who had reflected on his irrelevance to the reproduction of society. Despite his particularity, Hayek was yet able to maintain the promises of modernity by saying that thanks to the operation of processes like the market, things would turn out for the best *in any case*. He did little other than establish modernity as its own myth.

Whereas a modern legislator like Lenin wanted to make sure that *improvement* would take place, and whereas he occupied a specific situation of detachment and attachment to a garden situation which enabled him to make sure that some things and not others indeed happened, the double strangers of allotment-type situations had no ability of their own to *make sure* of anything. Moreover, their attempts to go shopping for an agent tended to be at best desperate, at worst farcical, because they had nothing to offer in any exchange relationship. Consequently, they often tended to make their mundane marginality an event of world-historic significance. For some, that involved the most desolate pessimism (Adorno), for a few it meant anger (Ortega y Gasset), but for others it involved precisely the route which Hayek mapped.

Not infrequently in allotment situations, the double strangers who followed the Hayekian path, who (by their own standards) should have been but were not indulging in projects of social improvement and the deepening of reflexivity, came to terms with their weakness by turning it into a proof and a vindication of freedom. Whether they did that in good or bad faith was, of course, quite a different matter. As such, W.E.H. Lecky was happy to identify an on-going process of increasing morality and reciprocity, Marshall told a reassuring tale of increasing citizenship, and someone like a Herbert Spencer rationalized his irrelevance by turning it into a prime illustration of a law of societal development.

In allotment situations the double strangers could *only talk about* the emergence of an increasingly distinct and moral realm of the societal. Some told the stories with great enthusiasm, others told them with deep gloom. But in the garden situations the relationships confronting the double strangers were rather different. There, the double strangers could take up the full burden, and the full possibilities, of their legislative capacities, and actually *go about creating* the homogeneous and free realm. As such, they could read certain passages of Plato as something approaching a policy document rather than a historical artifact. (In both the garden and the allotment situations of course, anything which was seen as inadequate to the demands of the societal entity was put into an invidious bucket category called the natural. As I hope to have shown, it was the boundary-drawing activities of modernity which established nature as the unreflexive and reified *other* of society.)

However, that fairly fundamental distinction between the social and hermeneutic position of the double strangers in gardens and allotments, and, therefore, between the rather different meanings of sovereignty and freedom, became less stark as the gardens increasingly came to look like allotments. It was increasingly impossible for the legislators of modernity to treat certain social situations as if they were mute and incapable of indigenous reproduction without assistance. After all, the projects to free those mute realms from passive reification were successful to the extent that they made the silent speak with their own voices. Moreover, through a mixture of oversight, stupidity, and illusions, alternative meanings of freedom and sovereignty were allowed some, however small and tenuous, foothold in the garden situations. *The garden situations which occasionally confronted European modernity were themselves rendered incapable of reproduction by the very projects of modernity. Had they not been made thus incapable, their very continuation would have been an offence to, and a mark of the failure of, the central tenets of modernity.*

It is on this basis that it seems reasonable to identify processes towards some kind of convergence between the institutional arrangements and the principles of sovereignty expressed in the two paradigmatic versions of European modernity. However, it should be stressed that since the basis of the different experiences was totally contingent, the pressures and processes suggesting convergence were similarly in no way *necessary.* Moreover, the tendencies which implied some kind of coming together went hand in hand with other tendencies which suggested a more serious scenario of *divergence* and the stimulation of extremely aggressive conflicts. The convergence was not too deep; it tended to be fairly superficial. It was driven by the attractiveness which surrounded some institutional arrangements, the repellence which surrounded others, and by the simple fact that one version of modernity was able to reproduce its meanings and practices of freedom whilst the other version was not. Once more, the discussion returns to the market.

After 1989, Europe ceased to live by utopian anthropologies which announced that the perfect men and women of the perfect future could be forged out of the flawed and pliable stuff bequeathed to the project by the reifications of habit, tradition, time, and place. Instead, the market stressed a definition of going on which had no place for any profound standards of *being*, however laudable they might have been (the only standards of being which market arrangements could allow were fairly vague; i.e. the emphasis placed on what are said to be the marks of individual selfishness). Rather, in those arrangements, the questions of individuality, sovereignty, and freedom, were understood purely in terms of the decisionist choices of *doing*. With the emergence and the consolidation of a consumerist decisionism throughout Europe, the improving programmes of modernity became, in a very real sense, quite useless and quite irrelevant.

The projects which had required such enthusiasm and sacrifice for the best part of two hundred years, were predicated upon vistas and arguments which the market had established to be little more than personal affectations. Consequently, the meanings and the practices of history, society, individuality, lost any quality of an ethical or existential imperative which they might have once possessed. As such, what it meant and what it involved to be a good member of society, or less rigidly an adequate member of social relationships, was also subjected to a quite fundamental transformation. Individuality ceased to be something which involved deferral and denial; rather it became something instantaneous and immediate.

The further point is that, thanks to the allotment situation which the market originally built upon and represented, the double strangers were absolutely unable to reinvoke transcendental categories of the meaning of individuality and freedom. Typically, the double strangers had been able to reproduce their magical exclusivity either at the expense of structural societal irrelevance, or, thanks to the consolidation of liberal democratic institutions which to some extent represented the intellectuals' last hopes of clinging on to the ability to make and remake the world, they had traded universality for partiality and particularity. And, of course, they had to face one overwhelming fact which could not be ignored in any honesty. From the perspective of the arrangements and imaginations which emerged out of modernity, it rather seemed that the intellectuals had been *proved wrong*. The market situation at least in part involved the realization that the erstwhile legislators had been wrong about the angel of history, wrong about self-sufficient society, wrong about their own abilities. As such, they traded something more than their universalistic pretensions. They were also forced to trade ambitions for apologies and enthusiasm for embarrassment. The double strangers were unable, and quite possibly perhaps even unwilling, to stake claims to universality in anything other than the most dishonest and marginal ways. It was precisely this social situation which spread throughout Europe.

The common position of the double strangers after 1989 had extremely serious implications. The decline of the possibility of makeability meant also the decline of society. The combination of market arrangements which stressed only *doing*, and the sidelining of the legislative abilities of the intellectuals, meant that it was quite impossible to produce and reproduce the image of the bounded community. With the collapse of really existing socialism, and with the development of intrinsically open-ended milieux of participation which accepted the inclusion of anyone who looked the part, all hope of clear and coherent boundary-drawing evaporated. In the face of the rise of decisionism, the old interpretation of society as the distinctive and reflexive realm of freedom (because it was consequently so easy to identify and anathematize the unfree) could be no longer simply assumed and treated as second nature. As such, the image of society, and in particular the ideal of the nation-state, itself became little more than an obsolete historical memory. Instead, it was replaced by something else, something which ironically took on board the recollections of the lofty aims of the double strangers, and yet something which was imagined in circumstances which dictated that the intellectuals were not able to practise or achieve the ideals which were their legacy to the future.

This is to stress the hermeneutic failure of the image of society as a nation-state, but, of course, there were a number of other pressures which also implied the increasing redundancy of the bounded communities which had been established with so much effort during modernity. Not the least of these pressures was the ambitious project of the Single Europe which was promoted with such enthusiasm by the remarkably aptly named European Community. The move towards European unification was another process towards convergence, but it also entailed only further moves of divergence. The project of unification was an attempt to use the nation-state precisely to consign the nation-state to the wastebin of history. Culturally, it was an attempt to establish an imagined community of a Europe which was understood to be the unitary home of all that is finest in the world irrespective of the accident of particular national origin.

The identity of Europe converged around traditions of the finest literature (the literary heritage of Europe is said to involve a very clear genealogy linking, say, Cervantes, Goethe, Beckett), the most beautiful buildings, the most intense and transcendent music. But the history of Europe tells another story of virtually ceaseless war and hostility. The movements towards unification were about the creation of new supranational institutions which could claim to promote the former products of Europe whilst overcoming the latter. In important degree, all these cultural ambitions of convergence to some extent reflected the economic realities of multinational capital and pan-European markets of consumption and communication. Moreover, the identification of the cultural traditions and heritage fed back into the imaginations of Europe to make the case for unification even more pressing and incontrovertible.

The point was, of course, that as soon as someone like, say, Beethoven was made a representative of a *European* culture rather than of a *Germanic* culture, the meanings of German identity were made rather open-ended, insignificant and, at best, relatively unimportant. The bounded-community of 'being German' was, consequently, radically undermined in the name of all it was or is to be *European*. And to be European in these terms is to be able to speak universally, across the divide between one set of particularities (early-nineteenth-century Austria) and another set of particularities (late-twentieth-century Britain). Indeed, the case of Beethoven is rather interesting in the construction of the imagined world of Europe. After the Berlin Wall had been opened, a concert was held in understandable celebration. The Berlin Philharmonic Orchestra gave a performance of Beethoven's Ninth, in which Schiller's *Ode to Joy* was renamed the *Ode to Freedom*. However, the Ninth Symphony has around it a long tradition of being one of *the* expressions of the cultural identity and the self-consciousness of Europe itself. When the piece was performed in Berlin, those meanings could not of course be removed or denied. Consequently, as soon as the choir started singing in the final movement, an event in the history of Germany was being constructed as, simultaneously, the moment when Europe realized its own unity. The particular German meanings were certainly not swamped, but they were made to represent a greater transnational, universal significance.

The process of unification was legitimated by the not too unreasonable assumption that each nation-state could best protect itself, and attain the most efficient and reasonable forms of administration, through participation in a grand system of ostensible equals. In other words, the path to the unified Europe was signposted by a protection of the imagination of boundaries through incorporation in a supranational system which, ironically however, involved nothing other than the utter practical devastation of those boundaries. The common-sense (and historically extremely dubious) construction of canonical aesthetic traditions was, at least in part, held to be an illustration of the wonders which might be possible given the acceptance of the legacy of unity, but it was also an illustration of the insignificance of the old boundaries. To some considerable extent, all of these movements towards something called the Single Europe, which would overcome local conflicts in the name of a universal magnificence, represented nothing other than an embodiment of the wildest hopes which the intellectuals had projected for Europe ever since they became aware of the existence of their strange colleagues in other cities and other countries (an awareness which Goethe registered in the 'Dedication' to the first part of his *Faust*).

At last, with the European Community's plan of the unified Europe, the double strangers were within reach of the pan-European culture of reflexivity which they had promoted and struggled so hard to achieve. Unfortunately, their plans approached fruition at precisely the moment when they were themselves too marginal, too tied to their own irrelevance, to reap any benefit from it. They could only participate in the plans as particular *professionals*. Instead, the ability to make universal cultural expressions was vested in different kinds of strangers, like Leonard Bernstein (an American). More than that, the project was to be completed at exactly the moment when the historical conditions of its realization slipped away.

The blueprint of the unified Europe was drawn up (as something more than armchair speculation), and made the goal of a fairly plausible project which accepted the lack of utopian anthropological alibis, in a specific historical situation when it was relatively easy to know which nation-states were to be rendered obsolete through incorporation within the grand allotment. In the period between the 'normalization' of the post-War settlement and the collapse of really existing socialism, there was a more or less direct match between the political and cultural identity of Western Europe, military organizations, and the open-endedness of market arrangements. For a while, Western Europe for all intents and purposes *was* Europe (or at least, that was the claim that it could make without stirring up too much opposition). That is, the universalization of an essentially extremely particular definition of the European identity was a distinct possibility to the extent that some kinds of particularity were readily accepted and, indeed, already practically integrated into a wider entity (such as, but not only, the European *Economic* Community).

Quite simply, in the period of the Soviet-type system, it was not too difficult for Europe to be identified as that area which was bounded to the West by the sphere of influence of the United States of America, to the East by the sphere of the Soviet Union, and to the South by an Africa which had been historically constructed as resolutely heterogeneous and, therefore, utterly beyond the compass of the new community of universality. The Soviet-type nation-states were not included in this particular imagination of Europe for a number of reasons. Firstly, and due to the originating garden situation of the system, those nation-states lacked the economic and the social linkages which would have enabled them to make sustainable claims to inclusion ('we' did not need 'them'). Secondly, they tended to operate through institutions which were more concerned to build up the indigenous garden more than peer over the fence to see the other side (such as Comecon which was entirely concerned with what went on inside, whereas the European Community was also always obsessed with relationships with the outside). Thirdly, even if the Soviet-type system could muster the energy and the self-belief, it tended to play a rather different game of universality than that which was played in the West. Fourthly, the nation-states of Central and Eastern Europe were under the sway of what used to be called Russia, and Russia was itself long suspected of only an ambivalent European pedigree.

As such, the spaces and the system beyond the allotment situation of Western Europe could be, and indeed were, easily constructed as outside of the reasonable boundaries of the community of universality. As the other, inclusionary, side of that coin, any differences between the different nation-states which were defined as inside, were identified as less important than whatever apparent or hidden features they might share in common (this is something approaching an international rendition of the stories of Lecky and Marshall). The boundaries of the imagined community which was able to call itself Europe were thus equated with *Western* Europe and, for some thirty or forty years, left entirely unquestioned. By way of a fairly trite example, it was always perfectly obvious to me that my world had nothing whatsoever in common with activities in Leipzig (other than football matches which *their* teams always seemed to win), but that my world was closely related to the festivals and folk culture of Sardinia. And, of course, the system which dominated Central and Eastern Europe actually did very little to alter or upset that facile and yet clear and comfortable division of the continent into a glorious 'us' and a miserable 'them'.

It was, then, in a very precise historical moment that the achievement of the universal and homogenizing ideals of European modernity could be realized. For a few decades little or no attention was paid to the meaning or the extent of the European identity. As such, Europe could be realized as a universal community of diverse particulars (as the well-established allotment), as the truth of a plurality of truths (an acceptance of the professional particularity and possibly even self-interest of the intellectuals). Religious festivals in Seville were things of wonder and legitimate expressions of cultural diversity, but religious festivals in Cracow were superstitious tomfoolery. For the period between the establishment and the collapse of the Soviet-type system, it seemed as if the goals of the globally benevolent and improving project called Europe were indeed within reach.

But the collapse of really existing socialism changed all that.

The move of convergence towards the practical realization of a clear identity was made extremely doubtful. As soon as the Soviet-type system fell apart, the previously taken-for-granted boundaries of Europe were reinserted into a history from which it seemed as if they had been removed and, consequently, they were made again the context for certain practices of reflexivity. As really existing socialism wobbled and toppled, the historical moment of the achievement of the Single Europe slipped away. Some people waved it goodbye, others drowned in its wake. The double strangers who should have wept as their hopes finally sank without a trace did not know what to do. Perhaps they were even *unable* to know what to do. The blueprint of unification no longer fed off social and historical conditions of possibility. And there was no social group with the mixture of detachment and involvement which could either restate the old hopes or create new ones.

The superficial movement of Central and Eastern Europe to institutional arrangements which were based more or less deliberately on the ideal of the arrangements which existed in the West meant nothing other than the disappearance of the Eastern boundary of what was to have been the unified Europe. As such, a new and previously quite unforeseeable set of ambivalences emerged to bedevil social relationships and constructions of order. In particular, to the extent that after 1989 the Eastern boundary of any unified Europe was made more than a little vague (*is* Kiev European?), the whole process of defining the magical and the filthy strangers was resuscitated. With the collapse of the post-War division of Europe into *their* garden and *our* allotment, the clear dividing line which separated the West (which had appropriated for itself the tradition of Europe, and which had the resources to confirm that appropriation) from the East (the other Europe – Europe's other), were fundamentally blurred. The possibility of the construction of universality out of a restricted set of particularities was destroyed. Consequently, the historical moment which nourished the ambitious plans of European unification were turned into little more than recollections.

The events which could have meant the true convergence of all Europe (and thus the redundancy of the *problem* of Europe) ironically meant that the identity of Europe was kept alive through reconstruction around new imaginations of community and inclusion. But since Western Europe possessed a level of organization and wealth which was entirely absent in Central and Eastern Europe, the West inevitably had the greatest role in the creation of those new identities (the prime example here is the fate of the German Democratic Republic, whatever and wherever that might have been). Indeed, it did not take too long at all for the attempts to re-establish the order of the community called Europe to involve increasingly vigorous, and increasingly desperate, bureaucratically motivated attempts to reconstruct the old Eastern boundary against illicit heterogeneity. Whilst Czechoslovakia, Poland, Hungary, might have *wanted* to demonstrate some convergence with Britain, France, and Germany, the latter nation-states, who accepted (however grudgingly) the legitimacy of each other, made sure that what Central and Eastern Europe wanted, it could not have.

That is perhaps the deepest meaning of the great fear of immigration from the East which flourished in the capitals of what was meant to be the unified Single Europe, after the realization of the wider implications of the collapse of really existing socialism. Typically, given the primacy of market arrangements, the blueprint of unification crucially involved formally unrestricted internal movement; all individuals could be practical strangers because the problem of strangers posed few problems. The *extent of strangeness* had been established and ordered in advance. The commitment to free internal movement, to open-endedness, was made in a context where the parameters of that open-endedness were obvious, extremely secure, and acceptable. But with the collapse, the parameters were blurred. Millions of people gained some way of entering the open-ended market arrangements, an access which was in no way accounted for by the blueprints of universality. Inevitably, attempts were very quickly launched to redefine the boundaries of the Single Europe with new barricades to keep out the filthy strangers. Illicit heterogeneity was constructed around such *activities* as the predilection for driving desperately unfashionable motor cars, a predilection which was fairly rapidly taken to be a sign of the driver's *intrinsic and immutable* difference or inability to fulfil the demands of consumerist participation and reciprocity ('no one in their right mind would have a car like that').

Of course, the attempts to reinvigorate the blueprint of

205

Europe by holding the flow of the haemorrhage on the Eastern boundary were doomed to failure at a practical level (leading to an explosion of racism in the West and to stronger annihilations of *them*). The attempts were most certainly doomed at a hermeneutic level. The imagination of Europe has been unable to exclude cities and symbols like Prague and Budapest. Those places, and their people, to some extent have to be included within the community of Europe (because of a cultural heritage and the legacy of Cold War rhetoric), and yet they pose nothing but problems. Firstly, they take the open-endedness of market arrangements strictly at their own word and, thus, threaten to turn what should be an establishment of order into a context of chaos. Secondly, Prague and Budapest after 1989 were obsessed with attempts to forge legitimate and reproducible interpretations of society which were assumed to be *already solved prior to* the moment of the realization of unity (that is, they were not mature enough for inclusion, they had not yet dealt with *their own* strangers). Thirdly, Central and Eastern Europe was living by myths of the universal legislator which were already fading memories in the professionalized West. Whereas someone like Vaclav Havel could talk about the 'primordial "I"' and keep a straight face, or where Lech Walesa could promise to solve all problems everywhere by the stroke of a moustache, the West maintained itself through the utterly mundane and routine practices of the technicist problem solvers.

The imaginations of Europe had no place for heroic individuals who would 'change the world'; they had a place only for accountants, personnel managers, and computer specialists. Political and hermeneutic styles directly reflected interpretations and practices of sovereignty, freedom, and order. Where sovereignty had been pluralized, and forged into an order through an emphasis on arrangements like the market, that is, *where freedom took the form of a consumerist decisionism, the legislators of order were also decisionist specialists.* This has a very serious implication because whereas someone *like* Havel could do what he did out of a sense of ethical obligation, the emphasis on decisionism increasingly meant that social life was denuded of an ethical dimension beyond legal restraint, habit, and reification. Consequently, that life could have no 'heroes of ethical obligation' (so that the death of Socrates, for example, proves not his integrity and courage, but rather his cantankerousness and foolishness. For a profound reflection on the changing ethical meaning of death, a reflection which is not incompatible with the story of this book, see Redner 1982.).

The problem is that our canonical ethical narratives are predicated upon precisely the recognition of bounded communities which decisionism, with its emphasis on the adequacy of the individual moment of doing, combined with the process towards the realization of the Single Europe, was rendering obsolete. Hans Jonas has noted that all of the conventional and accepted ethical principles assume an immediacy of time and place. The ethical codes which framed the debates on duty, responsibility, and commitment in the social relationships of modernity were all predicated upon the assumption of a *bounded universe*. As Jonas writes, the agents and the subjects invoked in the conventional ethical maxims, 'are sharers of a common present. It is those who are alive now and in some relationship with me who have a claim on my conduct as it affects them by deed or omission' (Jonas 1984: 5).

Consequently, in the terms of Hans Jonas's very suggestive and helpful comment, a principle such as that systematized by Kant as the categorical imperative, which said that we should treat others as an end in themselves and never as a means to our end, was predicated upon a double confinement of time and place. Firstly, Jonas says that the ethical universe as conventionally conceived is composed only of contemporaries (I can only treat you as anything because we are simultaneous). Secondly, the universe is confined in its, 'horizon of place within which the agent and the other meet as neighbor, friend, or foe, as superior and subordinate, weaker and stronger, and in all the other roles in which humans interact with one another' (Jonas 1984: 5). The symbol and the milieu of that confinement of ethics around the immediate was *the city*.

For Hans Jonas, the city is much more than a place where women and men happen to live. For him, cities allow individuals and societies to determine their self-images and self-identity freely of natural reification. Certainly, the city can be seen as a restricted world, but it is nevertheless a world of *freedom*. On the basis of a discussion of the Chorus from Sophocles' *Antigone*, Jonas suggests that thanks to the rise of the city as the free realm of women and men, 'life was played out between the abiding and the changing'. Jonas continues: 'the abiding was Nature, the changing his own works. The greatest of these works was the city, and on it he could confer some measure of abiding by the laws he made for it and undertook to honor' (Jonas 1984: 3). The city was the site of social reflexivity, self-sufficiency, and self-creation.

Certainly, Hans Jonas is making an important statement. Essentially, it lends quite a lot of support to the analysis of modernity which I have been trying to develop in this essay although Jonas takes the time-span of urbanization back to Sophocles, whereas I take it back to as recently as the seventeenth and eighteenth centuries. However, when he draws on Sophocles, Jonas is making a typically modern move. He is implicitly constructing a hermeneutic heritage reaching back to the ancients which serves to add extra layers of legitimacy to the ideas and practices of those who are, in fact, indubitably modern. Jonas is saying that the ethical maxims which played such a fundamental role in shaping our interpretations of sovereignty, and which placed such definite and ostensibly invariant limits on our activities, were all founded upon the production and the reproduction of an orderly world which fitted into clearly defined categories. For Jonas, ethical systems as conventionally established unproblematically assumed the significance and the maintenance of *boundaries*. It was those boundaries which established the extent of the universe of others relevant to me, and the greatest of those boundaries was signified by the city.

However, Jonas's diagnosis of the contemporary situation is that technology has fundamentally blurred if not erased the definite universes, inside of which all is simultaneous, immediate, and relevant, and outside of which all is distant, removed, and possibly irrelevant (that is, strange and dangerous). In a fairly similar narrative vein, it might be suggested that the boundary lines which made ethics possible were destroyed by the rise of open-ended market arrangements which had as one of its consequences the obsolescence of the nation-state. Consequently, Europe after 1989 was not just a place of a complex mixture of convergence and divergence, it was also a place of little or no ethical content (as conventionally understood), outside of legality or a personalism which directly reflected the interpretations of sovereignty applauded and enhanced by consumerism.

With the collapse of the bounded classifications of order, with the irrelevance of the modern projects and their ultimate inability to deal with the problem of those strangers who come today and stay tomorrow, social and cultural activity lost any inherent and intrinsic ethical value. Such value was rather derived from time-honoured codes (modernity created new reification). Instead of living through demanding appeals to our duties towards history, humanity, or heaven, we live through demanding appeals to precisely ourselves. All others are only relevant to us to the extent that, despite an entirely legitimate appearance of heterogeneity, they are in all important respects entirely homogeneous with us (invariably, the important respects turned out to be utterly trite).

At the risk of sounding at best melodramatic and at worst absurdly pompous, it can be said that such is the ethical condition of sovereignty and freedom in the Europe which has no boundaries.

The basis of conventional, modern ethics collapsed along with the dreams of the projects of modernity. As such, the age of the heroes was also consigned to the wastebin of history; Europe became a world without heroic exploits or heroic struggles because there came to be little or nothing for individuals to be heroic about. For that matter the sovereign individuals of contemporary Europe probably do not even know who or what it is that ought to be heroic. Instead, consumerist decisionism locates the moment of heroism and the identity of the hero in the otherwise ethically neutral acts of consumption and in the transient *representations* of adequacy.

Indeed, and as Max Weber saw so clearly, whilst the technicians and professionals attempt to manage problems according to the most strict codes of bureaucratic efficiency and whilst, to some extent, administration becomes the basis of an occupational ethic, the initial *choice* of that way of procedure was based on nothing more than an assertion (Weber 1948). In this sense, then, Weber's bureaucracy goes hand in hand with consumerism to provide something of a diagnosis of what it is to make a commitment in contemporary Europe.

It seems quite reasonable to propose that, 'the peculiarly modern self . . . in acquiring sovereignty in its own realm lost its traditional boundaries provided by a social identity and a view of human life as ordered to a given end' (MacIntyre 1985: 34).

Instead, the individuals who are said to reign supreme in contemporary Europe are guided by little or no idea as to where the universe of their obligations begins and ends. (Do I have obligations towards the beggar in London? Do I have obligations towards the famine victim in Ethiopia?) Consequently, the practice and the hermeneutic of individuality is inclined towards no *end* as, of course, it was in the city-based maxims of the likes of Immanuel Kant and, much earlier, Sophocles (according to Jonas). On this basis it could be said that decisionist individuality is truly pointless. All a contemporary individual can know is what she or he is and what she or he does. *My universe of obligations is constructed around nothing more than an extension to others of my criteria of adequacy and sovereignty.* In Alasdair MacIntyre's terms, this is a situation of *emotivism* (MacIntyre 1985).

The impact of emotivism, which MacIntyre sees as a product of the inherent failures of the Enlightenment project of trying to ground morality on universally valid principles, is profound indeed. It means that the horizons of moral utterance and practice have collapsed to such an extent that they encompass nothing other than the actions and beliefs of the individual. In the emotivist condition, 'evaluative utterance can in the end have no point or use but the expression of my own feelings or attitudes and the transformation of the feelings and attitudes of others' (MacIntyre 1985: 24). There would seem to be no chance of an escape from this condition without the construction of a new and viable universal grounding. Yet there would seem to be no realistic possibility of any such universality because there is no social group occupying a suitably strange and magical social position.

Alasdair MacIntyre continues to explore some of the features of the contemporary ethical condition: 'I cannot genuinely appeal to impersonal criteria, for there are no impersonal criteria. I may think that I so appeal and others may think that I so appeal, but these thoughts will always be mistakes.' He continues to point out that solidarity between individuals is thus largely a political problem rather than an ontological condition: 'The sole reality of distinctively moral discourse is the attempt of one will to align the attitudes, feelings, preference and choices of another with its own. Others are always means, never ends' (MacIntyre 1985: 24). So, given that I am simply one stranger in a world which I experience as full of strangers (everyone is strange to me except those I love; the *need* to love becomes greater as the strangeness of others is attenuated; similarly the imagination of the nation-state becomes increasingly powerful as the nation-state as an institution becomes increasingly obsolete), I reduce morality to the strategic question of getting others to think that I should be treated as possibly magical, or at the very least as not filthy.

I try to make sure that I am seen and treated as an acceptable stranger by surrounding myself with the signs and significations of societal adequacy and, less benevolently, by utterly repudiating any connections between myself and those who are unable to make reproducible claims of societal adequacy. As such I treat the beggar as someone of no significance to me, and avert my gaze which might invite reciprocity, lest some of her filth tarnishes my purity. Like everyone else, she is a means to my ends. (To some extent a reflection on this situation, and an enthusiastic attempt to make some good out of it, informs the work of Richard Rorty; see in particular, Rorty 1989).

As such, when the social constructions of order are unable to deal with the matter of establishing the parameters of inclusion and exclusion, there can be no *obligations* which demand treatment as essential and, even more, no *individual identities* which demand treatment as if they are essential (in any case, given that the individual is the paramount sovereign, how can any one individual condemn the choices of other individuals, so long as they accord to her or his assertions of adequacy?). In modernity, individuals could only avoid the fate of evacuation into the sewers if they could change their identities with ease and frequency. Hence, again, the poignancy of the beggar; she is filth precisely because she lacks the resources which would enable her to change her identity. Hence also the strength of the threat which is said to be posed by 'ethnic minorities'. Their inadequacy defines them; they lack the resources to define themselves. *They are defined and, therefore, they are not sovereign.*

In contemporary Europe, individuality is, and can only be, created and identified on the basis of surface appearances and temporary alliances. The stress on the transient, and the importance of it, is a prime reflection of the paradoxical contemporary ethical and existential situation that, 'we simultaneously and inconsistently treat moral argument as an exercise of our rational powers and as mere expressive assertion' (MacIntyre 1985: 11). Consequently, the predominant basis of grouping in contemporary Europe tends to be not around the time-honoured bounded imaginations of immutable belonging. Rather, grouping, and the strategic alliances to make ethical principles and standards of adequacy reproducible, tends to occur around *neo-tribalist identifications*. These neo-tribalist affiliations reflect the emotivist moral condition, and the near impossibility of the development of any universalistic bounded communities (universalistic in either a garden or an allotment-type context).

The idea of neo-tribalism has been discussed by Michel Maffesoli. According to his very rich interpretation, our world is typified by the development of an awareness that the stakes of individuality are vested neither in common identities nor an 'ongoing and developing history' (Maffesoli 1988: 141). Rather, ours is a world where social participation and social identity is created around affiliations which are inherently volatile and in a state of perpetual flux (that is, these are identities which boil down to little more than decisionist assertion). According to Maffesoli, with the notion and for that matter the practical social activity of neo-tribalism, 'we are dealing less with aggregating into a group, a family, or a community, and more with zipping from one group to another.' Maffesoli continues: 'In fact, contrary to the stability induced by classic tribalism, neo-tribalism is characterized by fluidity, by punctuated gathering and scattering. This fluidity best describes the spectacle that goes on in the streets of modern metropolises' (Maffesoli 1988: 148).

Neo-tribalist affiliations are especially strong in contemporary Europe precisely because there are no other meaningful kinds of affiliation which can respond in any constructive (and not just retrogressive, pre-modern) way to the problem of living in a world without boundaries. As such, identities are now constructed around professional roles (such as computer experts, and, given the collapse of any grounding of humanity, the aptly-named human-resource planners, who communicate through highly cosmopolitan networks in languages which are extremely efficient internally and quite impenetrable to outsiders). Meanwhile, subcultural styles tend to be transnational in their content and their hold. For example, there is now something of an international neo-tribalist identity surrounding certain kinds of youth culture which can bring together into meaningful communities individuals who have absolutely nothing else in common. Moreover, it is fairly easy for any individual to take on or revoke the identity of a particular kind of international youth simply as a matter of choice, without consideration of any over-riding ethical obligations (which of course in any case no longer exist). However, the enhancement of the temporary has a peculiar effect. Since neo-tribalist arrangements are embedded only in the momentary, their grip is extremely tenacious. Neo-tribalist arrangements have no form; they are all content (they are tracks which follow no direction) and, so, the vigour and rigour of the content has to be utterly powerful if it is not to be swept away by the wind. As such, *a world without boundaries is a world which experiences an explosion of fundamentalism*. Moreover, these fundamentalisms are more dangerous and more ambitious than any of their pre-modern ancestors simply because of the technology which is at their disposal.

The location of individuality is reduced to the immediacy of the here and now. It has little or nothing of that transcendent component which was so important to the narratives which informed European modernity. As such, and by extension, it has become increasingly pointless, if not wholly fictitious, to talk about that abstract, orderly, clear thing called *society* (and so the structure/agency debate which was predicated upon the problematic of society also becomes more than a little meaning-less). Instead, if the product of European modernity called social science, or less grandly sociology, is to have any hermeneutic value in the conditions of emotivist, *postmodern* Europe, perhaps new concepts are needed which do not emphasize the intrinsic order of some synthetic entity; seemingly vague concepts like *social relationships* or Maffesoli's preferred *sociality* (Maffesoli 1988). The advantage of those concepts is that neither of them is indebted to the myths of society and its improvement.

Modernity, which involved the promise of improvement and which struggled to achieve that promise, also projected its hopes and dreams into the future. The bounded communities constituted so many firm launching pads into the new begin-ning. But, 'the essential characteristic of the points just made is a new concept of space-time relationship. The emphasis is on the immediate and the affectual, that is, that which is tied to a given place, a place shared with others' (Maffesoli 1988: 142). All in all, that is rather more than an ironic end to the hopes of modernity which precisely involved a denigration of the embedded.

All of this implies a radical reformulation of what it is to be a sovereign individual in open-ended market arrangements, what it is to be an individual in social relationships rather than an agent in the structured society. In so far as individuals now belong to collectives purely through a combination of personal (that is, sovereign) decisions and entirely transient alliances, which are useful and binding only in the immediate situation, individuality can have no intrinsic core which implies the possession of the qualities of some transcendental humanity. That is why it would be very hard for anyone in a market situation (or, previously the allotment-type context) in all honesty to talk like Vaclav Havel about primordial qualities without an embarrassed, self-conscious, giggle. Instead, the paradigmatic sovereign individual of convergent and divergent, imaginable and unimaginable, postmodern Europe is perhaps best seen as simply a 'papier-mâché Mephistopheles': 'if I tried I could poke my forefinger through him, and would find nothing inside but a little loose dirt, maybe'. (These quite wonderful and resonant words come from Joseph Conrad's *Heart of Darkness*. Certainly it is a story with extremely dubious connotations but, also, it is certainly a story with a lot to say about the heart of Europe (Conrad 1967: 81).)

But undoubtedly the death of the heroes, and the rise of the hollow men and women which pessimistic and disgruntled moderns like Eliot (and Conrad) so bewailed can be seen as an immensely liberatory event. Certainly, it seems quite reasonable to speculate that the decline of the bounded communities can in the end only lead to a collapse of the frequently nightmarish imaginations which they nourished. And, perhaps, it is possible for the sovereigns of the postmodern condition to practise solidarity, reciprocity, and responsibility on an open-ended terrain and, thus, finally attempt to forge some linkages with the beggar, who is as contingent in her exclusion as I am contingent in my inclusion.

After all, if individuality and responsibility is a problem which can only be addressed to the here and now, if these are matters about which it is ultimately impossible to honestly say anything definite, then the meaning and the identity of the beggar precisely becomes *indefinite*. As such, there is *no reason why I should not* engage in reciprocal relationships with her. If I cease to reconfirm through the turning away of my gaze the now-obsolete, redundant, fictitious boundaries of the societal body which no longer exists, I might indeed see that when she looks back at me she is creating some reciprocal tie between us and making claims upon me. Since our inadequacy or our adequacy is entirely contingent, we could have been in each other's situation (my embeddedness in consumerism will be thus undermined: I will have to admit that she might not look good, but still she *looks*). However, to point to a *possibility* is in no way to point to a *probability*, and if my analysis is right, it will not be possible for the extension of reciprocity to include the beggar to be established as anything other than so many individual choices, perhaps, even, so many moments of nausea. More than that, the explosion of fundamentalism would seem to imply nothing other than so many deliberate blindings of the beggar. There is an essential dilemma at the core of the postmodern treatment of the filth of modernity, a dilemma which is, undoubtedly, as horrible as it is hopeful.

It was the processes, the networks, and the commitments to improvement and freedom which constituted the marks of European modernity. Those processes, networks, and commitments also established the critically detached God's-eye perspective of the double stranger, so that she or he could make disinterested evaluative judgements on the adequacy of the activities and ambitions of individuals and societies. But the conditions upon which the legislative role was predicated no longer exist. Contemporary Europe no longer lives and experiences the contradictions of European modernity. Instead, contemporary Europe and its imaginations are now haunted by the new ghosts and for that matter the new opportunities of postmodernity. The era and the attitude of the two sovereigns have disappeared, just like its boundaries.

BIBLIOGRAPHY

Adorno, T.W. (1989) 'Perennial Fashion – Jazz', trans. S. and S. Weber, in S.E. Bonner and D.M. Kellner (eds) *Critical Theory and Society: A Reader*, New York: Routledge.

Adorno, T.W. and Horkheimer, M. (1972) *Dialectic of Enlightenment*, trans. J. Cumming, New York: Herder & Herder.

Anderson, B. (1983) *Imagined Communities. Reflections on the Origin and the Spread of Nationalism*, London: Verso.

Andrzejewski, J. *et al* (1978) 'Movement for the Defence of Human and Civil Rights in Poland', in B. Szajkowski (ed.) *Documents in Communist Affairs 1977*, Cardiff: University College Cardiff Press.

Arendt, H. (1963) *On Revolution*, London: Faber & Faber.

Balcerowicz, L. (1990) 'The Price of Polish Economic Reform', in W.M. Brinton and A. Rinzler (eds) *Without Force or Lies. Voices from the Revolution of Central Europe 1989–1990*, San Francisco: Mercury House.

Barbalet, J.M. (1988) *Citizenship*, Milton Keynes: Open University Press.

Baudrillard, J. (1983) *In the Shadow of the Silent Majorities*, trans. P. Foss, P. Patton, and J. Johnston, New York: Semiotext(e).

Bauman, Z. (1987) *Legislators and Interpreters. On Modernity, Postmodernity and Intellectuals*, Oxford: Polity.

—— (1988) 'Strangers: The Social Construction of Universality and Particularity', *Telos* no. 78: 7–42.

—— (1989) *Modernity and the Holocaust*, Oxford: Polity.

—— (1990) 'Modernity and Ambivalence', *Theory, Culture and Society* vol. 7 (2–3): 143–169.

Bellow, S. (1975) *Humboldt's Gift*, London: Secker & Warburg.

Benjamin, W. (1989) 'Theses on the Philosophy of History', in S.E. Bonner and D.M. Kellner (eds) *Critical Theory and Society. A Reader*, New York: Routledge.

Berlin, I. (1981) *Against the Current. Essays in the History of Ideas*, Oxford: Oxford University Press.

Borges, J.L. (1970) *Labyrinths. Selected Stories and Other Writings*, trans. D.A. Yates and J.E. Irby, Harmondsworth: Penguin.

Braudel, F. (1973) *Capitalism and Material Life 1400–1800*, trans. M. Kochan, New York: Harper & Row.

Bryson, N. (1988) 'Representing the Real: Gros' Paintings of Napoleon', *History of the Human Sciences* vol. 1 (1): 75–104.

Buck-Morss, S. (1977) *The Origin of Negative Dialectics. Theodor W. Adorno, Walter Benjamin, and the Frankfurt Institute*, New York: The Free Press.

Burke, E. (1968) *Reflections on the Revolution in France*, Harmondsworth: Penguin.

Charter 77 (1978) 'Charter 77 Complete Text', in B. Szajkowski (ed.) *Documents in Communist Affairs 1977*, Cardiff: University College Cardiff Press.

Chartier, R. (1988) *Cultural History. Between Practices and Representations*, trans. L.G. Cochrane, Oxford: Polity Press.

Clark, K. (1977) 'Utopian Anthropology as a Context for Stalinist Literature', in R.C. Tucker (ed.) *Stalinism. Essays in Historical Interpretation*, New York: Norton.

Connerton, P. (1989) *How Societies Remember*, Cambridge: Cambridge University Press.

Conrad, J. (1967) *Youth, Heart of Darkness and The End of the Tether*, London: J.M. Dent.

Dahrendorf, R. (1990) *Reflections on the Revolution in Europe*, London: Chatto & Windus.

Douglas, M. (1966) *Purity and Danger. An Analysis of the Concepts of Pollution and Taboo*, London: Routledge & Kegan Paul.

—— (1975) *Implicit Meanings. Essays in Anthropology*, London: Routledge & Kegan Paul.

Elias, N. (1978) *The History of Manners*, trans. E. Jephcott, Oxford: Basil Blackwell.

Feher, F. (1987) 'Freedom and the "Social Question" (Hannah Arendt's theory of the French Revolution)', *Philosophy and Social Criticism* vol. 12 (1): 1–30.

—— (1990) 'Soviet-Type Societies: The Need for New Theory', *Problems of Communism* vol. xxxix: 95–98.

Feher, F. and Heller, A. (1983) 'Class, Democracy, Modernity', *Theory and Society, vol 12: 211–244*.

Feher, F., Heller, A., and Markus, G. (1983) *Dictatorship Over Needs. An Analysis of Soviet Societies*, Oxford: Basil Blackwell.

Foucault, M. (1970) *The Order of Things. An Archaeology of the Human Sciences*, London: Tavistock.

—— (1977) *Discipline and Punish. The Birth of the Prison*, trans. A. Sheridan, London: Allen Lane.

—— (1982) 'The Subject and Power', Afterword in H.L. Dreyfus and P. Rabinow (eds) *Michel Foucault: Beyond Structuralism and Hermeneutics*, Brighton: Harvester.

Garton Ash, T. (1989) *The Uses of Adversity: Essays on the Fate of Central Europe*, Cambridge: Granta.

Gellner, E. (1983) *Nations and Nationalism*, Oxford: Basil Blackwell.

—— (1990) 'Rethinking the Revolution', *Partisan Review* vol. LVII (2): 309–312.

Giddens, A. (1990) *The Consequences of Modernity*, Stanford, California: Stanford University Press.

Gierek, E. (1978) 'Socialist Poland has Created Conditions for Genuine Implementation of Human Rights', in B. Szajkowski (ed.) *Documents in Communist Affairs 1977*, Cardiff: University College Cardiff Press.

Gouldner, A. (1975) 'Prologue to a Theory of Revolutionary Intellectuals', *Telos* no. 26: 3–36.

—— (1979) *The Future of Intellectuals and the Rise of the New Class*, London: Macmillan.

—— (1985) *Against Fragmentation. The Origins of Marxism and the Sociology of Intellectuals*, New York: Oxford University Press.

Gramsci, A. (1971) *Selections from the Prison Notebooks of Antonio Gramsci*, trans. Q. Hoare and G. Nowell Smith (eds) London: Lawrence & Wishart.

Habermas, J. (1974) *Theory and Practice*, trans. J. Viertel, London: Heinemann.

Haraszti, M. (1987) *The Velvet Prison. Artists Under State Socialism*, trans. K. and S. Landesmann, New York: Basic Books.

Harvey, D. (1985) *Consciousness and the Urban Experience*, Oxford: Basil Blackwell.

Haug, W.F. (1986) *Critique of Commodity Aesthetics. Appearance, Sexuality and Advertising in Capitalist Society*, trans. R. Beck, Oxford: Polity.

Havel, V. (1975) 'Letter to Dr Gustav Husak' in J. Vladislav (ed.) Vaclav Havel, *Living in Truth*, London: Faber & Faber, 1987.

—— (1981) *The Memorandum*, trans. V. Blackwell, London: Eyre Methuen.

—— (1984) 'Politics and Conscience', trans. E. Kohak and R. Scruton, in J. Vladislav (ed.) Vaclav Havel, *Living in Truth*, London: Faber & Faber, 1987.

—— (1990) 'The Art of the Impossible', *The Spectator* 27 January: 11–13.

Hayek, F. (1944) *The Road to Serfdom*, London: Routledge.

Heller, A. (1990) *Can Modernity Survive?* Oxford: Polity Press.

Heller, M. and Nekrich, A. (1986) *Utopia in Power. The History of the Soviet Union from 1917 to the Present*, trans. P.B. Carlos, London: Hutchinson.

Ibsen, H. (1988) *An Enemy of the People, The Wild Duck, Rosmersholm*, trans. J. MacFarlane (ed.) Oxford: Oxford University Press.

Ignatieff, M. (1984) *The Needs of Strangers*, London: Hogarth Press.

Jarv, H. (1987) 'Citizen *versus* State', in J. Vladislav (ed.), Vaclav Havel, *Living in Truth*, London: Faber & Faber.

Jonas, H. (1984) *The Imperative of Responsibility. In Search of an Ethics for the Technological Age*, trans. H. Jonas and D. Herr, Chicago: University of Chicago Press.

Kant, I. (1970) *Kant's Political Writings*, H. Reiss (ed.) Cambridge: Cambridge University Press.

Kerr, C. (1973) *Industrialism and Industrial Man*, 2nd edn, Harmondsworth: Penguin.

Kerr, C. (1983) *The Future of Industrial Societies*, Cambridge, Mass: Harvard University Press.

Konrad, G. (1984) *Antipolitics. An Essay*, trans. R.E. Allen, London: Quartet.

Kosztolanyi, D. (1987) 'The Place of the Hungarian Language on the Earth', in E. Toth (ed.) *Today. An Anthology of Contemporary Hungarian Literature*, Budapest: Corvina.

Kracauer, S. (1989) 'The Mass Ornament', trans. B. Connell and J. Zipes, in S.E. Bonner and D.M. Kellner (eds) *Critical Theory and Society. A Reader*, New York: Routledge.

Kundera, M. (1982) *The Book of Laughter and Forgetting*, trans. M.H. Heim, London: Faber & Faber.

—— (1984) *The Unbearable Lightness of Being*, trans. M.H. Heim, London: Faber & Faber.

Lash, S. (1990) 'Learning from Leipzig – Or Politics in the Semiotic Society', *Theory, Culture & Society* vol. 7 (4): 145–158.

Lecky, W.E.H. (1911) *History of European Morals from Augustus to Charlemagne*, London: Longmans Green.

Lenin, V.I. (1964) 'How to Organise Competition?' in *Collected Works. Volume 26. September 1917–February 1918*, Moscow: Progress Publishers.

—— (1967) 'On Co-Operation', in *Selected Works in Three Volumes*, volume 3, Moscow: Progress Publishers.

—— (1973) *What is to be Done? Burning Questions of Our Movement*, Peking: Foreign Languages Press.

Lévi-Strauss, C. (1969) *Conversations with Claude Lévi-Strauss*, with G. Charbonnier, trans. J. and D. Weightman, London: Jonathan Cape.

Lienesch, M. (1988) *New Order of the Ages. Time, the Constitution and the Making of Modern American Political Thought*, Princeton, New Jersey: Princeton University Press.

Luhmann, N. (1979) *Trust and Power*, Chichester: Wiley.

Lukács, G. (1970) *Lenin. A Study on the Unity of His Thought*, London: New Left Books.

MacIntyre, A. (1985) *After Virtue. A Study in Moral Theory*, 2nd edn, London: Duckworth.

Maffesoli, M. (1988) 'Jeux De Masques: Postmodern Tribalism', *Design Issues* vol. IV (1–2): 141–151.

Mannheim, K. (1960) *Ideology and Utopia: Introduction to the Sociology of Knowledge*, London: Routledge & Kegan Paul.

Marshall, T.H. (1973) *Class, Citizenship and Social Development*, Westport: Greenwood.

Marx, K. (1942) 'The Eighteenth Brumaire of Louis Bonaparte', in *Karl Marx. Selected Works in Two Volumes*, volume 2, London: Lawrence & Wishart.

—— (1942a) 'Address and Provisional Rules of the Working Men's International Association', in *Karl Marx. Selected Works in Two Volumes*, volume 2, London: Lawrence & Wishart.

Marx, K. and Engels, F. (1942) 'Manifesto of the Communist Party', in *Karl Marx. Selected Works in Two Volumes*, volume 1, London: Lawrence & Wishart.

—— (1970) *The German Ideology*, C.J. Arthur (ed.), London: Lawrence & Wishart.

Mill, J.S. (1910) *On Liberty*, London: J.M. Dent.

Ortega y Gasset, J. (1932) *The Revolt of the Masses*, London: George Allen & Unwin.

Orwell, G. (1962) *The Road to Wigan Pier*, Harmondsworth: Penguin.

Plato (1974) *The Republic*, 2nd edn, trans. D. Lee, Harmondsworth: Penguin.

Redner, H. (1982) *In the Beginning was the Deed. Reflections on the Passage of Faust*, Berkeley: University of California Press.

Ricoeur, P. (1977) 'Patocka, Philosopher and Resister', *Telos* no. 31: 152–155.

Rizzi, B. (1985) *The Bureaucratization of the World. The USSR: Bureaucratic Collectivism*, trans. A. Westoby, London: Tavistock.

Rojek, C. (1986) 'Convergence, Divergence and the Study of Organizations', *Organization Studies* vol. 7 (1): 25–36.

Rorty, R. (1989) *Contingency, Irony and Solidarity*, Cambridge: Cambridge University Press.

Rousseau, J.J. (1931) *The Confessions of Jean Jacques Rousseau*, volume 1, trans. J. Grant, London: J.M. Dent.

—— (1979) *The Indispensable Rousseau*, J. Hope Mason (ed.), London: Quartet.

Rybakov, A. (1988) *Children of the Arbat*, trans. H. Shukman, London: Hutchinson.

Salisbury, H. (1977) *Black Night, White Snow. Russia's Revolutions 1905–1917*, London: Cassell.

Sartre, J.P. (1958) *Being and Nothingness. An Essay on Phenomenological Ontology*, trans. H.E. Barnes, New York: Philosophical Library.

Schmitt, C. (1985) *Political Theology: Four Chapters on the Concept of Sovereignty*, trans. G. Schwab, Cambridge, Mass: The MIT Press.

Scruton, R. (1988) 'The New Right in Central Europe I: Czechoslovakia', *Political Studies* XXXVI: 449–462.

—— (1988a) 'The New Right in Central Europe II: Poland and Hungary', *Political Studies* XXXVI: 638–652.

Simmel, G. (1950) *The Sociology of Georg Simmel*, trans. K.H. Wolff (ed.), New York: The Free Press.

Skvorecky, J. (1990) 'Czech Writers: Politicians in Spite of Themselves', in W.M. Brinton and A. Rinzler (eds) *Without Force or Lies. Voices from the Revolution of Central Europe in 1989–90*, San Francisco: Mercury House.

Smart, C. (1990) 'Gorbachev's Lenin: The Myth in Service to *Perestroika*', *Studies in Comparative Communism* xxiii (1): 5–22.

Solzhenitsyn, A. (1974) *The Gulag Archipelago 1918–1956. An Experiment in Literary Investigation*, trans. T.P. Whitney, London: Collins & Harvill.

Spencer, H. (1940) *The Man versus The State*, London: Watts.

—— (1969) *Principles of Sociology*, S. Andreski (ed.), London: Macmillan.

Stalin, J. (1973) 'Report to the Seventeenth Congress of the Communist Party of the Soviet Union (Bolshevik) on the Work of the Central Committee', in B. Franklin (ed.) *The Essential Stalin*, London: Croom Helm.

—— (1973a) 'Speech to the Nineteenth Congress of the Communist Party of the Soviet Union', in B. Franklin (ed.) *The Essential Stalin*, London: Croom Helm.

Tester, K. (1991) *Animals and Society. The Humanity of Animal Rights*, London: Routledge.

Touraine, A. (1989) 'Is Sociology Still the Study of Society?' *Thesis Eleven* no. 23: 5–34.

Trotsky, L. (1972) *The Young Lenin*, trans. M. Eastman, Newton Abbot: David & Charles.

Weber, M. (1930) *The Protestant Ethic and the Spirit of Capitalism*, trans. T. Parsons, London: George Allen & Unwin.

—— (1948) *From Max Weber. Essays in Sociology*, trans. H.H. Gerth and C. Wright Mills (eds), London: Routledge & Kegan Paul.

Yeo, E. and Yeo, S. (1981) *Popular Culture and Class Conflict 1590–1914: Explorations in the History of Labour and Leisure*, Brighton: Harvester.

Zinoviev, G. (1973) *History of the Bolshevik Party. A Popular Outline*, trans. R. Chappell, London: New Park.

NAME INDEX

SUBJECT INDEX